"This is a good introduction to the hist
not just for evangelical readers. In the a
Madison without explaining Locke; I could not explain Locke without explaining Aquinas; and I could not explain Aquinas without explaining Augustine,
Peter, Paul, Aristotle and Plato.' Well done!"

Michael Novak, author of *On Two Wings: Humble Faith and Common Sense at the American Founding*

"Greg Forster recognizes that political philosophy is older than Christianity and
independent of the Old Testament. This fact does not deny that both Testaments
have something to say about politics. He has avoided the temptation of trying to
explain the Christian tradition as if it began in the twentieth century, or even in
the sixteenth. The very existence of revelation as its own coherent whole implies
that the public square at some points should be 'contested,' even for it to be itself.
In the beginning, he cites C. S. Lewis's coy devil to warn us that 'social justice'
can well be our first step away from God. That step is a very current temptation
that defines in large part the real 'crisis' that Forster sees in the public square.
The book is well worth a careful read."

James V. Schall, S.J., professor, Department of Government, Georgetown University

"This is a learned and lucid exploration of the origins, development and contemporary state of the political ideas of natural law, church and state, and religious
toleration. To understand how the public square became what it is today, Forster's
book follows the twists and turns in the triumphs and disappointments of these
political ideas in Western civilization. By concentrating on certain Christian
themes and thinkers in a sweeping historical analysis, Forster's *The Contested
Public Square* provides a much-needed correction for the introductory study of
Western political theory."

Lee Trepanier, associate professor, Saginaw Valley State University

"A quarter-century after Richard John Neuhaus's *Naked Public Square,* Greg Forster has given readers the *The Contested Public Square.* Like Neuhaus, Forster has
documented the decline of natural law thinking. But beyond that declension,
Forster offers an ambitious survey of the rise of Christian political thought from
its inception some two millennia ago to its present 'crisis.'"

Jeffry H. Morrison, Regent University

"*The Contested Public Square* is a comprehensive and readable history of Western political thought that gives particular attention to the influence of Christianity. A major theme is the importance of natural law for the development of ideas of religious freedom, constitutionalism and human rights. Students and teachers of political theory will be particularly interested in Professor Forster's controversial but convincing argument that Augustine, William of Ockham, Luther and Calvin were natural law thinkers."

Paul E. Sigmund, professor of politics, Princeton University

THE
CONTESTED
PUBLIC SQUARE

THE CRISIS OF CHRISTIANITY AND POLITICS

GREG FORSTER

IVP Academic

An imprint of InterVarsity Press
Downers Grove, Illinois

InterVarsity Press
P.O. Box 1400, Downers Grove, IL 60515-1426
World Wide Web: www.ivpress.com
E-mail: email@ivpress.com

InterVarsity Press® is the book-publishing division of InterVarsity Christian Fellowship/USA®, a student movement active on campus at hundreds of universities, colleges and schools of nursing in the United States of America, and a member movement of the International Fellowship of Evangelical Students. For information about local and regional activities, write Public Relations Dept., InterVarsity Christian Fellowship/USA, 6400 Schroeder Rd., P.O. Box 7895, Madison, WI 53707-7895, or visit the IVCF website at <www.intervarsity.org>.

Scripture quotations, unless otherwise noted, are from The Holy Bible, English Standard Version, *copyright © 2001 by Crossway Bibles, a division of Good News Publishers. Used by permission. All rights reserved.*

Design: Cindy Kiple

Images: The Munt Tower with a Quack Praising his Merchandise, Amsterdam *(oil on panel) by Sybrandt van Beest (1610-74) ©Private Collection/ © Lawrence Steigrad Fine Arts, New York/ The Bridgeman Art Library ©Private Collection/ © Lawrence Steigrad Fine Arts, New York/ The Bridgeman Art Library ISBN 978-0-8308-2880-7*

Printed in the United States of America ∞

Library of Congress Cataloging-in-Publication Data

Forster, Greg, 1973-
  The contested public square: the crisis of Christianity and
politics / Greg Forster.
    p. cm.
  Includes bibliographical references and index.
  ISBN 978-0-8308-2880-7 (pbk.: alk. paper)
  1. Christianity and politics. I. Title.
BR115.P7F673 2008
261.709—dc22

                                                                                    2008022659

| P | 21 | 20 | 19 | 18 | 17 | 16 | 15 | 14 | 13 | 12 | 11 | 10 | 9 | 8 | 7 | 6 | 5 | 4 | 3 | 2 | 1 |

| Y | 26 | 25 | 24 | 23 | 22 | 21 | 20 | 19 | 18 | 17 | 16 | 15 | 14 | 13 | 12 | 11 | 10 | 09 | 08 |

This book is dedicated to

Anya Katerina Forster

with hope that you will one day

live in a just world

Certainly we do not want men to allow their Christianity to flow over into their political life, for the establishment of anything like a really just society would be a major disaster. On the other hand we do want, and want very much, to make men treat Christianity as a means; preferably, of course, as a means to their own advancement, but, failing that, as a means to anything—even to social justice. The thing to do is to get a man at first to value social justice as a thing which the Enemy demands, and then work him onto the stage at which he values Christianity because it may produce social justice. For the Enemy will not be used as a convenience. Men or nations who think they can receive the Faith in order to make a good society might just as well think they can use the stairs of Heaven as a shortcut to the nearest chemist's shop. Fortunately it is quite easy to coax humans around this little corner. Only today I have found a passage in a Christian writer where he recommends his own version of Christianity on the ground that "only such a faith can outlast the death of old cultures and the birth of new civilizations." You see the little rift? "Believe this, not because it is true, but for some other reason." That's the game.

His Abysmal Sublimity, the demon Screwtape
Undersecretary for Temptation, English Sector
via C. S. Lewis, in *The Screwtape Letters*

CONTENTS

Acknowledgments 11

Introduction 13

1   WELCOME BACK TO BABYLON
    How Persecution Permanently Shaped
    Christian Political Ideas 19

2   THE WISDOM OF THE GODS
    Theology Encounters Philosophy. 43

3   CITIES OF GOD AND MAN
    Augustine Formalizes the Idea of Dual Citizenship 62

4   NATURAL LAW
    The Medieval Church Develops the Most Important
    Political Idea in History 84

5   *REGIO* VERSUS *RELIGIO*
    The Reformation and the Nation-State. 107

6   ON THE ROAD TO JERUSALEM
    The Emergence of Religious Freedom 142

7   AN APPEAL TO HEAVEN
    Revolution and Liberal Democracy. 172

8   THE FIERY TRIAL
    Christian Responses to Totalitarianism 209

Conclusion 243

Index 250

ACKNOWLEDGMENTS

I CAN HARDLY BEGIN TO THANK ALL THE PEOPLE to whom I am indebted. What follows is only a down payment; perhaps in eternity there will be an opportunity to compile a complete list.

InterVarsity Press took a chance on a young and unestablished author who sent them, unsolicited, a very ambitious book proposal. My editor, Gary Deddo, and everyone else at InterVarsity Press has been a blessing to work with.

Many people read drafts of this book, or portions of it, and offered their critiques. Their help has improved the book immeasurably; all remaining faults are of course my own responsibility. Special thanks go to Caroline Stack, Stan Hoke, and two anonymous reviewers for InterVarsity Press, each of whom gave me detailed suggestions on the entire manuscript. Other readers include, in alphabetical order: Gary Deddo, Mark Graham, Pam Miller, Glenn Moots, Kim Ian Parker, Stephen Phillips, John Seaman, Paul Sigmund and Larry Wilson.

Glenn Moots has generously extended to myself and many others the benefits of his networking talent. His ability to connect scholars with similar interests who are well situated to help one another has been a tremendous blessing to this book and to the field of political theory.

The book was substantially easier to write because from 2003 to 2005 I taught adult Sunday school classes, mostly on Christianity and politics, at Coral Ridge Presbyterian Church in Ft. Lauderdale, Florida. The church gave me extensive freedom to design my own courses and, as a result, my class notes provided a foundation for the book that I ultimately wanted to write. Adding grace to grace, my next church home, Christ Covenant Orthodox Presbyterian Church in Indianapolis, Indiana, allowed me to teach a Sunday school class on Augustine.

Kyle Bode of the Kern Family Foundation compiled the index to this book, and the Foundation will be supporting my work, starting shortly before this book goes to press.

The Friedman Foundation for Educational Choice and my boss there, Robert Enlow, accommodated me as I wrote this book on my own time while also holding down a full-time job at the foundation.

Speaking of which, I owe thanks beyond expression to my wife Beth for putting up with this book for the last two and a half years. I had to do almost all the writing on evenings and weekends, even while we were raising a rambunctious toddler, and she supported me all the way. "An excellent wife who can find? She is far more precious than jewels" (Prov 31:10).

This book is dedicated to our daughter Anya, who was five months old when I sent the initial proposal to InterVarsity Press and will be turning three years old as the first copies go on sale. Her presence constantly reminded me, as I struggled to get this book written, why I had decided to take the job on in the first place. Sometimes it was hard to remember! And of course, to all my other family and friends: I couldn't have gotten here without you.

Above all, of course, I owe everything to God, from whom all blessings flow. "God is light, and in him is no darkness at all" (1 Jn 1:5). *Soli Deo Gloria.*

A WORD ABOUT SOURCES

All of the primary sources discussed in this book are available in multiple editions. Most are also available free on the Internet, if only in older translations. To provide compatibility across editions, I have cited standardized reference points (chapter numbers, section numbers, etc.) rather than page numbers from a specific edition. Secondary sources I have cited in the usual way.

I take seriously my scholarly responsibility to convey the ideas of my sources accurately. However, this includes the responsibility to convey those ideas clearly. I have therefore not scrupled to modernize the texts in such matters as spelling, punctuation and capitalization. In some of the older translations, I have also updated a few obsolete grammatical and linguistic practices.

InterVarsity Press has set up a website with links to online resources related to this book, including online editions of the primary sources. Direct your browser to <www.ivpress.com> and search for the title of this book.

INTRODUCTION

IN ITS PRESENT FORM, THIS BOOK IS AN INTRODUCTION to Christian political thought. However, it was originally going to be a completely different book. In 2002, as I finished the main writing for my first book and had to start thinking about what I would write next, I set out to write a book about the role of religion in the political thought of the American founders. As I saw it, most people held one of two views: either that the founders saw religion as dangerous and wanted to restrain it, like many in Continental Europe at the time, or that the founders wanted a government based on the Bible, like Calvin's Geneva or Winthrop's Boston. Though some facts support each of these descriptions, on the whole I thought that both of them were seriously misleading. I hoped to show that while all but a handful of the founders believed in Christianity and did not think it was dangerous, most of them wanted government to be based on God's "natural law" of justice, known by all people everywhere, rather than on the Bible. They thought that forcing people to obey the Bible against their wills was inconsistent with what the Bible itself said; their study of the Bible led them to conclude that God did not want them to enforce Christianity by law.

However, I ran into a problem. I found that I could not make a persuasive case for this interpretation of the founders unless my audience had a firm grasp of what the concept of natural law had come to mean for Christians in the late eighteenth century. So before I could explain the founders to my audience, I had to explain the serious changes that had occurred in Christian political thought during the seventeenth and eighteenth centuries. But I soon discovered that to explain those changes, I had to show how they grew out of the political thought of the Reformation and the rise of the nation-state in the sixteenth and seventeenth centuries. And then it dawned on me that those developments in turn made no sense unless we understand how natural-law thought had developed during the Middle Ages—which in turn required an understanding of how medieval political thought had itself been fundamentally shaped by Christianity's tumultuous encounter with classical Greco-Roman political philosophy during its first five centuries. In other words, I could not explain Madison without explaining Locke; I could not explain Locke without explaining Luther; I could not explain Luther without explaining Aquinas; and I could not explain Aquinas without explaining Augustine, Peter, Paul, Aristotle and Plato.

The result of this intellectual train wreck is the book you now hold. This one covers such a broad scope of history—just shy of two and a half millennia in about 250 pages, or roughly a decade per page—that the original subject of the American founding is now only a marginal part of it. I am content with that; since I first set out to write that other book, some new and quite good historical scholarship has made great strides toward setting the record straight about the American founders' political thought. And in any case I am now convinced that this, a general introduction to the history of Christian political thought, is the book that really needed to be written. However good the scholarship on the founders or any other Western political figures may be, it cannot effectively correct popular misunderstandings so long as the larger context of the development of Christian political thought is neglected. Without that essential background, there is not much hope for a clear understanding of any subject in the foreground.

Knowing the history of Christian political thought is not only important to interpreting historical figures like the founders but also to understanding where our civilization stands now and how we got here. If you were to wake up in an unfamiliar location, not knowing how you got there, you could find out where you were by asking around or by looking at a map. In human history, however, there are no maps and no bystanders to help us. The only way to make sense of where we are now is to know the path we took to get here.

To see why the broad historical context is so crucial to understanding political ideas, it is helpful to look at how the same problem arises from neglecting the history of theology. The church's ideas about God did not just fall out of the sky fully formed in the first century; they underwent a historical process of development. For example, there is good evidence that Christians were already confessing the divinity of Christ not long after his death, but these confessions were extremely simple—not much more than "Jesus is God." It took centuries for theologians to work out the detailed implications of this idea. The complex and highly developed doctrine of the incarnation that we find in the Nicene and Athanasian Creeds ("although he is God and man, yet he is not two, but one Christ; one, not by conversion of the godhead into flesh, but by taking of the manhood into God; one altogether, not by confusion of substance, but by unity of person," etc.) was the result of a long, painstaking historical process of reasoning and argument among theologians. Even after these creeds were formulated, there were still many important issues that remained to be resolved by later theologians (e.g., that the one Christ has two natures, a human nature and a divine nature). Similar historical processes took place for virtually every other aspect of theology, such as the church's consideration of which manuscripts were of authentic apostolic origin and should be included in the canon of Scripture.

Unfortunately, popular ignorance of this historical process leads to all kinds of confusion and misunderstandings and facilitates the spread of inaccurate historical assertions. Examples of this include the claim that Christians did not confess the divinity of Christ until that doctrine was imposed by Emperor Constantine for political reasons in the fourth century, or that priests in the early church distorted or manipulated the texts of the Bible for their own purposes. In the absence of firm background knowledge of the real history of theology, these propositions sound plausible to many people, but a serious consideration of all the available evidence decisively compels us to reject them.

The same principle applies to the history of Christian political ideas. Just as it took many years for Christians to work out the detailed implications of their theology, there has been a similar process of historical development in Christian political thinking. The understanding of a concept like natural law was different in the fifth, thirteenth, sixteenth, eighteenth and twentieth centuries, as Christian thinkers responded to changing circumstances and worked out the consequences of their ideas in greater detail. Where people do not know the context of that historical development, it is easy to misinterpret the political ideas of historical figures like the American founders.

Political thought is also called political theory, and any introduction to it must begin with a justification of theory itself. Many people dismiss formal theorizing as unimportant for practical matters, or they fear that it will shackle us to rigid ideologies. In defense of theorizing, theologian R. C. Sproul likes to say that "behind every practice, there is a theory." He means that in every area of life, our behavior is always shaped by our understanding of the way things work, even when we do not realize it. When I am hungry and I reach for the potato chips, I may not consciously think, "Eating food relieves hunger," but nonetheless that theory is unconsciously guiding my actions. There is always some theory guiding our behavior, so if we do not consciously develop a rigorous and well-tested theory, we will just end up unconsciously following a sloppy and unproved one. Perhaps if I had spent more time theorizing about my eating habits, I would have developed a more sophisticated set of principles to guide my eating and bought a less-fattening snack on my last grocery trip. There is no avoiding theory; if we do not have good theory, we will have bad theory.

Political thought is the theory that stands behind the practice of politics. Its goal is to develop better principles of action for our political life. While political thought is not the only factor that shapes the real world of politics, it is one of the most important factors. Political thought alone could not have won American independence from Britain; it also took lots of blood, sweat and tears willingly sacrificed to the cause. But the Continental Congress could never have persuaded the people of the thirteen colonies to make those sacrifices if it had not offered a convincing political theory to justify the revolution. And after independence was won, the radical American experiment in representative democracy and individual liberty was made a success as much by the ingenious political thought of Madison as it was by the personal magnetism of Washington and the practical political savvy of Jefferson and Hamilton.

Christian political thought is far too enormous a subject for one book to cover completely; this book is only an introduction. Like any introduction to a subject, it has to leave out a lot of information because there is just no room to cram it all in. I have done my best to focus on the areas that will be the most relevant and enlightening for the contemporary reader.

For example, I have left out a great deal of political thought from the ancient and medieval periods that is less relevant for us today so that I would have more space to cover the ideas from these periods that have a larger continuing impact. Augustine devoted long sections of *The City of God* to refuting the moral and social philosophies of important Roman thinkers like Varro, Plotinus and Porphyry; Aquinas and Ockham deliberated at length on the constitutional role of the pope in the Holy Roman Empire; fully half of Locke's *Two Treatises of Government* is devoted to demolishing the absolute monarchism of Robert Filmer. These matters are important and deserve our attention; indeed, some of them deserve more attention than they are now receiving even from specialized scholars. But there is no place for them in a general introduction to Christian political thought. As a result, any book of this type must give an inadequate picture of the real mental lives of the thinkers it portrays. The best I can do about this is warn you: this book is only opening a door into a room. I hope that you will be interested in what you see, but you will not see everything in the room until you walk in for yourself.

Also, the focal point of my story is the political effects of the Reformation and the Enlightenment in Western Europe, for the simple reason that I am writing in English and those were the defining political events in the history of the English-speaking world. If I were writing a history of Christian political thought for Russian or Brazilian or Chinese readers, the focus would be different.

What this book does provide is the story of how we got to where we are now. It covers the most important of the various political ideas we have tried in the past; it shows the reasons we took the paths we did rather than pursuing other possibilities. I have also tried to convey a sense of why I find it such a thrilling story. It is full of dramatic twists, exciting hopes, bitter disappointments and glorious triumphs—and this is true regardless of which characters you think are the heroes and which the villains. The story is all the more gripping because it is our story, and we still have a chance to help write the ending.

1

WELCOME BACK TO BABYLON

HOW PERSECUTION PERMANENTLY
SHAPED CHRISTIAN POLITICAL IDEAS

Bless those who persecute you;
bless and do not curse them. . . .
Let every person be subject to
the governing authorities.

PAUL, IN THE EPISTLE
TO THE ROMANS

AT THE BEGINNING OF THE BOOK OF REVELATION, the resur-
rected Christ instructs John the apostle to convey messages to seven local
churches in Asia Minor. One of them was the church in Smyrna, an important center of trade in the region. Christ's message for the Christians
in Smyrna was a warning: they were going to face severe persecution. "Do
not fear what you are about to suffer," Christ told them. "Be faithful unto
death, and I will give you the crown of life" (Rev 2:10).

In approximately A.D. 155, an eighty-six-year-old man was dragged into
an arena in Smyrna before an angry mob. He was Polycarp, bishop of the
church in Smyrna and one of the most important Christian leaders alive

at the time. He had apparently been a disciple of John the apostle and was considered the church's strongest remaining link to the apostles. Christians relied on Polycarp as a trustworthy judge of which teachings were consistent with Christ's message and which were not, making him a crucial figure in a time when Christians were still struggling to understand the revelations that had been delivered to them in the previous century. He was also a key opponent of the fraudulent gospels being promoted by Gnostic polytheists.

As Polycarp stood and ignored the jeers of the crowd, the Roman proconsul warned him that he would be executed if he did not repudiate Christ and make a sacrifice to the emperor. Under Roman law, Christianity was considered a form of atheism because it refused to acknowledge the divinity of the emperor, so the standard formula for repudiating Christianity in court was to say, "Away with the atheists!" The crowd demanded Polycarp's death, but the proconsul expressed reluctance to execute a man whose advanced age ought to entitle him to respect. He repeatedly implored Polycarp to say the required phrase, "Away with the atheists!"

Polycarp was more than willing to oblige. He pointed to the crowd and said, "Away with the atheists!"

So they tied him up and burned him alive.

Discussions of the history of Christianity and politics often begin with the events of the fourth century A.D., when the persecution of Christians was brought to an end, the church became increasingly influential, and eventually the Roman Empire adopted Christianity as its official state religion. But the story does not begin there. By the time the empire was converted, Christianity had already developed an understanding of the purpose of civil government and its relationship to the church. This understanding of politics continued to serve as the foundation of Christian political thought well after the empire's conversion. Telling the story of Christianity and politics from the fourth century onward is like telling the story of Romeo and Juliet without ever mentioning the feud between the Montagues and the Capulets: the plot makes no sense if we leave out the backstory.

The earliest and most fundamental influence on Christian political thought was its experience of persecution during its first three centuries.

The books of the New Testament mention politics almost exclusively in connection with political persecution. In the four Gospels, we find Jesus responding to the Roman persecution of the Jews; in the book of Acts and the apostolic epistles, we find the apostles responding to the persecution of Christians. Both Jews and Christians were oppressed by Rome during this period for their refusal to acknowledge the divinity of the emperor. Rome's persecution of Judaism was significantly more severe than its persecution of Christianity. Rome had political conflicts as well as religious conflicts with Judaism, but the conflict with Christianity was solely over religion, so the suppression of Christianity was a less urgent priority. On the other hand, in addition to suffering Roman persecution, Christians were also persecuted by the Jewish authorities as heretics and blasphemers. They were cast out by society, and then they were cast out by their fellow outcasts.

This double persecution had left first-century Christians with no refuge. They had no institutions of their own, as the Jews did, to help them stand against the emperor. If they wanted an institution, they were going to have to build it themselves: in the New Testament we find the apostles giving Christians their marching orders to get busy and build it. By the time the empire was converted three centuries later, the Christian church was not only fully built; it also was thriving beyond even the most hopeful first-century expectations. Persecution was certainly not the only reason Christians built the church. It is not even the most important reason they built the church. But it is one of the reasons they did, and it had a profound influence on both the structure and the doctrine of the church they built.

Because the Christian church was built under these unique conditions, it is a religious institution unlike any that has ever existed. One of the ways in which the early persecution of Christianity made the church unique was in shaping Christianity's understanding of the church's relationship to political institutions. This unique understanding of the church-state relationship did not simply vanish when the persecution of Christianity stopped; by that time it had long since been hard-wired into the intellectual and institutional life of the church. To this day the church remains an institution designed to serve a politically persecuted religion.

Politics in the Old Testament

The Old Testament, considered as a whole, is the story of how God saves and preserves a chosen people for himself after the great catastrophe of the Fall of humanity: protecting his chosen people from destruction, chastising them for their disobedience and promising them that in due time one of their own descendents would fulfill their salvation by permanently reconciling them with God. As part of his providential care for his people, God guides them through a series of political situations. These situations change over time as God provides for his people's changing needs and fulfills his plans for them: tribal patriarchy from Adam to Joseph, exile in Egypt from Joseph to Moses, the rule of "judges" before the monarchy, the united monarchy from Saul to Solomon, the divided monarchy after Solomon, the Babylonian exile and finally the restoration of at least some autonomy through the return from Babylon to Jerusalem.

The common thread running through all these political conditions was their connection to the ethnic nation of Israel. Though those who were not physically descended from Abraham could become part of God's visible people, they could do so only by formally joining the nation of the Jews. They could not visibly and outwardly be people of God while also remaining members of some other nation. Because of this, all aspects of social life for those who followed God—including their political systems—were subordinate to, and dependent upon, the

existence of the distinct Jewish nation.

This changes in the New Testament, where God allows people to be visibly and outwardly people of God without joining a particular nation. As part of this extension of God's visible people to all nations, the New Testament no longer requires believers to obey the special political and ceremonial laws of the Old Testament (see esp. Eph 2:14-15). Christians are no more obliged to live under the Davidic monarchy or the Mosaic legal code than they are required to abstain from pork or circumcise their sons, and for the same reason—because God no longer requires people to belong to a distinct political nation in order to be God's distinct people.

However, this is not to say that the Old Testament has no influence over Christian political thought. Although the specific political and legal ordinances given to God's people before Christ are no longer considered binding, the general worldview of the apostles and the early Christians was defined by the Old Testament. One particularly important influence of the Old Testament on Christian politics is the principle that government authority cannot be absolute or unlimited because all things are subordinate to God; rulers have duties as well as rights. In Jeremiah 18:1-11 God tells Jeremiah that his power over nations and kingdoms is as absolute as the potter's power over the clay. Psalm 2 warns that God's anointed one will be given the whole earth for his possession, so kings must "serve the LORD with fear" or fall under divine wrath. Christians have always disagreed about what it means for government to "serve the LORD" in the context of the New Testament era, where political and religious authority are not interdependent as they were in the Old Testament. However, the Old Testament teaching that all things are subordinate to God is one of the underlying foundations of Christian political thought.

WHAT IS THE CHURCH?

Christianity's unique conception of the relationship between religious and political institutions begins with its unique conception of what its religious institution is. When responding to the claim that all religions believe essentially the same thing, Christian apologists often stress that Christianity is the only major religion whose founder claimed to be divine.[1] Something similar could be said about the uniqueness of the Christian view of the church. People today speak of churches, synagogues, mosques and other religious institutions as though they were all the same kind of thing. This is true on a superficial level in that they are all religious institutions, just as there is a superficial similarity between the teachings of Christianity and the teachings of other religions because they are all religious teachings. But just as Christianity's beliefs about its founder are fundamentally different from other religions' beliefs about their founders, Christianity's view of the church is fundamentally different from anything found in other religions.

Christianity claims that the church is more than just a social organization in which people with similar beliefs engage in religious activities. It even claims that the church is more than just a sacred institution created by God to administer the rules and rituals he has ordained for his people. Christians would surely agree that the church does fit both these descrip-

---

[1]C. S. Lewis writes: "There is no parallel in other religions. If you had gone to Buddha and asked, 'Are you the son of Bramah?' he would have said, 'My son, you are still in the vale of illusion.' If you had gone to Socrates and asked, 'Are you Zeus?' he would have laughed at you. If you had gone to Mohammed and asked, 'Are you Allah?' he would first have rent his clothes and then cut your head off. If you had asked Confucius, 'Are you Heaven?' I think he would probably have replied, 'Remarks which are not in accordance with nature are in bad taste'"; from "What Are We to Make of Jesus Christ?" in *The Collected Works of C. S. Lewis* (New York: Inspirational Press, 1996), p. 406.

tions, but this alone would not make the Christian understanding of the church any different from what many other religions claim for their religious institutions.

What sets the Christian idea of the church apart is the idea that the church is eternal. For Christians, the church does not exist simply to engage in certain activities, impose certain rules and provide certain services; nor is it merely a conduit through which believers can commune with God while they are separated from him in this world. On either of these views, the church would no longer be needed once believers are directly reunited with God after death. A dead man would no longer need the church, and once all people had died, the church would cease to exist. But according to Christians, the church is the everlasting temple within which God will live with his people forever. "We are the temple of the living God," Paul wrote to the church in Corinth (2 Cor 6:14-18). In the heavenly life, individuals will not have their own separate relationships with God, with each person's relationship standing apart from everyone else's and independent of any social organization. The whole of redeemed humanity will come together to form a single social structure, just as stones came together to form the temple of the Old Testament, and the heavenly life will be lived only in this composite social structure. "You are no longer strangers and aliens," Paul wrote to the church in Ephesus, "but you are fellow citizens with the saints and members of the household of God, built on the foundation of the apostles and prophets, Christ Jesus himself being the cornerstone, in whom the whole structure, being joined together, grows into a holy temple in the Lord. In him you also are being built together into a dwelling place for God by the Spirit" (Eph 2:19-22). The distinctness of individuals will be preserved, but at its core the redeemed life of those individuals will be social rather than solitary.

This idea of the church as an eternal institution is less noticed than it should be. One reason is that people sometimes associate it exclusively with Roman Catholic and Eastern Orthodox theology. But Protestantism has historically confessed the idea of the eternal church just as much as every other part of Christendom. Protestants' disagreements with Roman Catholic and Eastern Orthodox ideas of the church have to do with the way the eternal church should be organized during its temporary residence here in the fallen world, especially the way it should be institutionally structured and the kind of authority it can rightfully exercise. That the church is a single, eternal institution established by God to serve as the everlasting vessel of humanity's redeemed life is not in dispute. All branches of Christianity agree that the church is an eternal institution and that its worldly organization should reflect its eternal qualities. What they disagree over is what kind of worldly organization rightly reflects those qualities. These disagreements are very important, but on the question of whether the church is eternal, as distinct from questions about the social and institutional implications of its eternality, all the major branches of Christianity are in agreement.

The Christian claim that the church is eternal ought to be as shocking to us as the Christian claim that God became a human being. The idea that individuals will not each have their own independent lives with God in eternity—that eternal life means life as a member of an eternal social institution—is just as alien to our natural religious expectations as the notion of God becoming a helpless infant, nursing from his mother and soiling his diaper just like any other baby. It is no wonder that there is nothing like the Christian view of the church in any other religion, just as there is no parallel to the incarnation. It is an idea that cuts against the grain of everything we naturally want to believe about our relationship with God.

What Is the State?

The equally shocking implication of this idea is that the church is radically more important than the state. In the political thought of other religions, religious institutions are almost always less important than political institutions. Wherever both religious and political institutions are seen as worldly rather than eternal, the civil government takes precedence because it obviously has a larger degree of worldly importance. Religious and political institutions are sometimes treated as equally important in cases where they are closely identified or interdependent, such as in theocratic systems. However, no other religion makes religious institutions radically *more* important than political ones, as Christianity makes the eternal church radically more important than the merely temporal state.

That the apostles view the state as relatively unimportant compared to the church is clear enough, not only from the way they talk about it (see sidebars) but, more importantly, also from the way they do not talk about it. Surprisingly, the New Testament contains almost no discussion of politics. It goes on for pages and pages about the church, but about the state it says virtually nothing. Almost the only political teaching it provides is that a person's ordinary political duties (behaving peacefully, obeying the law, paying taxes, etc.) continue to apply when rulers deny God and persecute believers. The apostles were speaking narrowly to a single political issue—whether Christian subjects must obey rulers who deny and even persecute Christianity—rather than offering a broad teaching about politics in general. The New Testament offers nothing that can even remotely be called a general theory or philosophy of politics.

The apostles even seem to bend over backward to avoid taking political positions where we would expect them to do so. They offer no guidance on what kind of political system is best. When they require Christians to obey and even "honor" the Roman emperor, one might expect them to provide some comment one way or the other on the desirability of dictatorship as a form of government, but they neither endorse it nor condemn it (1 Pet 2:17; see also 1 Tim 1:12–2:7). They also take no position on other political and economic institutions. For example, they require Christians who are slaves to obey their masters, but they neither endorse nor condemn slavery as such (See Eph 6:5-9; Col 3:22-25; 1 Tim 6:1-2; Tit 2:9-10). The command for slaves to obey masters is no more an endorsement of slavery than the command to obey the emperor is an endorsement of dictatorship; the basis of both commands is precisely the apostles' refusal to use their authority to interfere with political and economic institutions by taking a position one way or the other on these questions. Their guiding principle is not that slavery or dictatorship is good, but that converting to Christianity does not change one's legal status. If you were the emperor's subject before you came to Christ, you are still his subject afterward; if you were a slave before, you remain one. The question of whether dictatorship or slavery is a good thing is simply not raised.

The New Testament's almost total refusal to engage with politics except on one narrow issue (obedience to rulers who persecute Christianity) is a great frustration for Christians. They naturally desire God's guidance for their political lives, just as they desire his guidance in all other matters. The political ordinances laid down in the Old Testament were applicable only to ancient Israel; the apostles declared that believers in the era of the new covenant need not obey the political and ceremonial laws of the old covenant (see Eph 2:11-22, esp. vv. 14-15; also Gal 2:11–5:12). The New Testament's silence on politics combined with the apostles' setting aside the political order of the Old Testament leaves the faithful with no revelatory instruction as to how their political affairs are to be ordered.

In cases like dictatorship and slavery, the Christian's frustration at having no revealed guidance for shaping the political order intensifies into a deep sense of disappointment. The Christian heart cries out, "Why did you not speak, Lord, and condemn these wicked institutions?"

However, we must bear in mind that the Bible was not written for political purposes, nor was it written to answer all our questions about all subjects. If anything is clear about the intentions of the biblical authors regarding the purpose of their work, it is clear that they did not intend for Scripture to settle all or even most of the questions that human beings ask. Every theologian knows that there are plenty of questions about God—and not just trivial ones but gravely important ones—to which the Bible simply does not provide answers. And if the biblical authors did not intend to settle all theological questions, still less did they intend to settle all questions about human affairs such as politics. The New Testament's silence about politics is in keeping with the broader silence of the Bible on all kinds of questions that people naturally want and expect the Bible to address. The biblical authors indicate that they intend to tell the faithful what they need to know, not necessarily all that they want to know.

But, someone might object, is not the right way to conduct politics something that we really need to know, not just something we want to know? This is a fair question, and to answer it we must introduce a little more theological history.

Most Christian theologians have drawn a distinction between *general revelation* and *special revelation*. General revelation includes the knowledge that God has provided to everyone through reason and conscience; special revelation includes the additional information that God has revealed to some but not others, especially in the Bible. Though this distinction was not formally and explicitly drawn in the apostolic era, it was not long before Christian thinkers started drawing it; as we will see in chapter three, in the early fifth century, Augustine was already taking the distinction for granted.[2] Theologians drew this distinction because they concluded that it was implicit in the apostles' teachings, especially in the first two chapters of the epistle to the Romans.

The distinction between general and special revelation should not be oversimplified. They are not ultimately independent; God is the source of both. Nor do they provide the basis for two distinct spheres of knowledge; there is not one "rational" truth and another, distinct "revealed" truth. Christianity holds that there is only one truth, that all truth is rational (that is, it is not contradictory or illogical), and that all of it is divinely revealed. Only the mode of revelation differs. Nor do general and special revelation apply separately to separate spheres of life: both apply equally to all of life. Nor is special revelation obligatory only for those who choose to accept it: if God speaks, everyone has an obligation to hear him.

This distinction also gives rise to some difficult problems that Christian thinkers have always struggled with. Mapping out what we can know from general revelation is difficult. Moreover, the two are never as distinct in practice as they are in theory. Those who accept both will interpret what they learn from general revelation in light of what they know from special revelation, and vice versa. These and other problems lead some thinkers to prefer conceiving of a continuum between general and special revelation, rather than a simple dichotomy between the two, or even abandoning the terminology of general revelation and special revelation altogether. But thankfully this book need not tread into such deep waters; for our limited purposes, we need only draw a simple distinction between the things the Bible says and the things we can know even though the Bible does not say them.[3]

---

[2]In *The City of God* 19.1, the book that contains the bulk of that work's political thought, Augustine casually remarks that he will make his case "not merely by appealing to divine authority, but also by employing such powers of reason as we can apply for the benefit of unbelievers." I rely on Henry Bettenson's translation (New York: Penguin, 1984). For online resources see <www.ivpress.com>.
[3]The case for a clear distinction between general and special revelation has always seemed to me to be extremely strong. We cannot receive revelation that comes to us through the senses until we

Knowing right from wrong is one of the main things Christian theology has historically attributed to general revelation rather than to special revelation. So while it is certainly true that knowing right from wrong in political matters is something we need to know, not just something we want to know, the traditional response is that we already do know it—or at least we already posses all the faculties we need to provide a basis for figuring it out.

When confronting the problem of figuring out what is right and wrong in politics, it is worthwhile to step back and look at how the Bible treats right and wrong generally. The Bible does not at any point present a philosophical argument that there is such a thing as right and wrong, for the benefit of readers who may be ignorant of this fact. Rather, the Bible consistently assumes that the reader is already aware of right and wrong without needing the Bible to establish that distinction. This is one reason Christianity developed the concept of general revelation in the first place; a distinct mode of revelation was needed to explain how people could know right and wrong without having been told about them. Paul was making precisely this point when he wrote the remarks in his epistle to the Romans that have formed the basis of the Christian doctrine of general revelation: God is just in requiring everyone to obey the moral law because he has made it known to everyone by reason and conscience (see Rom 1–2).

It appears that the authors of the New Testament thought about politics in the same way. This is not to say that the apostles say nothing about politics; they do make it clear that government should enforce

---

first have a capacity to perceive truth, and we cannot have a capacity to perceive truth without already possessing some knowledge of truth. (This is the subject of some of Augustine's profoundest reflections in the *Confessions*.) We could not recognize truth as true unless we came to it already possessing a standard of truth. If, for example, we did not already know that two contradictory statements cannot both be true, we could never learn this from experience, because we cannot learn anything at all without first assuming that two contradictory statements cannot both be true. We could not read the Bible if we did not come to it already possessing the knowledge and the mental faculties necessary to understand language. A person who truly knew nothing would be unable to learn anything; he would have no way to interpret and assimilate new input. Therefore there must be some truth that we do not receive through the senses; if we are to know any truth at all, some truth must come hard-wired into our very nature as human beings. We do not "receive" this truth; we always already know it. This does not mean that it does not come from God, but it comes from him in another mode. It is revelation, but revelation that God provides in human nature itself rather than through the medium of the senses. This is why general revelation is sometimes called "natural revelation."

justice. Peter writes that government's job is "to punish those who do evil and to praise those who do good" (1 Pet 2:14). Paul says government is "an avenger who carries out God's wrath on the wrongdoer" (Rom 13:4). But although they affirm that government should enforce justice, they provide little or no guidance as to exactly what social rules are required to enforce it. They seem to be assuming that the reader already knows all about the rules of justice, and only needs to be exhorted to follow them faithfully. Readers are left to discover political right and wrong the same way they discover other kinds of right and wrong: from general revelation.

So Christianity does include divine guidance for politics, just not the kind of guidance we might expect. "God already gave you reason and conscience: go and use them!" is the implicit political theory of the New Testament.

All attempts to find a broader political theory in the Bible are cases of eisegesis (bringing a preferred theory to the text and interpreting the words in whatever way makes them endorse the preferred theory) rather than exegesis (allowing the text to determine our interpretation of its meaning). The dangers of eisegesis are familiar to anyone who has studied the history of biblical interpretation; countless errors and absurdities have resulted from people's determination to find in the text of the Bible a teaching that they are sure it must contain. All the various views claiming that the Bible endorses a particular form of government fall into this category. Over the past two thousand years, various people have claimed the Bible's endorsement for aristocracy and for democracy, for capitalism and for socialism, for one-man rule and for separation of powers, for compulsory religious uniformity and for total religious freedom, and for countless other contradictory political systems and principles. In some times and places these theories have achieved great power and influence. Yet none of them has stood the test of time: not one of them has achieved a lasting place in the history of Christian political thought. Later generations of Christians, looking back on these ideas from the perspective of different historical situations, have not judged them to be worth emulating.

This is not to say that the Bible provides absolutely no specifics about justice that are relevant to politics. The Bible forbids theft, so a political system based on outright theft would be inconsistent with the Bible. Numerous other specific examples of this kind could be listed.

However, all of the Bible's specific ethical injunctions do not add up to a general theory of politics, just as the items on a grocery list do not add up to a general theory of nutrition. The Bible forbids theft but does not, for example, endorse capitalism over socialism. Even if we happen to think that capitalism does a better job of protecting private property than socialism, the biblical text does not justify claiming that the Bible endorses capitalism. Such broad, complex questions simply do not receive a general treatment anywhere in the Bible.

The only explicit political program in the New Testament, if it can be called that, is to reaffirm the foundational purposes of government that all civilized societies have always recognized: to keep the peace, enforce justice, preserve the community and its members, and so forth. If anything in the New Testament can be called a political innovation, it is the explicit endorsement of the Christian God for these long-recognized foundations of politics, along with the claim that the moral laws that government enforces—do not kill, do not steal, and so forth—ultimately come from God, so the government's authority is ultimately derived from God's authority. "There is no authority except from God," Paul writes to the church in Rome, "and those that exist have been instituted by God. Therefore whoever resists the authorities resists what God has appointed, and those who resist will incur judgment" (Rom 13:1-2). Likewise, Peter declares that government is "sent by him," meaning God (1 Pet 2:14). This claim has certainly provided later Christian thinkers with a great deal of food for thought, but we cannot call it a political theory in its own right; it amounts to no more than this: when government is doing its proper job, keeping peace and enforcing justice, it is doing God's work. The New Testament does not raise questions such as how this work ought to be carried out and what kind of government is best for doing it.

This is why all the Christian political theories that have stood the test of time are ones claiming only that a given political system or policy is the best way to secure the proper purposes of government, not that the text of the Bible actually endorses that system or policy. This is the kind of

The Authority of Government

The most important discussion of political authority in the New Testament is Paul's letter to the Romans. The first five verses of Romans 13 contain the key teaching:

> Let every person be subject to the governing authorities. For there is no authority except from God, and those that exist have been instituted by God. Therefore whoever resists the authorities resists what God has appointed, and those who resist will incur judgment. For rulers are not a terror to good conduct, but to bad. Would you have no fear of the one who is in authority? Then do what is good, and you will receive his approval, for he is God's servant for your good. But if you do wrong, be afraid, for he does not bear the sword in vain. For he is the servant of God, an avenger who carries out God's wrath on the wrongdoer. Therefore one must be in subjection, not only to avoid God's wrath but also for the sake of conscience.

However, it is important to read these verses in the context of the entire passage, starting at least as far back as 12:14 and continuing at least to 13:10, in order to see what Paul's concerns and purposes were when he wrote those crucial verses. In Romans 12, Paul delivers a series of exhortations: verses 1-8 concern a Christian's proper attitude toward him- or herself, verses 9-13 concern Christians' proper behavior toward each other, and verses 14-21 concern their proper behavior toward the larger world. In the third section, Paul's top priority is to forbid vengeance: "Repay no one evil for evil. . . . Never avenge yourselves, but leave it to the wrath of God, for it is written, 'Vengeance is mine, I will repay, says the Lord.'" This provides crucial context for the command to obey the government in 13:1-5, where Paul calls government "an avenger who carries out God's wrath on the wrongdoer." God claims the exclusive right to avenge all evil (12:17-21); but at least in cases of injustice between individuals, he has delegated some of this authority to government (13:1-5). On this point see also Genesis 9:5-6.

This passage need not imply limitless obedience to anyone who happens to seize political power in any possible way. As we will see in later chapters, historically most Christian political thinkers have rejected that reading of the passage because it would imply that might makes right. In commanding obedience to government, Paul emphasizes three principles: government's authority is for the purpose of promoting justice (v. 3); government exists to serve the community (v. 4); and obedience to government is based on conscience (v. 5). Just how far these caveats can be stretched has always been deeply controversial, but at least Paul's command to obey government has usually been interpreted as applying only to governments that meet some standard of being lawfully or legitimately constituted. To express this view in another way, when Paul tells us to obey "government," he means government properly so called; he does not mean that if a gang of criminals assassinates the rightful rulers and starts calling themselves "the government," we would therefore have to obey them.

The minority of thinkers who argue that the Bible does command limitless obedience to anyone who seizes power often point to 1 Peter, in which the command to obey government (2:13-17) is presented just before a command for slaves to be subject to their masters, in which obedience is commanded "not only to the good and gentle but also to the unjust" (2:18-25). The minority view argues that since the two commands (obedience to government and obedience to masters) are parallel, the explicit command to obey "unjust" masters implies that the command to obey rulers includes unjust rulers. However, others read the passage in the opposite way: obedience is explicitly extended to unjust masters but not explicitly to unjust rulers; therefore it is due to unjust masters but not necessarily to unjust rulers. The very nature of a master/slave relationship excludes the possibility of maintaining justice between master and slave, whereas historically most Christian thinkers have held that justice is precisely what the subject/ruler relationship is based on (a claim we will be reviewing in some detail in future chapters).

political thought that continues to be judged important and relevant even as historical circumstances come and go through the ages.

CHURCH AND STATE TURNED UPSIDE DOWN

Christianity believes that its religious institution (the church) is eternal and will survive intact after the destruction of the universe and the end of time itself; however, it believes that political institutions (the state) are merely temporal agencies that keep the peace and enforce justice in this world: they will vanish when this world does. Given this, it is no wonder that political and other worldly concerns have never been a central part of the meaning of human life for Christians. When a professional baseball player breaks his leg and is unable to play, he still spends more time thinking about baseball than he does thinking about his cast and crutches. He may be very thankful for the medical paraphernalia that allow him to get around while his leg heals, but he does not give them any more thought than he has to, and he will toss them aside the moment he is able. The game is what he cares about. For the Christian, the state is merely the cast and crutches that we lean on while we wait for the wound in our souls to be fully healed, so that we can get back into the game of divine joy in heaven.

Christianity's exclusion of politics and worldly things from the center of human life contrasts sharply with most other religions and thought systems. As we will see in chapter two, political life was the center of human fulfillment in the mythological worldview that preceded Christianity in the West. It was only in the shared life of the city that those seeking honor, strength, beauty, glory and similar values were able to accomplish their greatest achievements. For similar reasons, political and worldly things have continued to stand at the center of human life for most civilizations. And those who do not share this worldly orientation have still generally counted politics as one of their central concerns. First-century Judaism, although more rigorously moral and otherworldly than the mythological culture around it, still expected the coming Messiah to be a worldly king who would liberate the Jews from Roman rule. Even the philosophers, with their emphasis on living for personal wisdom and goodness, often felt compelled to acknowledge a central role for politics in the philosophic life. Aristotle and Confucius both saw the political community as the fulfillment of a moral design in human nature, so politics ought to be the highest activity of human life— or at least it would be in a well-ordered society made up of morally good people, if such a thing ever really existed. Of all non-Christian systems of thought, only the most severely world-negating, such as the Stoics of ancient Rome or the stricter forms of Buddhism, have managed to keep politics out of the center of human life as completely as Christianity has.

This certainly is not to say that Christian societies have always practiced what they preached. Christian societies have regularly succumbed to the temptation to value the worldly over the spiritual. But in principle if not always in practice, Christianity's commitment to the vast superiority of the things of the spirit over the things of the world has nonetheless shaped the political history of Christian societies in important ways.

The impact of these conceptions of church and state on Christian politics has not been what one might have expected it to be. The view that the church is eternal and the state merely temporal would seem to suggest theocracy: that the church should control the state. If the church is God's eternal temple and the state is merely a temporary apparatus for keeping justice and peace in the fallen world, the conclusion that the state should bow to the church would seem to follow naturally.

But once again the New Testament defies our expectations. Far from endorsing theocracy, the apostles insist that all Christians—which is to say, the church—rightly owe their obedience to the state, even a state that persecutes Christians. They do not just say that Christians must obey a non-Christian emperor for the present because there are no feasible alternatives at the moment (as a matter of temporary strategy). Such a position would imply that theocracy could legitimately be established at a later time when the opportunity arose. On the contrary, the apostles describe the church's obedience to the state as a permanent duty always required by God's law. After declaring that government is instituted on God's authority, Paul draws the conclusion that "one must be in subjection, not only to avoid God's wrath but also for the sake of conscience" (Rom 13:5). The context makes clear that by "God's wrath," Paul means the punishment that the civil authorities would impose on rebels; he is saying that one should obey government not only to escape civil punishment ("to avoid God's wrath") but also because moral law requires it ("for the sake of conscience"). In his first epistle, Peter states that obedience to government is an integral part of living a morally good life, so that the obedience of Christians would refute those who claimed that Christianity was a danger to society: "This is the will of God, that by doing good you should put to silence the ignorance of foolish people" (1 Pet 2:15). Just as the apostles shocked us with their bizarre claim that the church is eternal, and disappointed us with their refusal to articulate a political theory, they also confound us by telling the infinitely more important church to obey the infinitely less important state.

The apostles surely do make it clear that the church's obedience to the state is limited by the higher duty to obey God. Luke recounts what Peter said when the apostles were ordered not to preach Jesus: "We must obey God rather than men" (see Acts 5:17-42). If the state orders the church to commit murder or worship an idol, the church must refuse to do that. This is an important principle, since Christians believe that God has given the church both the duty and the authority to preach the gospel, preserve the written word of God, conduct worship, administer the sacraments, maintain order in the church, provide services of mercy to those in need, and perform other ecclesiastical functions. If the state tries to interfere in the church's administration of these functions, the apostles clearly authorize the church to disobey.

But where the state's laws do not interfere with the things God has entrusted to the church or otherwise come into direct conflict with God's commands, the church must obey the state. As we have already seen, Peter and Paul both say that conscience demands such obedience. Peter does not elaborate the point, but Paul goes on to specify why good conscience demands obedience to the state: because this is necessary for the state to do its job. "Rulers are not a terror to good conduct, but to bad," he writes to the Romans. "Would you have no fear of the one who is in authority? Then do what is good, and you will receive his approval, for he is God's servant for your good" (Rom 13:3-4). He struck a similar note in his letter to Timothy, asking the church to pray for blessings upon the government "that we may lead a peaceful and quiet life, godly and dignified in every way" (see 1 Tim 2:1-4). While the church only requires cooperation from its own members to do its job, the state needs everyone's cooperation to do its job: the very nature of its function, to keep the peace and enforce justice, presupposes that all members of society must obey it.

In accordance with their general silence on broader political issues, the apostles leave two big questions unanswered: Why did God define the relations between the church and the state in this surprising way, calling on the church to obey the state even while indicating that the church is radically more important than the state? And if the church must submit to the state in worldly matters, must the state submit to the church in spiritual matters? These questions are even more complicated than they sound. In fact, for most of the rest of this book we will be looking at the various ways in which Christians in different periods of history have answered them. For now, the important thing to note is that the apostles themselves are not concerned with these questions. They say nothing about them—which is why Christians have struggled so hard with them and have come up with so many different answers to them, as we will be seeing for the rest of this book.

SOJOURNERS, EXILES AND AMBASSADORS

The immediate practical effect of the command to obey the state, as the apostles themselves affirmed, was that the church would have to endure the persecution of both the Roman Empire and the Jewish authorities. In his letter to the Romans, almost immediately before his command to obey the state, Paul declares: "Bless those who persecute you; bless and do not curse them" (Rom 12:14). Christians could not organize an armed resistance. They were called to glorify God by patiently enduring the hardships of persecution.

This command to obey rulers even when they persecute Christians is often troubling for modern Christians, many of whom have been raised to believe that rebellion against oppressive governments is a God-given right. The history of Christian thought on the legitimacy of revolution is a difficult subject; we will look at it more carefully in future chapters, especially in chapter seven. For now it is sufficient to say that since at least the fifth century most (though not all) Christian thinkers have made a distinction between lawfully constituted governments and unlawful usurpers and tyrants, who may call themselves "rulers" but are really just powerful criminals. As we will see, they justify this distinction on grounds that the failure to draw it leaves us with no difference between citizenship and slavery, two concepts that the Bible clearly treats as distinct, and ultimately implies that might makes right. Historically, the predominant position has been that Christians must obey lawfully constituted governments whenever such obedience does not directly conflict with God's express commands, but obedience is not due to usurpers and tyrants.

On the other hand, all we can say from the text of the New Testament itself is that the apostles clearly forbade rebellion in the particular time and place of ancient Rome. They command the church to submit to the Roman government. This must mean that policies like dictatorship, religious persecution, military aggression and so forth do not always justify rebellion. If Christians are going to draw a distinction between lawful governments and usurpers, it cannot be based simply on the presence of oppressive policies—and most Christian thinkers who support the right to rebellion have not in fact based it on that. In later chapters we will see what they do base it on.

Submission to Persecution

As the apostles lay the foundations of the church in their epistles, almost the only concern they show for politics is in their efforts to shape the church's response to persecution. For example, many Christians today diligently obey Paul's command in 1 Timothy 2:1-2 to pray for those in positions of authority, but few remember the context of this command. In the first chapter of 1 Timothy, Paul has reflected on how God showed grace to him even though "formerly I was a blasphemer, persecutor, and insolent opponent," and even "the foremost" of all sinners. Just after this reminder of how Paul once held a position of authority and used it to persecute the church, he instructs Christians to pray "for all people, for kings and all who are in high positions." Paul seems to be commanding Christians to pray for their rulers specifically out of concern that Christians may hate and resent their rulers for persecuting them. After reminding his readers that he himself was once a persecutor and God showed him unmerited favor rather than hate, Paul then exhorts Christians to pray for all people—*even* for their rulers.

Why did the apostles command the church to submit to persecution rather than resist? They did not provide a detailed analysis of the issue; they do not seem to have thought that much explanation was required. In the most explicit passage on this question, Romans 13:1-5, Paul writes that God has ordained government as the means to uphold justice in the community. This mandate can only be carried out if all members of society obey government, so Paul equates resistance to government with rejection of the divine ordinance from which government receives its authority.

Paul takes the same position for granted when writing to Timothy that submission to government is part of the general duty to live "a peaceful and quiet life, godly and dignified in every way," so that others will see the goodness of Christianity and be drawn to Christ (1 Tim 2:2). Peter also takes the same position for granted in his first epistle, where he writes that Christians should submit to government "that by doing good you should put to silence the ignorance of foolish people"—that is, silence those who would otherwise claim that Christians are bad citizens (1 Pet 2:15). In both cases, Peter and Paul see submission to government, and even to persecution, as a form of Christian witness through holy living. The church's obedience to government is a necessary element of its holiness.

As a result of the apostles' command, Christianity endured persecution for the first three centuries of its existence. The church was not only driven away from the state; it was also driven out of the political community altogether. Christianity was illegal; it could only be practiced surreptitiously, in secret and peaceful defiance of the law, following the command that we must ultimately obey God above all human authority while also obeying the command to submit to the state as far as possible. The intensity of the persecution varied over time: the ban was not always strictly enforced, and Christians were often able to live and worship more or less unmolested. But they were never allowed to profess their faith publicly as equal citizens. Even in times when the ban was not being strictly enforced, there were limits to how openly Christians were allowed to acknowledge themselves. And the enforcement of the ban was not always so relaxed: the possibility of a crackdown against their faith was constantly lurking in the background of Christian life.

This ostracism forced the early church to develop an apolitical sense of its own identity. Almost nothing political was included in the idea of what it meant to be a Christian. It was surely understood that a Christian should uphold peace and justice, do good to his or her neighbors, and so on. But becoming a Christian did not mean, for example, adopting a specific political ideology or supporting one political group or faction over another one.

On a deeper level, the specific activities of the Christian life, and above all the Christian church as an institution, were seen as distinct and set apart from the broader community. Though Christians did think that they should be active in the world and interact with it in a Christian way, they also thought that Christianity itself was something that God had set apart from that world. Even while advising Christians on how to live "among the Gentiles," Peter reminded them that they were "sojourners and exiles" (1 Pet 2:11-12). To put it another way, Christians were to live in the world, not because they were a natural part of that world, but because they were serving as representatives of another world. Paul tells the Corinthians that Christians are "ambassadors for Christ" who have been sent on a "ministry of reconciliation" to tell the world that "in Christ God was reconciling the world to himself" (see 2 Cor 5:11-21). This principle is where we get the old saying that Christians are supposed to be "in the world but not of the world" (see Jn 17:11, 16 KJV). Christians are *in* the world in order to bring *to* the world a message of reconciliation that comes from *beyond* the world.

Several centuries of development in this apolitical direction, driven by
the necessity of living under persecution, produced a church with an extremely strong conception of its own independence from government and
the political community at large. The writings that have survived from
the leaders of the church in the first few centuries after Christ are quite
similar to the New Testament in this regard: no general theory or philosophy of politics is evident and politics usually comes up only in connection
with the persecution of the church (even then the authors say little beyond
stressing that Christians must obey the law, pay their taxes and accept the
other normal obligations of subjects). For example, the Christian leader
Justin Martyr, who wrote extensively against the suppression of Christianity, makes a lengthy case that Christians are better citizens because they
are under a religious obligation to obey the law, honor the emperor, do
justice, keep peace with their neighbors, and so on.[4] This kind of analysis, tightly focused on the issues raised by the church's immediate situation, is as far into the realm of political thought as he and the other early
Christian leaders would go. And for all their emphasis on good Christian
citizenship, they speak of the church itself as something independent of
the political community; their conception of the church places it firmly
outside the realm of politics.

To get a sense of how significant this turn of events was, consider
how the church might have developed if either the Roman or Jewish
authorities had embraced Christianity rather than persecuting it. The
idea that the church's foundations could stand apart from the political
community might never even have occurred to Christians. After all, this
was not how things had been arranged in the Old Testament system. The
Levitical priesthood could not possibly have existed independent of the
broader Jewish political community. Why would things be any different now? The apostles' command for the church to obey the state in all
worldly matters could just as easily have been fulfilled in a society where
church and state continued to exist as interdependent parts of a larger
whole, rather than as distinct spheres of authority. If the Jewish rulers
had accepted Christianity, the interdependence of church and state that

---

[4]See Justin Martyr *First Apology* chaps. 12, 15-17. For online resources see <www.ivpress.com>.

prevailed during the Old Testament era could have simply continued in the New, even after the obligations of the Old Testament's ceremonial and judicial laws were lifted. Or if the Roman authorities had accepted Christianity in those earliest centuries, the same fusion of political and religious institutions that had once existed in Jerusalem could have been reproduced in Rome. That would probably have seemed like the only natural thing for Christians to do.

Instead, the persecution of Christianity, combined with the apostles' command to obey the state, led the church to develop an apolitical identity. It immediately became clear that there would be no reproducing the Old Testament system of political and religious institutions whose existence was subordinate to the larger social whole. After being violently driven out of the political community, the church had to either stand on its own or fall. And to stand on its own, it had to abandon the Old Testament social model and come to a new, apolitical understanding of its foundations and legitimacy.

But while the church was developing and strengthening a sense of its own independence from politics, its slow but steady growth in numbers was silently setting it on a collision course with the political world. In the third and fourth centuries, as the bulk of the Roman population embraced Christianity, the church gradually came out of the shadows of persecution and increasingly became a legitimate part of Roman life. As part of this process, the church played an increasingly significant role in Roman politics, culminating with its legalization in 313 and its establishment as the state church of the Roman Empire in 380.

If Rome had been converted to Christianity in the first or even the second century, the Old Testament model of church and state as interdependent parts of a larger social unity could simply have been transplanted to Rome. But coming as it did in the fourth century, the conversion of Rome brought about a major intellectual crisis for the church. Three hundred years of development under conditions of persecution had produced a church with a thoroughly—and irreversibly—apolitical understanding of its own existence and mission. This identity now had to be reconciled with the church's increasing entanglement with imperial power and Roman political affairs.

However, we must postpone our account of that crisis until chapter three. Before we examine it, we must first look at something else that happened to Christianity in the centuries before it was legalized: its encounter with the mythology and philosophy that had shaped the Roman world.

2

THE WISDOM OF THE GODS

THEOLOGY ENCOUNTERS PHILOSOPHY

Jews demand signs and Greeks seek wisdom,
but we preach Christ crucified.

PAUL, IN THE FIRST EPISTLE
TO THE CORINTHIANS

MORE THAN FOUR HUNDRED YEARS BEFORE the time of
Christ, an Athenian named Chaerephon set off on a pilgrimage to the
city of Delphi. Few modern Christians have heard of Chaerephon, but
Christian thinking has been fundamentally affected by the results of
Chaerephon's pilgrimage. Surprising as it may sound, Chaerephon's trip
to Delphi turned out to be as important to the history and development of
Christian thought as Paul's trip to Damascus.

A contemporary described Chaerephon as "bold," remarking that he
was "very impetuous in everything he did."[1] His behavior at Delphi was

---

[1]Plato *Apology of Socrates* 21a. In references to Plato's works, I cite the Stephanus numbers. I have
primarily relied on Benjamin Jowett's translation of the *Apology* (in *Dialogues of Plato*, rev. ed. [New

no exception. Delphi was the home of the famous Delphic oracle, the priestess of Apollo who was believed to predict the future and provide insight into mysteries. The oracle's knowledge was in very high demand, and pilgrimages to Delphi from all over the Greek world were common. When Chaerephon's turn came to question the oracle, he asked, "Is there anyone wiser than Socrates of Athens?" It was a bold question, because Socrates was not yet a philosopher. He was just another member of the Athenian working class, the son of a stonecutter. In fact, "bold" hardly begins to cover it. To travel all the way to the holiest city in Greece, stand before its most revered religious icon and suggest that some obscure Athenian laborer was wiser than all the world's leading lights—this was nothing short of outrageous.

The oracle's response was even more shocking. When asked whether anyone was wiser than Socrates, her answer was "no." That answer turned out to be the opening shot in a cultural civil war. Society's religious and political authorities were soon to be challenged by a new, rationalistic intellectual class that stood apart from them and criticized their beliefs. Before long this war would lead Athens to execute Socrates on charges of blasphemy and corrupting the youth; his trial took place on a sacred hill known as the Areopagus. But Socrates' disciples carried on, and their disciples did so after them. The civil war over Socrates was still raging when another famous blasphemer, Paul, stood on the very same Areopagus four hundred years later and proclaimed the gospel of Christ to the Athenians.

When Christianity first encountered philosophy, the two came into major conflict. The pre-Christian philosophers held some views that were flatly incompatible with Christianity, and the church's early theologians eagerly took up the task of debating them. They had great success, and non-Christian philosophies declined radically in power and influence.

However, even as philosophy outside of Christian thought was withering, within Christian thought philosophy was already beginning to grow. Though Christianity had to reject some of the philosophers' views, their

---

York: Colonial Press, 1900]) because of its easy readability, making a few corrections based on G. M. A. Grube's translation (in *The Trial and Death of Socrates*, rev. John M. Cooper, 3rd ed. [Indianapolis: Hackett, 2000]), as well as some further adjustments of my own that are intended to clarify some of the more difficult idiosyncrasies of the Greek language. Readers interested in seeing a more literal rendition should consult Grube's translation. For online resources see <www.ivpress.com>.

Homer

Homer was the greatest of all the ancient poets, and his two epic works, the *Iliad* and the *Odyssey*, were revered as the greatest of all myths. Attending a recital of Homer was simultaneously a religious, cultural and social experience: the epics offered a divine revelation in the form of poetry, a shared Greek cultural identity and an occasion for community fellowship. The epics were viewed as sacred and authoritative: quoting Homer was a common way to support one's position in an argument.

These two epics were both probably written in the period 725-675 B.C. The *Iliad* was almost certainly written before the *Odyssey*. They clearly rely on preexisting oral traditions, and the surviving manuscripts appear to include some changes and insertions by later editors. However, their linguistic and literary characteristics strongly suggest that each poem was originally composed, in more or less its final form, by a single poet, and there are no particularly strong reasons to challenge the ancient tradition that they were composed by the same man.

Both epics are huge—the *Odys-*sey runs to 12,109 lines, the *Iliad* to 15,693—and both incorporate an extensive array of supporting characters and interconnecting plotlines. Any attempt to summarize their content briefly must leave out so much crucial material that it cannot do justice to the originals. Virtually every theme that a work of literature can incorporate is powerfully conveyed and profoundly explored. In the *Iliad*, politics and warfare continually force the characters to make hard choices and accept hard consequences; in the *Odyssey*, the characters' loyalty and steadfastness are repeatedly tested by a chaotic world. The common theme in both epics is the human condition: what it means to be human as opposed to divine or animal, to be living but also mortal, to be an individual but also bound to a group, to have conflicting desires and conflicting duties that cannot be fully reconciled.

It is not too much to say that Homer's masterpieces were the foundation from which all subsequent literature in the Western world developed. Their influence still shapes our imaginative life.

fundamental commitment to reason and truth was compatible with the Christian faith. Later Christian thinkers found much profound insight alongside the errors in the thought of the pre-Christian philosophers. The earliest theologians focused on combating the errors of pre-Christian philosophy; yet after several centuries, theologians increasingly came to see philosophy as an essentially noble undertaking—although it had (like all human endeavors apart from God) gone wrong and embraced much error.

Athenian Tragedy

During the sixth and fifth centuries B.C., the public performance of stories about the gods gradually took on a radically new form in Athens. The singing of stories by a chorus gave way to individual performers acting out the parts of the story: theater was born. But plays were still religious rituals, performed as much for communion with the gods as for aesthetic and social reasons.

Aristophanes (ca. 446 B.C.–ca. 385 B.C.) was the greatest of the Greek comic playwrights and possibly the greatest satirist in all Western literature. He was fiercely conservative, and Athens around the turn of the fourth century B.C. was a target-rich environment for his satire, since it was teeming with new social movements and radical ideas. He is most famous today for *The Clouds*, an attack on philosophy, and *Lysistrata*, a satire of sex relations. But *The Birds*, his attack on utopian reformers, is at least as great a work; he also satirized Athenian litigiousness in *The Frogs* and *The Wasps*.

Aeschylus (ca. 513 B.C.–ca. 455 B.C.) was the first of the three great tragedians of classical Athens. Of the three, his works were the most reverent toward the gods and the least influenced by the radical new strains of thought that were on the rise in Athens during the fifth century B.C. His most important work is the trilogy *Oresteia*, which portrays a series of revenge killings taking place in Greece's ancient past. The cycle of revenge is ended when Athena institutes the first human judicial system. While the trilogy seems conservative and optimistic on the surface because it portrays the law as an instrument of divine order and justice, there is also a disturbing undertone to the work: Aeschylus never quite lets us forget that in any human judicial institution, the relationship between justice and revenge will always be murky at best.

Sophocles (ca. 495 B.C.–ca. 406 B.C.) represents the passing of the torch to a more humanistic generation of playwrights, for whom the gods are still revered but remote from human life. He is best known for his Oedipus trilogy, otherwise known as the Theban trilogy. The city is under a divine curse, and King Oedipus swears an oath to put out the eyes of whoever has caused it, refusing to listen to the prophet who tells him that he himself is the offender. He ends up fulfilling his oath upon himself. His daughter Antigone later resists the tyrannical rule of King Creon, Oedipus's successor, and pays for it with her life. The trilogy is an exploration of moral character: why people make the moral decisions they do and the enormity of the consequences.

Euripides (ca. 484 B.C.–ca. 407 B.C.) completes the transition from the reverent origins of the theater to open skepticism toward the gods. Many of Euripides' plays are extended critiques of the traditional myths, confronting us with the devastating human consequences of the "glorious" actions of the gods and heroes. For this reason, some scholars associate him with Socrates and the philosophers' moral criticism of mythology. Others argue that Euripides leans toward nihilism, equally skeptical of both the gods and human reason as sources of meaning. Either way, his plays were wildly popular, and many of them survive.

Rather than reject philosophy, they sought to restore it. In the court of Nebuchadnezzar, Daniel had studied the body of literature that the Babylonians called "the wisdom of the gods," even while he bore witness against the gods (Dan 5:11). After the conflict of the first four centuries was resolved, Christians continued to study the pre-Christian "wisdom of the gods," which in their opinion contained much that was erroneous. Many of them did so not simply to reject the philosophers' errors but also with a desire to develop philosophy that was not erroneous.

This choice had enormous consequences. Christ told his followers to do what they could to improve things in this corrupt and fallen world, but Socrates had a profound impact on the way Christians go about that work. Before Socrates, philosophy had been little more than a hobby for eccentric intellectuals. Socrates transformed it into a social movement: opposing the world's false wisdom and loose morals, exhorting it to seek true wisdom and sound morals. Much of the story of Christianity and politics is the story of Christians seeking to renew this movement and carry it forward in Christ's name. Because of Socrates, most Christians have historically believed that a political order cannot appeal exclusively to the Bible for justification. Christian societies have spent much of their time developing elaborate philosophical arguments for their political institutions, largely because they think they have a moral duty to justify them in such ways. This is one of Socrates' enduring legacies.

MORALITY AND RELIGION IN MYTHICAL SOCIETY

In the civil war over Socrates, on one side stood the religious conservatives of the day, the defenders of the traditional Greek gods, who are still so familiar to us: Zeus, Apollo, Athena and all the rest. In the religion of the ancient Greeks, as well as that of the Romans after them, belief and worship focused on stories about the gods—what we call "myths." Hearing, reading, reciting, singing and performing stories about the gods were acts of worship for them and even seem to have been the most important forms of worship. Those who memorized and recited the epics of Homer and the other poets were seen as religious figures; the original poets themselves, even more so.

This practice of making a religion out of poetry deserves its own name, to distinguish it from the other, less mythical polytheistic religions. We might call it "mythism."

It would be wrong to dismiss the depth and sincerity of traditional Greco-Roman religion. People often think of it as crudely superstitious or as a tool used by cynical rulers to keep the masses ignorant and obedient.[2] No doubt a significant amount of superstition about the supernatural world and cynical manipulation of religious beliefs were present, as they are in every society. But on the whole, Greco-Roman religion was neither stupid nor cynical.

The Greeks and Romans knew perfectly well that their myths were not factual records of events that took place in time-space history; in that sense the myths were not mere superstitions. However, just because they did not believe in the myths as factual accounts of historical events does not mean they did not "believe in" the myths in another sense. They seem to have felt that these myths put them in touch with a higher reality. The myths were "true," not as factual history, but as something like images or reflections of the deeper supernatural truth about the universe. They treated the myths as humanity's way of accessing this kind of truth. The origin of natural forces such as lightning was incomprehensible to them, but the picture of Zeus throwing lightning bolts was something they could grasp. Since it was the closest they thought they could get to the truth, on some level they believed in it, even knowing that it was a story they had made up themselves.[3]

The most important political and social consequence of mythism was its tendency to separate religion and morality. There was, on the one hand, the divine: an awareness that there exists in the universe something radically greater than humanity, before which the only appropriate thing to do is to fall down and worship. On the other hand there was the moral: an awareness that human behavior is subject to rules people ought

---

[2]Even classical scholars are troubled by this conundrum. A striking example: I once worked in an office with a man who studied classics in college. He said that some of his professors contemptuously dismissed the idea that the ancients really believed in their gods, while other professors would solemnly say, "Oh yes, they took this very seriously."

[3]See G. K. Chesterton, *The Everlasting Man* (Fort Collins, Colo.: Ignatius Press, 1925), chaps. 4-8. For online resources see <www.ivpress.com>.

to obey. The ancients did not always see a strong relationship between these two realms. They acknowledged that the gods were subject to moral flaws (pride, caprice, jealousy, lust, etc.), yet they did not see this as any reason the gods should not be worshiped. As for human virtue, the gods usually demanded only a limited amount of outward obedience: sacrifices, rituals, tribute and so on. They generally did not care much whether people were good in their hearts. Certainly a well-brought-up citizen would both worship the city's patron god and practice virtues like honesty and courage. But the citizen would not necessarily think of these two types of behavior as being specially connected.

This had a dramatic impact on ancient social and political life. Greco-Roman culture gave honor and esteem to aesthetic qualities as much as, or even more than, moral virtues. The ancient community placed just as high a value on physical strength, skill and beauty, and on personalities that were noble, refined, fierce and cunning, as it did on honesty, diligence and courage. A strong soldier who could kill many of the city's enemies in battle or a sculptor who could create a beautiful statue of Athena would have a much higher place in the city's honor than a man of mediocre talents who was merely a good person. The mythical heroes were admired not because they were good men—they were not, in fact, particularly good men—but because they won great victories and did heroic deeds.

To some, this description may not sound very different from any other society, including our own. Have not all societies valued strength and beauty, and honored those who win victories or produce cultural achievements? They have, but ancient societies prized these qualities much more highly than they prized personal goodness. For us, if someone is selfish, treacherous and spiteful, we are not inclined to admire that person no matter what desirable qualities that person also possesses or what great achievements that person has produced. The ancients simply did not feel that way.

The two major heroes of Homer's epics, Achilles and Odysseus, provide a perfect illustration. Achilles is the greatest of all warriors, but he is also outrageously resentful and cruel. Odysseus is the cleverest of all captains, but also self-absorbed and dishonest. Both are obsessed with their own fame. Modern audiences tend to have mixed feelings about these heroes because of their moral shortcomings, but ancient audiences do not seem to have been troubled by them. For us, the victories of Achilles and Odysseus are at best tarnished, and at worst spoiled, by the malice and dishonesty with which they are so often achieved, but ancient audiences did not have this reaction. This is not because they did not see, or did not disapprove of, the heroes' moral failings.[4] They were just much more willing than we are to let these failings slide in order to admire the heroes' great deeds.

Another result was that the members of a community placed much more importance on their shared communal life than on their separate individual lives. Home and family were valued distinctly less than the public spheres of activity like politics and social life, where all the glory and honor and great accomplishment took place. Supporting one's family was not nearly as important as supporting the city. Loving one's family was optional, and some even saw it as a sign of a weak or unserious character. But loving the city was mandatory. Men generally had stronger personal and emotional attachments to their male friends, who participated with them in the city's public life, than they did to their wives and children.

In short, an ancient citizen sought his personal identity and fulfillment primarily through participation in the life of the city, rather than through what we would call his "private" or "personal" life. And what he wanted for the city was not primarily that it should be good but that it should be great. Economic prosperity, cultural accomplishment, a flourishing religious and ceremonial life, diplomatic influence and military victory were the main purposes of human existence. To be sure, a certain baseline of moral goodness was one component of a truly glorious city: one could not be very proud of a city if its people were constantly stealing and lying and

---

[4]Ever since Nietzsche first proposed it, some people have always been attracted to the idea that the ancient Greeks had no conception of morality or virtue as we understand it and did not see dishonesty or cruelty as wrong. But there are a number of reasons we can conclude that the Greeks were well aware of, and disapproved of, the Homeric heroes' moral failings. Perhaps the most persuasive evidence is that the heroes themselves rebuke one another for their flaws. Achilles tells the dishonest Odysseus to his face: "I hate that man like the very Gates of Death / who says one thing but hides another in his heart" (Homer Iliad 9.378-79). And most of the other heroes are offended by Achilles' resentful arrogance: his adoptive father Phoenix scolds him that "it's wrong to have such an iron, ruthless heart" (9.602). I rely on Robert Fagles's translation (New York: Penguin, 1999). For online resources see <www.ivpress.com>.

stabbing each other in the back. But goodness was only one of many desirable qualities, and it was usually not considered the most important one.

SOCRATES, MARTYR OF IGNORANCE

This whole political and social order was shaken to its foundations by an ugly old man who had no money, no social standing and no political power. And the real irony is that he did it not with the power of superior knowledge, but with the power of superior ignorance.

At his trial, Socrates described to the jury the utter disbelief he had felt when he first heard that Apollo, speaking through the Delphic oracle, had called him the wisest man in Greece. He had thought: "What can the god mean, and what is the interpretation of his riddle? For I know that I have no wisdom, small or great." Consumed by a desire to understand the oracle's meaning, he sought out a politician with a reputation for great wisdom. The results were surprising: a little direct questioning revealed that the politician's opinions were not justified by any valid reasoning. Socrates tried to show the politician that his opinions were groundless, and this time the results were not surprising: the politician hated him. Socrates came away thinking: "Although I do not suppose either of us knows anything really noble and good, I am better off than he is. For he knows nothing, but thinks that he knows something; I neither know nor think that I know. In this last particular, then, I seem to have a slight advantage over him."[5]

Socrates went to another politician, then another and another. After running through all the supposedly wise politicians, he went to the poets, who were revered for both artistic and religious wisdom, but he got the same result from them: a little questioning revealed their "wisdom" to be fraudulent. Even the city's craftsmen, who obviously possessed some useful knowledge in their ability to take raw materials and turn them into manufactured goods, failed Socrates' test of wisdom. They did know some things he did not know, such as how to make a shoe or a table, but in all other matters he found that they were just like the politicians and the poets: they thought they understood everything when in fact they understood nothing. Socrates concluded that even in his ignorance, he was

---

[5]Plato *Apology of Socrates* 21b-21d. Although the account of Socrates' trial in the *Apology* was written by Plato, I have attributed quotations from it to Socrates himself (see sidebar "Plato").

Plato (ca. 428 B.C.–ca. 348 B.C.)

Plato was born into one of Athens's most prominent political families; he probably would have gone into politics himself if he had not fallen in with Socrates. Following the death of Socrates in 399 B.C., Plato left Athens and traveled abroad, returning around 385 to found the Academy, where he and other philosophers engaged in discussion and taught students. The rest of his life was divided between running the Academy and further travels in the Mediterranean world. The Academy continued to operate in Athens for over 900 years, until A.D. 529.

Most of Plato's works are dialogues in which Socrates discusses a subject (justice, truth, beauty, sex, economics, etc.) with one or more other characters. While they address an extremely wide variety of topics, the theme they return to most often is the nature of reason and truth. Plato was convinced that reason could not be explained as a merely natural function. To think at all, we must accept that there is such a thing as truth. However, for this to be the case, truth must really exist, and clearly truth does not exist as part of the natural world. Truth must exist on a higher metaphysical plane, and reason must be the faculty by which we perceive that higher reality. But it is difficult to perceive truth properly, and the process is fraught with all kinds of problems and limitations, which Plato explored at great length.

We cannot know to what extent the views of the character Socrates in Plato's dialogues represent the views of the ac-tual, historical Socrates. This is known as the "Socratic problem." Plato's *Apology of Socrates*, which records Socrates' speech in his own defense *(apologia)* at his trial, appears to have been published not long after the trial. It therefore is likely to be a fairly accurate record of what Socrates actually said. Beyond this, however, all attempts to disentangle the "historical Socrates" from the fictional "Platonic Socrates," along with related attempts to classify Plato's dialogues into "early," "middle," and "late" periods, have no basis in historical evidence and are purely speculative.

It would be difficult to overstate the influence of Plato's thought. Alfred North Whitehead summed it up well: "The safest general characterization of the European philosophical tradition is that it consists of a series of footnotes to Plato." Plato's theism made him particularly attractive for assimilation into the Christian philosophical tradition; Augustine reminds us that "Plato had no hesitation in asserting that to be a philosopher is to love God."[a]

A good place to start reading Plato is his *Republic*, in which Socrates takes up the question "What is justice?" He concludes that it is a harmonious ordering of the soul. It is important to realize—though some scholars disagree with this interpretation—that the ideal city described in the *Republic* is an allegory that illustrates the qualities of a just soul. It is not a proposal for real-world political reform.

---

[a]Augustine *City of God* 8.8.

wiser than they were. All this time he was earning the hatred of everyone he questioned, because his cross-examinations were exposing the ignorance of men whose positions of power and influence depended on their reputations for wisdom.

Socrates decided to devote his life to showing the world what he now thought was the true meaning of the oracle's message: the world was not wise. As he said at his trial:

> The truth is, O men of Athens, that it is the god [Apollo] who is wise, and by his answer he intends to show that the wisdom of men is worth little or nothing. He is not really speaking of Socrates; he is only using my name by way of illustration—as if he said, "O men, he is the wisest, who, like Socrates, knows that his wisdom is in truth worth nothing." And so I go about the world, obedient to the god, and search and make inquiry into the wisdom of any one, whether citizen or stranger, who appears to be wise. And if he is not wise, then I assist the god and show him that he is not wise.[6]

From then on Socrates spent his days in the marketplace and the other public spaces of Athens, talking to anyone who would listen about how wisdom was infinitely more important than money or glory or reputation, and the need to become aware of one's ignorance and the worthlessness of the opinions that the world considers wise. He attracted a small but fiercely loyal group of disciples, some of whom were sons of the city's most wealthy and powerful families.

The antagonism against Socrates grew more intense; he was seen as a dangerous teacher who would lead young men to doubt the shared religious beliefs that were the basis of the city's public life. In the end, Socrates was tried on charges of blasphemy and corrupting the youth. Socrates defended himself on grounds that he was obeying Apollo and also helping to prevent intellectual laziness in the city, just as the annoyance of a buzzing gadfly can prevent a horse from falling asleep on the job. The jury, however, narrowly voted to convict him. Even then, he could have escaped execution if he had chosen to do so; Athenian law allowed him to request a sentence of exile instead of death, and it

---

[6]Plato *Apology of Socrates* 23a-23b.

seems certain that the jury would have accepted the request given the narrowness of the vote to convict and the nonviolent nature of the crime. But Socrates flatly refused to request exile. It would go against his conscience, he said, to request a punishment—even a lesser punishment—when he believed he had done nothing wrong. He also pointed out that if he continued preaching his message, any other city he fled to would certainly convict him of the same charges all over again. After a long life in Athens, he had no desire to spend his last years wandering around the world, fleeing city after city. And he said that in any case he did not really mind dying—since he did not know what would lie beyond death, he did not know whether it would be good or bad for him, so it would be irrational to fear it.

The Athenians hoped that executing Socrates would end his troublesome influence, but it had exactly the opposite effect. His disciples were galvanized to carry on his work. Under the leadership of Socrates' greatest disciple, Plato, they formed a school called the Academy. Plato's greatest student, Aristotle, would later start a rival school, the Lyceum. Between them, Plato and Aristotle produced a body of philosophical writings covering almost every conceivable subject and doing so with a depth of reasoning and insight that has seldom been matched. Over the following centuries, these two schools and their prolific founders were succeeded by dozens of schools and hundreds of authors throughout the Greek and Roman world.

Socrates was not the first person to engage in philosophy (the word means "love of wisdom"). The earliest known philosopher was Thales, who lived roughly two centuries earlier than Socrates and was known for systematically studying the movements of the stars. By the time Socrates began his quest for wisdom, philosophy had long since developed as an intellectual alternative to mythism. However, the pre-Socratic philosophers kept quiet and rarely challenged the existing social order. Socrates threw down the gauntlet before mythism, challenging every person he met to defend his beliefs—whatever they were—rationally. He transformed philosophy into a permanent threat to the Greco-Roman religious and political order. So Socrates was something even more important than the first philosopher: he was the first proselytizing philosopher.

FROM IGNORANCE TO WISDOM

Socrates was not a skeptic in the strict technical meaning of that term: a person who thinks human beings can have no knowledge at all. All his talk about "ignorance" can easily lead to misunderstandings on this point. For skeptics, to realize your own ignorance is the culmination of the search for wisdom. For Socrates, it was just the starting point of that search.[7]

Socrates' point was that a person seeking wisdom must begin by realizing that people generally hold their beliefs for reasons that have nothing to do with whether those beliefs are true. Even if the beliefs happen to be true, that is not why people hold them. If people believe in the Greek gods, this is only because they were raised in Greece, not because there are good reasons to think that the Greek gods actually exist. If those people had been born in Egypt, they would have believed in the Egyptian gods. If people believe that the laws of Athens are good laws, this is because they were raised in Athens, not because they have objectively considered its laws and found stronger reasons to think that they are good than to think that they are bad. The realization that a person seeking wisdom must reach is not that all opinions are false: they may or may not be false. But people who have not examined their beliefs rationally do not legitimately know whether their opinions are true or false. While they may hold a great many opinions, they do not really know anything at all.

This process of discarding false wisdom produces a state of ignorance, but that is not the end of the story. The purpose of discarding false wisdom is to go on and discover true wisdom through reasoning. As we have seen, Socrates said that he bore witness against "the wisdom

---

[7]At his trial, Socrates only emphasized his embrace of ignorance, not the subsequent search for true wisdom. This was probably a strategic decision, to make it harder for others to convict him of blasphemy. However, Socrates actually preached much more than just ignorance. Certainly Plato does not give us a skeptical Socrates in the rest of his writings. However, the view that Socrates was not a skeptic does not depend on our accepting Plato's account of Socrates' teachings as historically accurate. Socrates' other chronicler, Xenophon, does not give us a skeptical Socrates any more than Plato does. More important, skeptical philosophy was already old hat in Athens by the time Socrates showed up, so it is unlikely that Socrates would have attracted so many disciples and had such a transformative impact if he had been preaching the same old skeptical message. We should also bear in mind that Plato was probably the greatest anti-skeptical philosopher in history, and it would be difficult to explain why he would adopt Socrates as the model philosopher in all his works if the historical Socrates had been a skeptic.

Aristotle (384 B.C.–322 B.C.)

Aristotle arrived in Athens at age seventeen to study philosophy at Plato's Academy, remaining there for the next twenty years. He left the city upon Plato's death, apparently because he was angry at having been passed over in favor of Plato's nephew to head the Academy. While away, he spent two years back in his native Macedonia, teaching Prince Alexander, later known as Alexander the Great. In 335, after returning to Athens, he founded his own school of philosophy, the Lyceum. He fled Athens in 323 B.C., apparently fearing for his life—possibly due to an anti-Macedonian political movement—and died the following year. The Lyceum probably closed permanently after the destruction of Athens in A.D. 267, giving it a run of just over 600 years.

Most of Aristotle's writings that have come down to us were not published during his lifetime; they were originally his papers at the Lyceum. They probably served as something like lecture notes. These papers were passed down among his students and admirers, then captured and carried to Rome after a sack of Athens in A.D. 86. Much of Aristotle's philosophy was lost in the West after the decline of Rome, but translations of his works appeared in the Arab world in the ninth century, where Aristotle's influence played an important role in the flourishing of Islamic philosophy. In the thirteenth century, as we will see in chapter four, Aristotle's lost works were reintroduced in the West, where they had an enormous impact on Christian philosophy (see sidebar "Thomas Aquinas").

His works cover subjects ranging from logic and epistemology (the study of knowledge) to physics and nature, ethics and politics, rhetoric and poetics. His mind was relentlessly analytic, breaking down each subject into its necessary components, then breaking down each component into subcomponents and so on. He and his students also conducted a lot of empirical investigation, cataloging everything from biological species to the histories and political constitutions of cities.

He identified ten "categories," the basic concepts that are the necessary preconditions of thought (substance, quantity, quality, relation, place, time, situation, condition, action, passion). He distinguished four types of causes: material (the elements *out of which* an object is created), efficient (the means *by which* it is created), formal (the idea of *what* it is) and final (the purpose *for which* it exists). He argued that all causes must be traceable back to a first cause, which he held to be a divine being in whom all potential was perfectly fulfilled.

The works known as the *Nicomachean Ethics* and the *Politics* are his most important analyses of morality and politics. He held that the key to virtue was to find the right balance, or "golden mean," between extremes. The *Ethics* and the *Politics* appear to have originally been a single document, which later editors divided into separate books. This reflects Aristotle's view of the intimate connection between morality and politics: the existence of political communities is the ultimate outworking of the moral plan in human nature.

of men" because "it is the god who is wise." Socrates discarded the false wisdom of humans in order to discover the true wisdom of the god. Plato would later make this point with his allegory of the cave, in which a tribe of people is raised in captivity underground. Kept totally immobile their whole lives, unable even to turn their heads, they are taught to believe that a series of shadows projected on the cave wall is the only reality that exists. In the allegory, one man breaks free of his restraints and crawls up out of the cave, into the sunlight, where he sees the real world. The point of rejecting the shadows on the cave wall is not to achieve a state of total darkness, but to take the first step toward climbing into the light.[8]

This quest for true wisdom led Socrates' disciples and their successors to construct their own explanations of truth and of the world around them. The philosophers' investigations challenged mythism along two distinct lines that came to be known as "natural philosophy" and "moral philosophy." Natural philosophy examined nature, including both events within nature and the metaphysical basis of nature's existence. Some of this was straightforward empirical investigation. Aristotle, for example, was the earliest known person to systematically catalog animal species and compare and contrast their traits, making him the first biologist. But more important than this were the philosophers' attempts to work out the first principles or conditions of reality that would have to exist for the natural world to be what it is. Pre-Socratic thinkers like Democritus, observing the behavior of objects, worked out detailed theories of the structure of matter. (Impressively, just from their everyday observations, they were able to deduce that all matter must be made up of billions of microscopic particles—that is, atoms.) Their investigations covered the supernatural as well as the natural. Both Plato and Aristotle have traditionally been categorized as theists because they argued that the world as we know it could not exist except through the work of an eternal divine mind—although their classification as theists has become controversial.[9] Other phi-

---

[8]See Plato *Republic* 514a-517e. For online resources see <www.ivpress.com>.

[9]Plato insists that an eternal "mind" or "reason" must be the ultimate source of reality (see esp. *Timaeus* and *Phaedrus*). But there is much disagreement over whether this amounts to theism, includ-

losophers held metaphysical views ranging from the mundane (materi-
alism) to the bizarre (Pythagoras and his followers believed that only
numbers really existed; they revered geometric shapes, especially the
twelve-sided dodecahedron).

Moral philosophy, on the other hand, showed that ethics had to be given
a far more central place in the scheme of human values than mythism could
give it. Plato and Aristotle held that the origin of moral behavior was in the
human personality: morality is the fulfillment of a structure or plan that
is inherent in human nature. Plato argued that moral goodness is the state
in which all parts of the soul (such as the desires) are under the control of
reason; they thus are all in harmony with one another, like the strings of
a well-tuned instrument. The morally good person is the happiest of all
people because of this inner harmony, while the evil person is constantly
torn by internal conflict among uncontrolled desires, and is therefore miserable.[10] Aristotle portrays goodness as a psychological balance: goodness
is following each desire to the correct length and no further. In battle, the
soldier who overindulges the desire for self-preservation is a coward, while
the soldier who overindulges the desire for glorious self-sacrifice is reckless.
True courage lies in finding the right balance between self-preservation and
self-sacrifice.[11] Other philosophers held a variety of moral views, ranging
from the sophists, who were relativists, to the Roman Stoics, who were so
severely moralistic that they thought virtue was the only good. So, for example, a proper Stoic should not particularly care if he were to get a ghastly
disease or have his legs crippled, since these events would have no effect on
his virtue and thus would not be bad for him.[12]

---

ing issues such as whether and to what extent Plato characterizes this "mind" as a personal being
and whether he sees it as transcending the natural world. Aristotle argues that events in the natural
world must be traceable to an eternal and divine first cause: an unmoved mover or uncaused causer
(see esp. *Metaphysics*). While Aristotle clearly saw this first cause as transcending the natural world
and probably saw it as a personal being (although some would dispute even this), it is not clear to
what extent this being takes any actual interest in what happens down here in the natural world.
For example, Aristotle says that God cannot love us because God is perfect and we are imperfect.
Thus, some think Aristotle should be classified as a deist rather than a theist. Other scholars defend the traditional characterization of both Plato and Aristotle as theists.

[10]See Plato *Republic*, esp. 443c-445b.

[11]See Aristotle *Nicomachean Ethics* 2.2. For online resources see <www.ivpress.com>.

[12]This is no exaggeration. The Stoic Epictetus solemnly declares that "sickness is a hindrance to the
body, but not to your ability to choose, unless that is your choice. Lameness is a hindrance to the
leg, but not to your ability to choose. Say this to yourself with regard to everything that happens,

It was moral philosophy that posed the real threat to the traditional order. While mythism encouraged people to seek fulfillment in their public and social lives, where glory and honor and great accomplishment were to be found, philosophy taught that the main purpose of human life was to become wise and good. Socrates defied all disapproval and even the death sentence itself to preach this message:

> Men of Athens, I honor and love you, but I shall obey the god rather than you. And while I have life and strength, I shall never cease from the practice and teaching of philosophy, exhorting anyone whom I meet and saying to him after my manner: "You, my friend, a citizen of the great and mighty and wise city of Athens—are you not ashamed of heaping up the greatest amount of money and honor and reputation, and caring so little about wisdom and truth and the greatest improvement of the soul, which you never regard or heed at all?"[13]

Soulcraft, not statecraft, was the path to real human fulfillment. All the things that mythological society held dear—strength, cunning, victory, beauty—had to be removed from the center of human life so that virtue, ethics and contemplation of the good could take their rightful place there. And wisdom and virtue were achieved first and foremost not in public life, but in private life. (Marriage and family were exceptions to the philosophers' turn toward the private life. The philosophers discounted marriage and family just as much as the mythists did, if not more so, mainly because most philosophers thought that women could not achieve a high degree of wisdom and virtue.)

The political implications of philosophy become clear as Socrates explains why he has never attended the regular city meetings where most political decisions were made in the Athenian democracy:

> Someone may wonder why I go about in private, giving advice and busying myself with the concerns of others, but do not venture to come forward in the assembly and advise the city. I will tell you why. . . . I am certain, O men of Athens, that if I had engaged in politics, I would have died long ago, and done no good either to you or to myself. Do not be offended at my telling you the truth, for the truth is that no man who goes to war with you, or any other

---

then you will see such obstacles as hindrances to something else, but not to yourself" (Epictetus *Enchiridion* 9). I rely on Thomas Higginson's translation (Whitefish, Mont.: Kessinger Publishing, 2007). For online resources see <www.ivpress.com>.
[13]Plato *Apology of Socrates* 29d-29e.

crowd, honestly striving against the many lawless and unrighteous acts that are done in a city, will survive. He who will fight for justice, if he would live even for a short time, must have a private position and not a public one.[14]

To philosophize is to "go to war" with the people of the city, at least in their collective political aspect, because it opposes the "many lawless and unrighteous acts" that inevitably take place in politics. Philosophy's uncompromising standards of wisdom and goodness inevitably bring it into regular conflict with the political system.

ATHENS MEETS JERUSALEM

When Christianity first encountered philosophy, it encountered an opponent. Some of the pre-Christian philosophers were closer to the Christian worldview than others, but all of them rejected at least some of its crucial elements. Probably the biggest source of opposition was the widespread belief among the philosophers that only supernatural things were pure and good. Nature, for them, was simply bad; it was a world that had fallen away from the supernatural. To be in the natural world at all was a curse. The true fulfillment of human longings, they thought, would be to leave nature behind altogether and exist purely in the supernatural. Likewise, the mind in and of itself was simply good, because it was supernatural, while the body in and of itself was simply bad. All vice was attributable to the body's evil appetites; even vices of the mind were attributed to the body's corrupting influence. Or as they sometimes put it, only the mind is truly the person: the body is not a part of the person, but a prison (or even a tomb) in which the person finds themselves trapped, and from which, if they are enlightened, they long to escape.

This view, sometimes called *dualism*, was an integral part of the whole worldview that developed among the pre-Christian philosophers. Obviously it put the philosophers directly in opposition to the Christians, with their claim that God not only made nature and called it good, but even drew a part of nature into union with himself and became a man. Much of the history of Christian theology in the first four centuries after Christ consists of the struggle to refute dualism and prevent its modes of thought from distorting Christian theology.

---

[14]Plato *Apology of Socrates* 31c-32a.

Nonetheless, after those first four centuries many Christians—and a substantial number of them even during the first four centuries—found much to admire in Greco-Roman philosophy. These Christians sought to renew the practice of philosophy, pursuing the original philosophers' goals of contemplating and explaining the truth while rejecting their dualism and other anti-Christian views. They argued that philosophy, once its errors were corrected, offered solutions to important intellectual problems on which the Bible was silent.

Once it became clear that some Christians were seeking to renew the practice of philosophy within Christianity, opposition arose within the church. Some objected to any use of Greco-Roman thought by Christians as a compromise with "the world" and a dilution of God's revelation. Tertullian, a leader of the church in the early third century A.D., famously asked, "What is Athens to Jerusalem?"[15] But gradually, over the course of many centuries, more and more Christian thinkers came to embrace the attitude of Tertullian's contemporary Clement of Alexandria, who argued that "philosophy is the handmaiden of theology."[16]

Christianity would have been a force for moral reform no matter what other ideas it encountered, but philosophy shaped the way in which this influence was exerted. In a sense, the whole subject of this book, Christian political thought, owes as much to Plato as to Paul. As we saw in chapter one, the Bible does not equip Christians with a detailed political theory. To address questions about government and politics, Christians had to think through matters not directly addressed in the Bible. And when discussing political questions with their non-Christian neighbors, they had to do so on grounds outside of the Bible if they were going to be persuasive. Critically and rigorously engaging with the Greco-Roman philosophical heritage helped them both to find answers to questions that the Bible did not answer and to address themselves on politics to those who did not believe the Bible. What they had to say when they first began to do so is the subject of chapter three.

---

[15]Tertullian *Prescription Against Heretics* 7. For online resources see <www.ivpress.com>.
[16]Clement of Alexandria *Miscellanies* 1.5. For online resources see <www.ivpress.com>.

3

CITIES OF GOD AND MAN

Augustine Formalizes
the Idea of Dual Citizenship

They glory in their shame,
with minds set on earthly things.
But our citizenship is in heaven.

Paul, in the Epistle
to the Philippians

THE ANCIENT PHILOSOPHER CICERO records the story of a pirate captain whose naval thievery was so successful that he attracted the attention of Alexander the Great. The disruption of commerce due to piracy was a constant problem in the ancient world, so serious that it sometimes forced even Alexander to take time out from conquering most of the known world. This particular pirate must have been an exceptionally skilled predator, because he managed to attract Alexander's attention while commanding only a single vessel, and a small one at that. In the end, however, even the most accomplished pirate cannot stand up to a sizeable empire, and the buccaneer was soon captured and brought before Alexander himself.

The man whose domain extended from Greece to Egypt to Persia to India sized up the lowly oceangoing thief and then demanded: "By what right do you dare to infest the seas with your puny brigantine?"

The pirate looked him squarely in eyes and replied: "By the same right that is your warrant for conquering the world."

Centuries after it was first recorded, this story was recounted by the first great Christian political thinker, Augustine of Hippo. Augustine's enormous work *The City of God* was the first real masterpiece of Christian political thought. Its analysis of the nature of politics has been one of the most prominent influences in Christian thinking, particularly in the West, in every era from its publication down to the present day. It is probably the most important work of Christian political thought ever produced.

When *The City of God* was completed in 426, Christianity had been legal for more than a century and had been Rome's official state church for almost half a century. As Christianity had come out of the shadows of persecution and into the limelight of the Roman political stage, the issues of political thought suddenly took on a new urgency: What, exactly, is the Christian view of government? How should Christian rulers rule? Could they legitimately permit other religions in their domains? Could they wage wars, and if so, under what conditions and within what limits? What role should the ruler play, if any, in settling doctrinal disputes?

While the church was outcast and persecuted, it had no need to develop a detailed set of views on these questions. Second-century Christians were no more worried about the need to develop guidelines for Christian rulers than they were about the need to put ceilings on all their pig stalls, just in case the pigs ever sprouted wings. It was all they could do just to keep the faith alive under the pressure of persecution and the proliferation of false teachings; preparing for the day when Christianity might rule an empire was not a top priority. However, as they took the reins of power in Rome, fourth- and fifth-century Christians realized that they had better develop some specific ideas about what to do with that power, and develop them fast. Their effort to wrestle with these questions found its greatest expression in the thought of Augustine, and especially in *The City of God*.

The key idea that animates Augustine's political thought is that each city is really a composite of two cities or communities: the City of Man and the City of God.[1] The City of Man is made up of all those who place themselves ahead of God; the City of God is made up of all those who place God ahead of themselves. The two "cities" therefore have different conceptions of "the good"—that is, what purposes are good for human beings to pursue. The City of Man seeks its good only in the present world, while the City of God seeks its highest good elsewhere, in heaven. However, even though the City of God does not seek its highest good in this world, it still has a responsibility to participate in political life and promote its proper good, which is civil peace. The two cities with their opposing purposes must learn to coexist while they sojourn together through this life, and the City of God has a duty to exercise its earthly citizenship and promote civil peace as far as is feasible. Thus the City of Man has only one citizenship, the citizenship of the present world; but the City of God has dual citizenship. Christians exercise citizenship both in the city of this world and in another city, which the New Testament calls "the city of the living God, the heavenly Jerusalem" (Heb 12:22). The City of God must perform a delicate balancing act, exercising citizenship in the earthly city but ultimately loyal to its higher citizenship in heaven.

Augustine argues that this balancing act is all the more difficult because the life of the city in this world is constantly being ruined and frustrated by the impact of human sin—both the sins of the City of Man and the sins of the City of God, whose members continue to struggle with sin. Because the entire world of politics is compromised by the sinfulness of all human beings, Augustine warned Christians not to expect too much in the way of godliness from the city in this world. Do what good you can in this life, he advised, and be content with that. You will have all eternity to exercise your citizenship in a truly holy political community; do not mistake this city for that one.[2]

---

[1]Augustine's Latin term *civitas terrena* would be more accurately translated as "City of the World" rather than "City of Man." But the traditional translation "City of Man" is used nearly universally, and it at least reflects Augustine's view that the members of the City of Man put themselves ahead of God.

[2]See Augustine *The City of God* 19.5-8; 19.27.

THE END OF THE WORLD

Augustine wrote *The City of God* in the aftermath of the sack of Rome in 410. Until it actually happened, the idea that Rome could be sacked and looted had been unthinkable. Rome was "the eternal city," the one thing in an uncertain world that would never fail. It had not been sacked in almost eight centuries. Rome's rule was unquestioned and unquestionable; its political power was the bedrock of civilized existence.

But the non-Italian tribes that lived within and around the empire had gradually grown stronger and had become increasingly discontent with Roman rule. In the early fifth century one of these tribes, the Visigoths, rebelled. As a result of political infighting, in 408 the Romans executed their own most brilliant general, a Christian named Stilicho. The Visigoths seized on this moment of weakness by besieging the city.

As part of a proposed deal for peace, the Visigoths gave the Roman Senate a gift of three hundred of their young men as slaves. But when the peace deal fell apart, the "slaves" inside the city attacked one of its gatehouses and succeeded in opening the gates. In poured the Visigoths, and the city was sacked.

By the standards of the day, the sack of Rome in 410 was relatively mild; there was less than the usual amount of killing, and most of the city's women were not molested. But the long-term impact was devastating, because the whole world had been shown that the impossible could be done: Rome was not invincible. The Romans were surrounded by tribes and nations that had resentfully paid them tribute and obedience for centuries from fear of their power; now all those tribes and nations were suddenly no longer afraid. Tribute stopped flowing in. Tens of thousands of Romans abandoned the city in fear and resettled in the countryside. The city was sacked again, by the Vandals, in 455, and yet again by an uprising of its own unpaid troops in 472. The last of the emperors of Rome was deposed in 476. Vestiges of Rome's glory remained for a long time: the empire's eastern territories, ruled from Constantinople, continued to call themselves the Roman Empire; in 800, Pope Leo III declared Charlemagne's kingdom in France and Germany to be the Holy Roman Empire and the rightful inheritor of the Roman crown. But the original Roman Empire, the empire that actually had its capital in Rome, was gone forever.

Augustine of Hippo (354-430)

Augustine led one of the most remarkable lives ever recorded. His *Confessions*, which tells his life story, is unique in human literature. One scholar remarks that the *Confessions* was written "not that we may know Augustine, but that we may know God: and it shows us Augustine only that we may see God."[a]

Augustine had a Christian upbringing, but as a child he never seriously embraced the faith. At age nineteen he read a book by the Roman philosopher Cicero praising the contemplation of truth as the best kind of life. Augustine decided to devote his life to discovering truth—a decision that he presents in the *Confessions* as his first real religious experience and the first step on his path to Christianity.

But that path would be long. He first joined the Manicheans, who claimed that orthodox Christianity was a small-minded superstition, while they themselves were independent thinkers who fearlessly sought truth. But a mind as powerful as Augustine's could not find satisfaction with the Manicheans' bizarre rituals, outlandish mythologies and simpleminded metaphysics. In his late twenties he gradually drifted away from them, toward classical Greco-Roman philosophy—though his disillusionment with Manicheism also left him wondering whether anyone could really know anything.

At age thirty he moved to Milan. He was a teacher of public speaking, and he heard that the local Christian bishop, Ambrose, was an excellent speaker, so he went to hear Ambrose's sermons out of professional interest. Ambrose, as it happened, was one of the foremost defenders of Christian doctrine in his day. His sermons made Augustine realize that he had never given Christianity a fair examination to determine whether it was true. He gradually became convinced that it was.

His heart, however, continued to resist conversion. He was strongly attached to his non-Christian life; he had kept a concubine for many years, whom he loved dearly and with whom he had had a son. In the end, he writes, he was resisting God even though he knew Christianity to be true, simply because he thought himself incapable of living a godly life.

The account of his conversion in the *Confessions* is one of the most famous passages in all literature. He writes that he felt as though God were on one side of him, and he desperately wanted to turn in that direction, but he was held back by his worldly lusts clutching at him from the other direction. Finally, as the agony became unbearable, he felt as though he were being asked, "Why are you relying on yourself, only to find yourself unreliable?"[b] Realizing that he had to trust in God's help to become good, he surrendered to God and found peace. "You have made us for yourself," he writes to God, "and our hearts are restless until they find rest in you."[c]

After his conversion, Augustine wanted to withdraw from the world. But Ambrose was not willing to let Augustine's extraordinary talents be hidden away. Augustine was eventually persuaded, very reluctantly, to become a priest and eventually a bishop. He published the *Confessions* in 398 partly in response to concerns over a man who had lived such a scandalous life being elevated to a position of authority in the church. In the three decades between his conversion and his death, he became one of the most important thinkers in the history of Christianity.

[a]B. B. Warfield, "Augustine and His *Confessions*," *Princeton Theological Review* 3, no. 1 (1905): 81-126, here citing p. 111, in sec. 3. For online resources see <www.ivpress.com>.

[b]Augustine *Confessions* 8.27. I rely on Henry Chadwick's translation (Oxford University Press, 1998). For online resources see <www.ivpress.com>.

[c]Augustine *Confessions* 1.1.

Christians in Rome could take solace in their God during these times, but for those who still worshiped the traditional Roman gods, the sack of Rome was the end of the world. This was not simply a loss of power and wealth for them, nor was it even just a matter of their home and their loved ones being attacked and conquered. It was the destruction of their whole universe. Everything reliable had turned out to be unreliable; everything certain had turned out to be uncertain; everything meaningful had turned out to be meaningless. It was as if they had awakened one morning to find themselves in a world where light was dark and heat was cold.

It is easy for us, who take it for granted that the flourishing of the political community is not the most important thing there is, to underestimate just how catastrophic the fall of a great city was for pre-Christian peoples. As we saw in chapter two, for the traditional mythological religions of the ancient world, the glory and accomplishments of the city were the highest good of human life. Their religious experience was essentially aesthetic rather than moral, so above all else they valued qualities like strength, skill, beauty, refinement, intellect and cunning—qualities whose highest achievements were found in the shared life of the city. Thus they invested all their religious hopes and desires in the political community. For the city to fall was not merely the loss of all worldly goods; it was also the loss of all goods whatsoever, the loss of goodness itself. It was, for them, the worst of all possible things—much worse than merely dying. The death of an individual person could be

Augustine's Theology

Augustine's contributions to theology and philosophy were as wide-ranging as they were influential. He lived at a time of extreme intellectual upheaval, when the Christian world was forced to confront a series of complex doctrinal issues. As the leading Christian intellectual of his time, Augustine left his indelible stamp upon Christianity's answers to the many questions it was confronting.

Probably his most important contribution was his writings opposing Pelagius, an Irish monk. Pelagius thought that existing Christian doctrine undermined human moral responsibility when it taught that because people are sinful, they are not able to do good works without God's help. Pelagius was outraged nearly to the point of physical violence when someone quoted to him the prayer from Augustine's just-published *Confessions:* "Require what you will, Lord, and grant what you require."[a] Determined to preserve the integrity of the human will at all costs, Pelagius began developing a sophisticated body of doctrine that diverged ever more sharply from mainstream Christianity—he taught that human beings are not sinful from birth, that heaven can be earned by good works, that death is not a punishment for sin, and so forth.

Augustine eagerly took up the challenge of vindicating the biblical claim that human beings are born at enmity with God and will never willingly submit to God unless God changes them. While people are "able" to do good in the sense that they possess all the natural faculties necessary for doing good, they are not "able" to do good in another sense, because they are immoral and consistently choose to reject God. They *cannot* do good, Augustine argues, simply because they *will not* do good.

Under Augustine's theological leadership, at the Council of Carthage in 418 the church declared that Pelagianism was not compatible with Christian belief. Over the next century, various forms of Semi-Pelagianism tried to reconcile portions of Pelagius's doctrine with Christianity. These efforts were also condemned in a series of church councils, culminating in the Second Council of Orange in 529, which declared that "it is wholly a gift of God to love God."[b]

Augustine also led the church in refuting the many other unorthodox teachings that were being put forward around the turn of the fifth century. Having been a Manichean himself before he was converted to Christianity, Augustine became the church's most accomplished critic of Manicheism. Another group, the Donatists—named for their leader, Donatus Magnus—had arisen after the persecution of Christians in the early fourth century. Many priests who had denied the faith during that persecution were received back into the church afterward, but the Donatists refused to recognize them or the validity of sacraments performed by them. A conference in Carthage in 411 declared Donatism to be inconsistent with membership in the church; heading this conference was Marcellinus—the same man who was to convince Augustine to embark on both his anti-Pelagian writings and *The City of God*.

[a]Augustine *Confessions* 10.40.

[b]Second Council of Orange, canon 25. For online resources see <www.ivpress.com>.

glorious, especially if he died in the service of his city; but the destruction of the city meant the loss of all glory.

Inevitably, many people lashed out in bitterness and rage, looking for something other than Rome itself to blame for Rome's destruction. In Christianity they found what they thought was a plausible target. If the city fell, it must be because the gods had abandoned it; and no wonder they had, for the city had abandoned them first, by embracing Christ. After the conversion of the empire, most of the temples of the traditional gods had been torn down or made into Christian churches. Naturally the gods were not going to put up with this insolence. The fall of Rome was their divine ultimatum: abandon Christ and return to the old ways.

These angry invocations of the traditional gods coincided with a more calm and rationalistic line of attack on Christianity. For some, the fall of Rome proved that the Christian faith was essentially weak and unsustainable. The doctrine of turning the other cheek and forgiving one's enemies, they said, was inconsistent with running a strong government and preserving the political community against its enemies. Christianity glories in a Savior who chose to become frail and weak in order to save his people, and it teaches its followers to imitate him, so naturally Rome had became frail and weak after adopting Christianity. No government could possibly survive for long if it were run by people who wanted to be Christlike.[3]

A TALE OF TWO CITIES

At first the sack of Rome did not have much impact on Augustine, at

[3]One of those who offered this line of argument was Volusianus, whose doubts about Christianity prompted the writing of *The City of God* (see below).

least as far as the historical record tells us.[4] He was the bishop of the north African city of Hippo, far from Rome and not immediately affected very much by the sack of the city. And while Augustine was an active participant both in the church's theological controversies and in academic philosophical debates, the historical record shows no great interest in political thought on his part up to and including the time when the sack occurred.

What drew Augustine into political thought was not political or military events, but the needs of a friend. While attending a church conference convened to oppose a heresy known as Donatism, Augustine had befriended the man running the conference, a Roman commissioner named Marcellinus. Their friendship was brief: they met in 411, and Marcellinus was executed in 413 by Roman officials sympathetic to the Donatists. However, the fleeting connection between these two men had enormous historic consequences. It was Marcellinus who first asked Augustine to respond to the legalistic teachings of a monk named Pelagius, touching off one of the most important theological debates in the history of Christianity (see sidebar "Augustine's Theology"). And it was the same Marcellinus who convinced Augustine to write his political masterpiece, *The City of God*.

Soon after they met, Marcellinus wrote to Augustine about a mutual acquaintance of theirs: Volusianus, a high Roman official. Volusianus had long been undecided about Christianity, but now he was in danger of decisively rejecting it in the aftermath of the sack of Rome. Marcellinus urgently requested Augustine's help in defending the faith. Augustine wrote letters to them both in which he addressed the arguments against Christianity, but Marcellinus felt that a more substantial intellectual investment in this question was needed. He urged Augustine to write an extended defense of Christianity.

---

[4]James O'Donnell, "Augustine's *De civitate Dei*" (manuscript, Georgetown University, 1983). "There is no sign here of any panic in Augustine or in his flock," O'Donnell writes of Augustine's sermons in the aftermath of the sack. "There is thus little reason to think that *The City of God* as we have it would ever have been written if things had remained as they stood a year after the sack of Rome: the rhetorical opportunity the calamity offered might have been neglected. But then Augustine was approached privately in ways that set his pen moving with greater ambition." For online resources see <www.ivpress.com>.

Augustine clearly took his friend's request to heart; he spent the next thirteen years writing *The City of God*. Modern editions of the book typically run to about 1,100 pages. One Augustine scholar remarks that it is "the longest single work presenting a sustained argument unified around a coherent single theme to survive from Greco-Roman antiquity."[5] The only ancient manuscripts that exceed it in length are composite documents such as collections of numerous smaller works or compilations of historical data. Augustine dedicated *The City of God* to Marcellinus, who had died by the time Augustine completed it.

In such a long work, Augustine finds space for many lines of argument. Where, for instance, had the supposed protection of the old gods been during the many previous military defeats and other disasters Rome had suffered over the centuries?[6] And why had the invaders refrained from looting the city's Christian churches or attacking anyone who took sanctuary there; if we are going to read higher meanings into the sack of Rome, Augustine asks, should we not read a higher meaning in that?[7] Augustine also presses more general critiques of traditional Roman religion, pointing out its numerous contradictions and absurdities. The traditionalists worshiped Jupiter above all other gods and considered the goddess Fortune a lesser deity, but at the same time they said Fortune determined all things.[8] They had also multiplied new gods to the point of ridiculousness; Augustine painstakingly lists the dozens of gods who supposedly watched over the various elements of daily human life.[9]

---

[5] O'Donnell, "Augustine's *De civitate Dei*." Augustine himself seems to have felt the extremity of the book's length. He ends it with these words: "And now, as I think, I have discharged my debt, with the completion, by God's help, of this huge work. It may be too much for some, too little for others. Of both these groups I ask forgiveness. But of those for whom it is enough I make this request: that they do not thank me, but join with me in rendering thanks to God. Amen. Amen."

[6] See Augustine *City of God* 3.17-31.

[7] See Augustine *City of God* 1.1-7.

[8] See Augustine *City of God* 7.3.

[9] In a particularly memorable passage, Augustine provides a partial list of the many separate gods and goddesses who supposedly oversaw and participated in the various elements of the sex act. Here Augustine's wit is at its sharpest: "Why fill the bridal chamber with a mob of divinities? ... Let the bridegroom himself do something! ... If there is any modesty in human beings (there seems to be none in the gods!), I feel sure that the belief in the presence of so many divinities of both sexes to urge on the business at hand would so embarrass the couple as to quench the enthusiasm of the one and stiffen the reluctance of the other" (Augustine *City of God* 6.9).

Augustine's Philosophy

Augustine is widely credited with having incorporated Plato's philosophical insights into Christian intellectual tradition. This view is somewhat oversimplified. As we saw in chapter two, Christian thinkers came to seek a renewal of philosophy within Christian thought through a long, gradual process, reaching as far back as Clement's debate with Tertullian in the early second century. Also, Augustine disagreed with Plato as much as he agreed with him; Augustine accepted Plato's arguments only after evaluating them for himself, in light of both natural reason and scriptural revelation, to see whether they were true.

Nonetheless, it is fair to say that Augustine was the key figure in solidifying and confirming the appropriation of Greco-Roman philosophy within Christian thought. In the late fourth century there had been a great revival of interest in Platonic philosophy, a movement that historians have labeled "Neo-Platonism." Augustine had learned a great deal while studying Plato and the Neo-Platonists during his pilgrimage toward Christianity; it was then that he was first confronted with a serious systematic analysis of the nature of the universe. Thus Augustine discovered (contrary to what he had thought) that Christianity did not contradict any of the truths established by natural reason. After his conversion, he found that the insights of the classical philosophers helped to solve some of the perplexing questions raised by Christian theology.

For example, Augustine writes in the *Confessions* that as he was gravitating toward Christianity, his last major intellectual objection was the problem of evil. How could evil exist in a world created by a good God? He found a way out of this quandary while studying the theistic philosophy of the Neo-Platonists. They argued that because God would not make evil, evil does not actually exist; the word *evil* refers to the absence of something (namely, goodness) rather than the presence of something. Once Augustine was satisfied with that solution to the problem, the last remaining intellectual barrier to his conversion was removed.

The City of God begins with an extended analysis of the two major non-Christian worldviews of the day. After dispatching traditional Roman religious thought—including both the crude, popular mythology of the masses and the more sophisticated pantheistic beliefs of the Roman elite—Augustine turns his attention to a sustained critique of Plato and Neo-Platonism. There can be no doubt that Augustine thinks much more highly of the philosophers than he does of the mythologists, but his attitude toward them is still distinctly critical. He seeks to keep whatever is true in Greco-Roman philosophy, while rejecting whatever reason or revelation shows to be false. At the beginning of book nineteen, the crucial book for political issues, Augustine says that he will make his case "not

merely by appealing to divine authority, but also by employing such powers
of reason as we can apply for the benefit of unbelievers."[a] Augustine's defense of this approach to philosophy
was extremely influential and helped

to ensure that the incorporation of
philosophy into Christian thinking
would last.

_____

[a]Augustine *City of God* 19.1.

However, the main argument of *The City of God* is that Christianity
appears bad to its critics because the critics conceive of "good" and "bad"
in the wrong way. Augustine divides humanity into two groups or communities, which he calls the "City of Man" and the "City of God." The
essential point of contrast between the City of Man and the City of God is
psychological: the two cities are distinguished from each another by their
different priorities. The City of God is made up of all those who put God
above all other things, while the City of Man is made up of all those who
put themselves above all other things. "In one city, love of God has been
given first place; in the other, love of self," Augustine writes.[10]

When Augustine describes members of the City of Man putting "self"
ahead of God, this does not necessarily mean that their behavior is "selfish" as we normally understand that word. The point is that they prefer
to satisfy their own preferences, whatever those happen to be, rather than
seeking God's will. This means that even "selfless" and "virtuous" behavior can be a form of putting oneself ahead of God. A mother who puts
her self-sacrificing love for her child ahead of God is really putting herself ahead of God; a patriot who puts his self-sacrificing love of country
ahead of God is really putting himself ahead of God. Augustine himself
drives this point home when he contrasts the more virtuous behavior of
the early Roman Republic with the widespread decadence and corruption
of Rome in his own time.[11] Both the early Romans and the later Romans
belong to the City of Man and put their own preferences ahead of God,
but the early Romans at least preferred honor, justice and self-control to
God, rather than preferring cruelty, wealth and self-indulgence to God.

_____

[10]Augustine *City of God* 14.13.
[11]See, e.g., *City of God* 1.15; 2.18-21.

However, even though the preferences of the early Romans were much less wicked than those of the later ones, both were putting their own preferences ahead of God.

Augustine's dualistic view of human psychology closely mirrors the view of human motivation expressed by the apostles in the New Testament. The apostles describe these two types of human personality in terms of the power of sin on the one hand, and the work of the Holy Spirit on the other. They teach that all human beings are born under the guilt and corruption of sin, and for this reason people put themselves ahead of God. But God sends the Holy Spirit to liberate people from the power of sin by drawing them to himself in Christ (see, e.g., Rom 8:1-17; Eph 2:1-10). Even Augustine's description of Christians having a distinct kind of "citizenship," owing to their different psychology, is taken directly from Paul's letter to the Philippians. "Their end is destruction, their god is their belly, and they glory in their shame, with minds set on earthly things," Paul writes. "But our citizenship is in heaven, and from it we await a Savior, the Lord Jesus Christ" (Phil 3:19-20).

Their different priorities cause the two cities to have different conceptions of the good. For the City of God, the only ultimate good is God; other things are good only to the extent that they look to God. For the City of Man, the satisfaction of one's own desires (whatever they happen to be) is good. And since you cannot satisfy your desires without having the power to satisfy them, the ultimate good for the City of Man, what it desires above all other things, is power. Augustine writes that the City of Man is "a city that aims at dominion, which holds nations in enslavement, but is itself dominated by that very lust of domination."[12]

There are two common misunderstandings to avoid regarding what Augustine means by the City of Man and the City of God. First, while Augustine labels these two groups "cities," in this context he is not talking about literal cities or distinct political units—as if, say, Los Angeles were a City of Man and Topeka were a City of God. He uses the word *city* metaphorically to refer to groups of like-minded individuals. Ac-

---

[12]Augustine *City of God* book 1, preface.

tual cities (like Los Angeles and Topeka) are composed of a mixture of people from both the City of Man and the City of God. Metaphorically speaking, the people in each city who have been redeemed by God form a city within the city, and the unredeemed likewise form another city within the city.

Second, Augustine is well aware that not all people who outwardly profess to be Christians, or who are members of the Christian church, are in fact true believers, who have embraced God in their secret hearts.[13] The City of God therefore does not include all people who outwardly profess to be Christians; it also is not identical with the institutional church.[14] Only those who have truly repented from sin and put God ahead of themselves in their hearts belong to what Augustine calls the City of God. This was a particularly important distinction in the early fifth century, since the new political prominence of Christianity was drawing more and more power-seeking opportunists into the church, especially into its leadership positions. When Christianity was outcast and persecuted, only those who really believed in Christianity wanted to belong to the church. Once it became the official state church of the Roman Empire, with the political power that went along with that role, it inevitably attracted an increasing number of "wolves in sheep's clothing" (see Mt 7:15).

WORKING ALL THINGS FOR GOOD

The overarching purpose of *The City of God* is to vindicate the Christian conception of the good by showing that the world is superintended by God, who is good and is guiding everything that happens in history for good purposes; thus any concept of "the good" is empty if it does not ultimately point to God. The introduction to one modern edition comments that "the great lesson of *The City of God* is that out of all things comes

---

[13]See, e.g., *City of God* 18.49.

[14]This is not to say that Augustine held a low view of the importance of the institutional church: quite the contrary. Like all the other theologians of the time, he thought that the righteousness of Christ was applied to believers through the sacramental system that had been entrusted to the institutional church. However, he did draw a crucial distinction between the institutional church, which contains many false Christians, and the City of God, which consists of all true believers.

good."[15] This echoes Paul's comment to the Romans that "for those who love God all things work together for good" (Rom 8:28).

The sack of Rome may have involved many things that were not good in themselves: people were attacked, possessions stolen, homes destroyed and many of the city's residents were raped, wounded, maimed or killed. In the traditional Roman worldview these things are the worst possible things that can happen. Members of the City of Man seek their good in the satisfaction of their worldly desires, which can only happen in the city of this world; consequently, the city of this world is, to them, the highest good, and its destruction is the worst evil. Augustine observes that even the philosopher Cicero, who preferred virtue and goodness over the glory of the city, sought virtue and goodness only for this world and thus elevated the survival of the city of this world to be the supreme good. He quotes Cicero: "For a man, death is not only inevitable but very often even desirable; whereas when a city is destroyed, wiped out, extinguished, it is (to compare small with great) as if the whole of this world should collapse and perish."[16]

But while the destruction of a city is bad in itself, Christianity teaches that God uses even bad things to serve the greater good: God's glory and humanity's salvation. Thus even the sack of Rome and the miseries that accompanied it, which in themselves are bad, should be seen as part of a plan that serves a higher good.

Augustine argues that the people who were attacked, plundered, displaced, raped, maimed and even killed in the sack of Rome actually lost nothing of essential value. "They lost all they had. Did they lose faith? Or devotion? Or the possessions of the inner man, who is 'rich in the sight of God'?"[17] The essential or ultimate good transcends the city of this world; this is the key insight that distinguishes the City of God from the City of Man.[18] The misfortunes of this life are nothing but an eyeblink compared to eternity. When the Roman people who suffered during the sack go to stand before God, they will find that all their sufferings in this world are irrelevant to whether they have gained or lost the eternal good, which is the only one that matters.

---

[15]John O'Meara, "Introduction," in Augustine, *The City of God* (New York: Penguin, 1984), p. ix.
[16]Augustine *City of God* 22.6; see also Cicero *On the Republic* book 3.
[17]Augustine *City of God* 1.10; see also chaps. 1.8-16.
[18]See, e.g., *City of God* 19.27.

Church and State in Early Christian Rome

In the fourth century, with the Roman population having largely converted to Christianity, Roman Christians did what every other people in history had done up to that point: they sought to integrate the church and the state. No society had ever drawn very sharp lines between the political life and the religious life of the community. There does not appear to have been any conscious decision about whether Christianity should behave any differently; this was just the way all societies had always been governed, and Christians naturally continued the same pattern.

Thus, when Constantine became the first emperor to profess Christ and legalized Christianity in 313, it was assumed that he would take an active role in church leadership. He did not by any means have as much power over the church as he had over the state, but he was considered an important authority figure. It was Constantine who convened the First Council of Nicaea in 325, where the church clarified and reaffirmed its long-standing commitment to the full deity of Christ.

Likewise, Christianity was made the official religion of the Roman Empire in 380, because it was simply assumed that the majority religion of the community would receive political favor. The temples of the traditional Roman gods, which had all along been quasi-government entities, were torn down or converted into churches. Even private worship of the traditional gods was legally constricted.

As Augustine's political ideas became more influential and later Christian thinkers worked out their consequences in more detail, his influence would eventually—many centuries later—prompt a greater separation between the activities of the church and the activities of the state. Augustine argued that in politics, those who truly accept Christ must work side by side with those who reject Christ, either openly or in their secret hearts, all working toward the common goal of civil peace. This implies that two very different sets of rules should govern politics and church life. We will see in chapter four how these ideas unfolded in the Middle Ages.

But Augustine does not stop at arguing that the sack of Rome did no essential harm to those who suffered from it; he goes on to argue that it will accomplish essential good. First, Augustine reminds us—at great length and in lurid detail—that Rome had a long history of wicked, murderous, oppressive behavior. By striking down Rome, he argues, God glorifies himself in the just punishment of evil and also provides a severe warning to others who practice wickedness.[19] Second, the fall of Rome will force people to confront

---

[19]See, e.g., *City of God* 1.33; 2.19-20.

the unreliability of all worldly things. Nothing in this world, not even the so-called eternal city, will last long; only God is really reliable. This will not only induce some people who are currently in the City of Man to join the City of God by abandoning their trust in worldly things; it will also help those who are already in the City of God to achieve a greater state of reliance on God alone. Augustine writes that "weaker" Christians, "who clung to their worldly goods with some degree of avarice, even if they did not prefer them to Christ, discovered, in losing them, how much they sinned in loving them."[20]

No doubt the sack of Rome was a rather extreme way of accomplishing these good ends. But that, according to Augustine, is only to be expected; he is forcing us to confront the fact that human evil is an extreme problem requiring extreme measures. The key concept he wants us to grasp is that worldly afflictions, however extreme, are always a small price to pay for eternal goods.

THE PHILOSOPHER-PIRATE

Augustine also responds to the view that Christian morality results in political weakness, forbidding governments to do what is necessary to preserve the community. He carefully distinguishes the use of violence for private revenge or oppression from the use of violence to uphold justice and civil peace. "There are some whose killing God orders," Augustine writes. The sixth commandment forbids only murder, not the lawful use of force. "For this reason, the commandment . . . was not broken by those . . . who have imposed the death penalty on criminals when representing the authority of the state in accordance with the laws of the state, the most just and reasonable source of power."[21] Turning the other cheek means suppressing your own prideful desire to avenge wrongs done to you or your loved ones, a desire that is motivated by the need to maintain your own superiority over others. Coming to your neighbor's aid when he is being attacked or oppressed, in order to vindicate justice and protect the innocent, is a different matter. Therefore Christian doctrine, if properly understood, does not weaken the state, because it does not forbid the state's legitimate use of force.

---

[20]*City of God* 1.10.
[21]*City of God* 1.21.

But then Augustine goes on to make a much bolder argument, and it is here that the story of the pirate who stood before Alexander comes in. In Cicero's *On the Republic*, published in 51 B.C., a group of friends are discussing justice. One of them, Philus, agrees to play devil's advocate and defend the view that politics should not be constrained by the rules of virtue and goodness. Philus recounts the story of the pirate who claimed that his piracy was no different from Alexander's conquest of the world. "This pirate was, truly, something of a philosopher in his way," Philus argues, "for worldly wisdom and prudence instruct us by all means to increase our power, riches and estates." The survival of the political community, Philus asserts, depends on successfully exerting power over your neighbors before they succeed in exerting power over you. The wise course is to do unto others before they do unto you. And to win the dog-eat-dog contest for survival, you must disregard justice, which "commands us to have mercy upon all; to exercise universal benevolence; to consult the interests of the whole human race; to give every one his due; and to injure no sacred, public or foreign rights." This is almost the same argument that Augustine was hearing from critics of Christianity almost four hundred years later: strict adherence to virtue will leave the state weak and helpless. Philus puts the point succinctly: "If we were to examine the conduct of states by the test of justice, as you propose, we should probably make this astounding discovery, that very few nations, if they gave back what they have stolen, would possess any country at all."[22]

In Cicero's book, the wise statesman Scipio and his friend Laelius refute Philus with two arguments. They briefly argue that a political community that practices justice is actually more likely to survive, not less likely, than one that practices unscrupulous theft and conquest. But more important, they argue that a political community that gives up on working for justice has abandoned its only reason for existing in the first place. The purpose of the political community, they assert, is not primarily to ensure its own survival at any cost, but to establish justice. They argue that this must be the case simply because the only thing that makes a group of people into a political community is that they share a common idea of justice:

---

[22]Cicero *On the Republic* book 3. I rely on Francis Barham's translation. For online resources see <www.ivpress.com>.

a group that lacks a shared sense of justice cannot be said to be a political community in any meaningful sense. "Justice is the very foundation of lawful government in political constitutions," declares Scipio.[23] The government's mission of establishing justice does include the preservation of the community against unjust violence by others, but to do so by the commission of its own unjust violence would defeat the whole point of having a government.

Cicero presses this line of thinking to a radical conclusion: in a society where justice is not enforced, there is, strictly speaking, no political community and no government. What we call the "government" in such a society is not really a government, because it does not do the one thing that governments exist to do: establish justice. Such societies have rulers but not governments. "Wherever I behold a tyrant," declares Scipio, "I know that the social constitution must be, not merely vicious and corrupt, as I stated yesterday, but in strict truth, no social constitution at all."[24] So a government that abandons justice to ensure its survival has, ironically, by that very act ended its own existence as a government.

Augustine, a profound devotee of Cicero's writings, quotes this passage with great approval. "Remove justice," he asks, "and what are kingdoms but gangs of criminals on a large scale? What are criminal gangs but petty kingdoms?"[25] He contrasts the political goals valued by the pre-Christian Romans—glory, conquest and so forth—with the political goals of justice and goodness favored by Christians. "Is it reasonable, is it sensible, to boast of the extent and grandeur of empire, when you cannot show that men lived in happiness, as they passed their lives amid the horrors of war, amid the shedding of men's blood—whether the blood of enemies or fellow citizens—under the shadow of fear and amid the terror of ruthless ambition?"[26]

So Augustine reverses the argument against Christianity on grounds of the need for political survival, turning it against the critics. Since it is justice that makes a political community what it is, the rise of

[23]Cicero On the Republic book 3.
[24]Cicero On the Republic book 3.
[25]Augustine City of God 4.4; see also 2.21; 19.21.
[26]Augustine City of God 4.3.

Christianity enhances, rather than detracts from, the real survival of the political community. Pre-Christian Rome, with its endless wars of conquest and exploitation of the weak, never lived up to the standard set for political communities by its own greatest philosopher, Cicero. Augustine argues that if Cicero is right that "a state cannot be maintained without justice," it follows that "there never was a Roman commonwealth."[27] The rise of Christianity, far from undermining the Roman political community, established it by establishing justice as the central purpose of its government.

A KIND OF COMPROMISE

The section of *The City of God* that has been the most influential on the political thought of future generations is book nineteen, where Augustine argues that all beings instinctively desire peace. "Just as there is no man who does not wish for joy," he writes, "so there is no man who does not wish for peace. Indeed, even when men choose war, their only wish is for victory; which shows that their desire in fighting is for peace with glory."[28] The desire for peace in its various forms drives most human behavior: religion is driven by the desire for peace with God, family life by the desire for peace in the family, economics by the desire for peaceful enjoyment of wealth, self-discipline by the desire for the peaceful absence of sinful desires, and so forth.

Political life is driven by people's desire to have peace with one another. While members of the City of Man cannot be at peace with God, they can be "at peace with the law by which the natural order is governed." Augustine defines this peace as a state of agreement: "Peace between men is an ordered agreement of mind with mind."[29] Obviously the members of the City of Man cannot fully agree with each other on all things, since they all seek to satisfy their own individual preferences. However, by negotiating compromises of their conflicting preferences, they can achieve agreement on a set of rules that will allow them to live together peacefully. The City of Man "limits the harmonious agreement

[27]Augustine *City of God* 19.21.
[28]Augustine *City of God* 19.12.
[29]Augustine *City of God* 19.13.

of citizens concerning the giving and obeying of orders to the establishment of a kind of compromise between human wills about the things relevant to the mortal life."[30]

The City of God, meanwhile, also desires to have peace in the city. It must "make use of this peace also, until this mortal state, for which this kind of peace is essential, passes away." Augustine writes that the City of God "leads what we may call a life of captivity in this earthly city as in a foreign land, . . . and yet it does not hesitate to obey the laws of the earthly city by which those things that are designed for the support of this mortal life are regulated."[31] Obviously the two cities will not agree about things that relate to eternity, such as worship, religion and observing rules of life and virtue as taught by Christianity. However, when it comes to "those things that are designed for the support of this mortal life," such as earthly justice, there is no reason the City of God should not seek the same peace as the City of Man. "Thus even the Heavenly City in her pilgrimage here on earth makes use of the earthly peace, and defends and seeks the compromise between human wills in respect of the provisions relevant to the mortal nature of man, so far as may be permitted without detriment to true religion and piety."[32]

For this reason, the city of this world can and should maintain a state of peaceful coexistence between the City of Man and the City of God within it. "Since this mortal condition is shared by both cities, a harmony may be preserved between them in things that are relevant to this condition." So it is the duty of Christians to participate in the life of the city and promote that harmony. Augustine writes that the proper purpose of all forms of authority (in the church, city, family and so on) is for the benefit of those over whom the authority is exercised. Thus, even when Christians exercise rule over their fellow human beings, they are really serving them, provided that they always act from the proper motives: "For they do not give orders because of a lust for domination but from a dutiful concern for the interests of others, not

---

[30]Augustine *City of God* 19.17.
[31]Augustine *City of God* 19.17.
[32]Augustine *City of God* 19.17.

with pride in taking precedence over others but with compassion in taking care of others."[33]

However, while all people desire peace and the two cities even desire the same kind of peace, the actual attainment of peace is extremely difficult, and even when it has been achieved, it is constantly being undermined and destroyed. This occurs because of the selfishness of human sin, not only in the City of Man but also in the City of God, whose members are still in the process of removing themselves from sinful behavior. Because of the universal presence of sin, the city of this world is constantly in a state of conflict. We may tend to focus on how this state of social conflict causes the frustration of our desires, but it would be better for us to remember that it is our sinful desires that cause the conflict.[34]

The politics of this life are therefore seriously deficient, and they will remain deficient as long as human beings continue to be sinful. So while Christians are called to participate in the life of the city and do what good they can, they must maintain realistic expectations for how much good can be done. They must not expect the earthly city ever to attain the kind of real peace that can only come to those who have peace with God.[35] Remember that for Augustine the peace of the city in this world is a state of "agreement," but not full agreement. It is "a kind of compromise." Real peace, that is, the peace of total agreement in a state of true virtue and goodness, will come only when God has banished the underlying causes of our disagreements: sin and ignorance.[36] Until then, Christians must work to promote the best "compromise" they can get and be satisfied with that. In chapter four we will look at the central political doctrines that emerged from this fundamental commitment to making compromises in the fallen world, rather than trying to build a heaven on earth.

---

[33] Augustine *City of God* 19.14.
[34] See Augustine *City of God* 15.4.
[35] See Augustine *City of God* 19.5-8; 19.27.
[36] See Augustine *City of God* 19.25.

4

NATURAL LAW

THE MEDIEVAL CHURCH
DEVELOPS THE MOST IMPORTANT
POLITICAL IDEA IN HISTORY

When Gentiles, who do not have the law,
by nature do what the law requires . . .
they show that the work of the law
is written on their hearts,
while their conscience also bears witness.

PAUL, IN THE EPISTLE TO THE ROMANS

THOMAS AQUINAS WAS BORN INTO an aristocratic family in Naples in the early thirteenth century. His father intended that Thomas would eventually take over his uncle's prestigious position as abbot of the original monastery of the Benedictine order. It was a perfectly ordinary career path for the European aristocracy. Positions in the church hierarchy were routinely filled by birth and wealth, with little concern for religious vocation. Aquinas was sent to the monastery at age five so he could be raised to take it over. But he grew to become an intensely devout young man and eventually decided he did not want an ordinary aristocratic life. At age sixteen he went to the University of Naples; when he left the university at age twenty-two and announced his intention to join the more world-renouncing Dominican order, his family kidnapped him. He was held captive in the family castle for more than a year, as his father tried every strategy to persuade him to change his mind. He was lavished with all the advantages and comforts he would have to give up if he turned away from the aristocratic life. His earliest biographers record that his father even brought in a prostitute to tempt him. But Aquinas was resolved to reject the life of wealth and power in order to live for God. Eventually the pope intervened and secured him a position with the Dominicans, from which he became one of the greatest Christian thinkers in history—partly through his meditations on the proper role of wealth and power in human society.

William of Ockham was born in England—in the town of Ockham, not surprisingly, about a day's ride from London—in the late thirteenth century. As a youth he was sent off to study in a school run by the Franciscans, another world-renouncing order. His academic career began ignominiously: he studied theology for a full twelve years without ever finishing a degree, earning himself the nickname "the venerable beginner." Nonetheless, he wrote extensively on theology and philosophy. He eventually clashed directly with the pope; Ockham argued fiercely that the life of poverty was the proper Christian life, while the pope insisted on a more wealth-friendly view. When his break with papal orthodoxy came to a head and he feared execution for heresy, he fled his order in the dark of night. Excommunicated for leaving without permission, he found refuge in the court of the German emperor, who was feuding with the pope and was happy to shelter the papacy's rivals. In exile, Ockham's writing naturally turned toward politics, in particular the need for limits on the exercise of authority and for greater freedom of conscience.

The key political concept that Aquinas and Ockham helped to develop is the idea of *natural law*. It holds that the only proper basis of political authority is the moral laws pertaining to life in the present world (do not kill, do not steal, keep your promises, help those in need, preserve the community, etc.) rather than laws pertaining to eternal matters. This idea was at least implicit, though embryonic, in the writings of many Christians going all the way back to the early church. But it was during the Middle

Scholasticism

For centuries the word *medieval* has been synonymous with close-mindedness and intellectual backwardness. In fact, while there are plenty of things to hate about the Middle Ages, almost the only thing one cannot accuse them of is a lack of intellectual activity—and bold, radical, innovative activity at that. The Middle Ages valued intellect for its own sake more than any age before or since; it was the Age of Scholarship.

As it happens, *scholasticism* is the name of the academic system that dominated the West from roughly the eleventh through the fifteenth centuries. Scholasticism was an attempt to formalize and systematize the process of advancing knowledge. In the first six centuries or so of Christianity's existence, intellectual investigation had been driven primarily by the immediate needs of the moment: Christian thinkers were mainly reacting to doctrinal challenges as they arose (the divinity of Jesus in the fourth century, the necessity of grace for salvation in the fifth century, and so forth). Later on, with the foundations of Christian doctrine settled, there were no more crises to react to. Christian intellectual activity died down, and Europe entered the Dark Ages. The scholastics sought to shake off this mental complacency by imposing self-discipline on Christian intellectual life. Early Christian thought had been like a fire brigade, rushing around to put out a series of doctrinal fires that threatened to burn down the church. When the

fires stopped appearing, the brigade got lazy. The scholastics reinvented the fire brigade as a team of expert architects who could systematically strengthen and improve the building.

The scholastics developed rigorous methods of investigation. Aquinas's *Summa theologica*, a typical scholastic book, is divided into a series of 3,125 "articles." In each article, Aquinas poses a question; states various alternative views, including quotations from Scripture and from famous scholars that might be used to support them; then gives his own preferred answer, followed by his reasons, followed by his point-by-point refutations of the alternative views he has rejected. And then on to the next article, and the next, and so on, for over three thousand pages.

In the end, the same systematization that was scholasticism's major strength proved to be its greatest weakness. Scholasticism pulled Europe out of the Dark Ages by forcing the Christian intellect to ask and answer questions in a methodical way. However, over time that very strictness of method lent itself to the growth of fossilized jargon and obsession with technicalities. Also, areas of study that do not lend themselves to scholastic methods, from literature to empirical science, were badly neglected. Scholasticism was eventually more of a hindrance to learning than a help to it. A famous joke depicts the scholastics arguing over "How many angels can dance of the head of a pin?" The scholastics declined in influence over the fourteenth and fifteenth centuries and were decisively surpassed by the new movement called *humanism* during the period now known as the Renaissance (see chap. 5, sidebar, "Sources of the Reformation").

Though we tend to think of the scholastics mostly in terms of their later decline, their accomplishments during their glory years were impressive. They advanced Christian knowledge considerably; one of the most important theological advances ever made, the realization that our guilt and Christ's righteousness changed places on the cross through a process of "imputation," was first proposed by Anselm, one of the early scholastics. Moreover, their investigations of subjects like logic, metaphysics, semantics (the study of language) and epistemology (the study of knowledge) imparted a new level of clarity and precision to Christian thought.

Ages that the doctrine reached full development. And after the thirteenth century, thinkers stressing natural law generally divided into two identifiable schools of thought: one following Aquinas's ideas, the other following Ockham's. The same division continues to this day, in a modified form, because the school following Aquinas has been the predominant influence on Roman Catholic political thought, while the school following Ockham has been predominant among Protestants—a fitting outcome, since the young Aquinas had to be rescued *by* the pope, while Ockham had to be rescued *from* the pope.

THE LAWS OF HIS NATURE, SO TO SPEAK

The concept of natural law had its origins in the thought of the early church. By the time Aquinas and Ockham arrived, Christian philosophers had been steadily building up the doctrine of natural law over the centuries since. So we should not think of it as something that medieval thinkers simply invented. The basic idea of what we now call natural law has been the driving force behind most (though definitely not all) Christian political thought for as long as Christianity has existed.

However, Christian political thinkers did not produce a fully developed understanding of the doctrine of natural law and its implications until the Middle Ages. As we saw in chapter one, the early church did not develop a detailed political philosophy; its attention was necessarily focused on other matters. Its only significant political thought was aimed at producing arguments against the persecution of Christianity. But, narrow as that concern may have been, there was the seed of an important political idea hidden inside it.

Justin Martyr and other early Christian apologists argued that the emperor should tolerate Christians, even though they did not believe in the shared religion of the Roman community, because Christians make good citizens. They obey the law, they help others, they pay their taxes, they pray for blessings upon the emperor, and so forth.[1] The whole basis of this line of argument is that a person need not believe in the shared religion of the community to be a good citizen. Justin and his contemporaries did not stop to develop that premise and realize all of its implications; they were too busy trying to avoid being executed for their faith. But with the benefit of hindsight, we can see that this argument implies a profoundly important conclusion: that the political system of a community does not arise from, or depend upon, its predominant religion. Otherwise how could religious dissenters, like the early Christians, make good citizens? The early Christians were not merely arguing (as many others had argued before them) that persecuting minority religions was unwise because it was more trouble than it was worth. They were arguing that Christians, as Christians, can make good citizens of a non-Christian society—an argument that had much more radical implications.

This seed, planted by the early church, began to sprout in the thought of Augustine, who gave a decisive formulation to the idea of natural law when he wrote that every human being is "drawn by the laws of his nature, so to speak, to enter upon a fellowship with all his fellow-men and to keep the peace with them, as far as lies in him."[2] Augustine had been greatly influenced by the Greco-Roman philosophical argument that there was a moral plan inherent in human nature and knowable by reason (see chap. 2). This idea, when combined with the view established by the early church apologists that good citizenship is not dependent on religion, produced a new perspective on politics and citizenship—that

---

[1]See Justin Martyr *First Apology* 12 and 15-17.
[2]Augustine *City of God* 19.12.

political systems arise from the moral plan that God has planted in every human heart.

The development of this idea in Augustine's thought was particularly prompted by two problems. The first, which he faced earlier in his career, was less directly political than religious. Augustine had to deal with critics of Christianity—especially the Manicheans—who attacked the laws and practices of the Jews in the Old Testament. Responding to them, he draws a distinction between the moral law of God's righteousness, which is eternal and unchanging, and the different kinds of behavior that law can require when it is applied to different circumstances. "By this law the moral customs of different regions and periods were adapted to their places and times, while that law itself remains unaltered everywhere and always." Relying on this premise, Augustine argues that the Old Testament laws and practices reflected the eternal moral law as applied to the particular circumstances of the ancient Jews. Those laws seem strange, primitive or even barbaric to us, he says, because if we instituted those practices in our own society, they would in fact be strange, primitive and barbaric. But that is exactly what we should expect, because our circumstances are so different from those of the ancient Jews; applying the moral law to our circumstances produces different requirements than applying it to their circumstances. When people denounce the Old Testament laws as evil, it is "as though something is allowed to happen behind the stables that is not permitted in the dining room, and a man were indignant because, though it is one house and one family, the same liberties are not given to all members to do what they please anywhere they like."[3] The premise Augustine develops here, that the laws of a society represent the application of a universal moral law to the particular circumstances of that society, became one of the crucial building blocks of natural-law theory.

The other problem Augustine had to deal with arose from his argument that Christians should cooperate with non-Christians in all things concerning the present world (see chap. 3). The problem for Augustine was that he had already argued that if a person is truly Christian, his desires and priorities will be fundamentally different from those of others.

---

[3]Augustine *Confessions* 3.13. For the sake of clarity, I have deviated a little here from the standard Chadwick translation.

If Christians put God first while all others put themselves first, how can the two types of people cooperate? Augustine needed to establish that in spite of their different psychologies, Christians and others want essentially similar things from politics. To do this, he argued that human social life is by its nature designed to work in a certain ordered and lawful way. Even those who reject God in their hearts generally do not reject the natural orderliness or lawfulness of society. "The earthly city, whose life is not based on faith, aims at an earthly peace," he writes; it can establish "a kind of compromise between human wills about the things relevant to mortal life."[4] So while sinful humanity, so long as it remains sinful, cannot have spiritual peace, it can nonetheless have earthly peace and thus be "at peace with the law by which the natural order is governed."[5] Hence, preserving the natural lawfulness of human society is a common area of endeavor for all people, whether they submit to God or not.

THE IMAGE OF GOD

Later Christian thinkers kept working out the further consequences of these ideas. This was a long and slow process of development; as a great historian of Christianity has remarked, we tend to forget that there were more centuries between Augustine and Aquinas than between Aquinas and ourselves.[6] The development of natural-law doctrine accelerated after the rise of scholasticism in the eleventh century (see sidebar "Scholasticism"), as Christian thinkers sought to fit all their political ideas together into a coherent body of teachings. In doing so, they developed the basic concepts inherited from the early church into the full-fledged doctrine of political authority that we now refer to as "natural law."

Although there are many different theories of natural law, on a broad level natural-law thought is defined by certain shared principles. It holds that there is an eternal moral law that is knowable to all human beings by reason and conscience, called the natural law. In other words, moral law is written into human nature through reason and conscience, and this is part of what the Bible means when it says that humanity was

---

[4]Augustine *City of God* 19.17.
[5]Augustine *City of God* 19.13.
[6]A professor of mine once told his class that he had heard Jaroslav Pelikan make this remark.

made "in the image of God" (Gen 1:26-27; see also Gen 9:6; 1 Cor 11:7; 2 Cor 4:4). This natural law remains influential, at least to some extent although not in a saving way, over the lives of fallen and sinful people. While sinners are not saved from their sins by their knowledge of the natural law, they do possess this knowledge, and their behavior is affected by it. Natural-law doctrine also holds that natural law is the proper source of political authority, and that it gives each human society the authority to establish a government by which it will govern itself. In particular, this last point means that government is not established directly by God. Rather, God authorizes the community to establish a government, and government's purpose under God's law is to serve the community that created it (we will look more closely at the importance of this point in chapter seven). Since government exists to enforce the natural law, government is itself subject to the natural law; government power is only to be used in accordance with the purposes for which it was created. The laws of each society should seek to apply the natural law to the particular circumstances of that society.

Basic Principles of Natural-Law Thought

1. Natural law is an eternal moral law revealed to all people through human nature.

2. Natural law influences (but cannot save) even fallen and sinful humanity.

3. Natural law is the proper basis of political authority.

4. Natural law authorizes society to establish a government.

5. Governments are themselves subject to the natural law.

6. Each society's laws should apply the natural law to that society's particular circumstances.

Obviously the claims made by natural-law theory go beyond the basic principles that are shared by all Christians, and as a result, not all Christians agree with the doctrine of natural law. As we have already mentioned in chapter one, Christian theology has historically taught that right and wrong are revealed to all people; this is the doctrine of

Thomas Aquinas (ca. 1225-1274)

If the scholastics were systematizers—bringing the many strands of Christian thought together into coherent intellectual systems—Thomas Aquinas was the systematizer of the systematizers. He took the various insights and analyses of the scholastics who came before him and unified them in a single body of theological and philosophical doctrine, whose breadth and depth are virtually unmatched by the works of any other theologian. However, as one would expect with any work of this nature, his theological synthesis has always been deeply controversial.

Aquinas wrote extensively but is primarily known for two major works. His *Summa contra Gentiles*, written between 1258 and 1264, is an apologetic work defending the truth of Christianity. It seems to have been aimed primarily at vindicating Christianity against Islam, which was the only major religious rival to Christianity that Western Europeans had to deal with on a regular basis. His *Summa theologica*, written between 1265 and his death in 1274, is an introductory textbook on Christian philosophy and theology. Before long it was being used widely throughout the West, not only as a textbook for beginners (its original purpose) but also as a summary of Christian doctrine that even advanced theologians would rely on.

Just as Augustine is widely credited with incorporating Plato's thought into Christian tradition, Aquinas is widely credited with doing the same for Aristotle after the works of Aristotle were "reintroduced" in the West in the thirteenth century, after having been lost. As we saw in chapter three, the reality of Augustine's treatment of Plato is different from the popular conception (see sidebar "Augustine's Philosophy"). Perhaps not surprisingly, the same is true of Aquinas and Aristotle.

It is true that Aquinas's moral thought owes a great deal to Aristotle's philosophy of ethics. However, this is not because Aristotle's ethics were reintroduced in the West; in fact, Aristotle's ethical thought had never been lost. Christian thinkers had always found much truth in Aristotle's account of the moral plan written in human nature, and most of the ethical thought of Christian philosophers had always been broadly Aristotelian.

What had been lost in the West, and was reintroduced in the thirteenth century, was not Aristotle's ethics, but much of his other thought, including especially his metaphysics. With the broader works of Aristotle now available, it became clear that Aristotle's thought was further from the Christian worldview than had originally been appreciated. For example, Aristotle's metaphysics held that matter was eternal and that the world had only been "created" by God in the sense that God was the first to give it form and motion. Suddenly, it was no longer clear whether Christian thinkers ought to be relying on Aristotle.

Aquinas's concern was to rescue the Aristotelian ethics of Christian tradition from Aristotle's metaphysics. He worked to show that Aristotle's account of the moral plan in human nature was broadly compatible with the Christian Scriptures, even if Aristotle's other thought was not. Thus, just as Augustine did not "incorporate" Plato into Christian tradition because that process had begun centuries earlier, but he did deepen and confirm the connection; so also, Aquinas did not "incorporate" Aristotle into Christian tradition, but he did deepen and confirm the connection.

"natural revelation." Thus Paul writes to the Romans, "When Gentiles, who do not have the law, by nature do what the law requires, . . . they show that the work of the law is written on their hearts, while their conscience also bears witness" (Rom 2:14-15). However, not all Christians agree that this natural revelation of moral law continues to play an active role in the life of those who are fallen and alienated from God. Some Christians are also concerned that affirming the authority of a moral law outside the Bible would compromise the Bible's authority. And some interpret the idea that natural law is "revealed in human nature" to mean that natural law is an autonomous or self-given law—that a person who followed natural law would be following his own nature rather than God.

Of these three major criticisms, the third is the least serious, because it reflects a misunderstanding of what natural-law doctrine actually teaches. No Christian natural-law thinker understands natural law as a law that human beings make for themselves; rather, it is a law that God makes for human beings and reveals to them through reason and conscience. Similarly, following a law that is known through human nature does not mean following a law other than God's law. After all, according to Christianity, human nature is made in the image of God; natural-law doctrine understands "the image of God" to include a natural knowledge of God's moral law.

The other two criticisms are more substantial. Against the view that natural law cannot be active among fallen and sinful people, defenders of natural-law doctrine argue that a knowledge of right and wrong plays an important role in the lives of all human beings. They interpret Paul's comments in Romans as teaching not only that all human beings were given a conscience but also that this conscience is never totally dormant in anyone's life no matter how deeply a person falls into sin. They point out that Paul does not say that the Gentiles "know by nature" the works of the law, but that they "do by nature" the works of the law: the Gentiles' knowledge of the law has an effect on their actions. In Romans 1, Paul comments that right and wrong are revealed to all people, "so they are without excuse" (Rom 1:20). Knowledge of right and wrong must continue to be active if people are to be without excuse for their sin. They also point to scriptural passages in which those who are alienated from God still evidence an awareness that there is such a thing as right and wrong. Saying that fallen people do not know right from wrong by nature, they argue, is tantamount to denying that they bear the image of God.

Against the view that natural-law compromises the authority of the Bible, defenders of natural law argue that the Bible itself affirms that natural law is the proper basis of politics. They point, for example, to Abraham's confrontations with various unbelieving rulers, in which it is taken for granted that in political life believers and unbelievers are bound together by a shared moral standard of rights and duties (see Gen 12:10-20; 20:1-18; 21:22-34; also 26:6-11; 34:1-31). Since the unbelieving rulers had received no special revelation from God, this common moral standard can only be the natural law. A similar presumption of a common political standard of right and wrong among believers and unbelievers is observable in the relations between the nations of Judea and Israel and their unbelieving neighbors, and in the relations of the Judean exiles with their Babylonian captors.[7] Finally, and perhaps most important, they point to the apostles' endorsement of the political authority of the Roman government (discussed in detail in chap. 1). The apostles teach that the Roman emperors

---

[7]See 2 Sam 10:2; 1 Kings 5:1-18; 10:1-29; Jer 29:1-14; Ezek 26; Dan 1:8-16; 3:8-30; 6:1-28. Natural-law defenders also point to differences between the way the Old Testament prophets condemn the wickedness of Judea and Israel and the way they condemn the wickedness of other nations. While Judea and Israel are condemned for violating God's specially revealed law, other nations are condemned for moral wickedness without any mention of the specially revealed law, implying that outside the context of the Promised Land, nations are held to a standard of natural law. E.g., compare Amos 2:4-16 with Amos 1:3–2:3.

ruled with authority derived from God even while they were persecuting Christianity; natural-law thinkers argue that this only makes sense on the premise that governments derive their authority from natural law rather than from Scripture.[8]

Objections to Natural Law and Responses

Objection: The natural revelation of moral law is obstructed by our sinfulness.

Response: Natural knowledge of right and wrong is damaged by sin, but not eliminated.

Objection: Affirming the authority of natural law compromises the authority of the Bible.

Response: The Bible itself teaches the authority of the natural law.

Objection: Natural law is a law made by human nature rather than by God.

Response: Natural law is a law made by God and revealed through human nature.

AQUINAS'S CONCEPT OF NATURAL LAW

The outline of natural-law theory given above is only a broad overview, and within it there is room for a great deal of disagreement about the details. The category of natural law encompasses a wide variety of different theories. Starting in the thirteenth and fourteenth centuries, however, most of the various accounts of natural law coalesced into two distinct intellectual schools: one following Aquinas, called the *Thomist* school after Aquinas's first name Thomas; the other following Ockham. These two approaches to natural law have remained more or less distinct ever since.

For Aquinas, all types of law—which includes the natural law known to all people through reason, the specially revealed law of God's verbal and written commands to his people, and the civil laws made by human governments—rest on the same two foundations: the eternal mind of God and the "end" or purpose for which God made humanity. The mind of God supplies the content of law, which is righteousness. In the case of natural law and the specially revealed law, the law's actual con-

---

[8]For further discussion of the natural-law response to these three objections, see David VanDrunen, *A Biblical Case for Natural Law* (Grand Rapids: Acton Institute, 2006)—an excellent short summary of the biblical basis of natural-law doctrine, to which my treatment here is much indebted.

tent always conforms perfectly to the mind of God, because these two types of law are made by God himself. In the case of civil law, which is made by human beings, the actual content of the law will differ from the mind of God (sometimes just a little, sometimes a great deal) due to the sinfulness and incompetence of human governments. However, righteousness as it is known in the mind of God is still the ideal or standard to which the civil law is supposed to conform. The righteousness of God is the proper basis for the content of civil law, if not always its actual basis.[9]

While the mind of God supplies the content of law, the obligation of law—the reason law is binding—arises because God made humanity to serve a specific end. Aquinas writes that this end is the beatific vision, the blissful life enjoyed by those who live "face to face" with God.[10] Obviously no one can live in full and direct communion with God and look directly on his divine glory without being righteous. God, who is himself righteous, will not take an unrighteous person into full communion with himself; for that matter, the very idea of an unrighteous person experiencing full communion with a righteous God is self-contradictory.[11] So obedience to law is obligatory because the purpose of human life presupposes it.

The natural law is distinct from other types of law in that it is "built into" human nature by God, while people receive both the specially revealed law and the civil law from outside sources (God and human government respectively). Aquinas identifies two specific elements of human nature that are the foundation of the natural law. The first is an awareness of right and wrong, which is derived from God's awareness of his own righteousness.[12] The second is a desire for happiness, which is the natural reflection of the purpose for which we are created.[13] All human beings possess these two elements.

However, a problem arises in the relationship between them. Reason shows us that goodness and happiness are inseparable—that our desire to

---

[9]See Thomas Aquinas *Summa theologica* First Part of the Second Part, question 93, art. 3. For online resources see <www.ivpress.com>.

[10]See *Summa theologica* First Part of the Second Part, questions 1-3, esp. question 3, art. 8.

[11]See *Summa theologica* First Part of the Second Part, question 4, art. 4.

[12]See *Summa theologica* First Part of the Second Part, question 91, art. 2.

[13]See *Summa theologica* First Part of the Second Part, question 1, art. 7; and question 5, art. 8.

be happy can only be truly and lastingly fulfilled by the beatific vision, which in turn we can only reach by pursuing righteousness. But sinful human beings refuse to equate the happy life with the good life. They refuse to be happy with righteousness. Only by the special regenerating work of God through the Holy Spirit do people overcome their sinfulness and reunite goodness with happiness.

This does not mean, according to Aquinas, that sinful people choose evil as such over good as such. A thief would not steal if he did not know that money was good. Instead, Aquinas argues that immorality consists of placing a lesser good (such as pleasure and wealth) above a greater good (such as obeying God and reaching the beatific vision).[14]

This state of affairs causes regenerate and unregenerate people to behave differently from one another in one sense, but similarly in another sense. On the one hand, a person who has been regenerated by God is pursuing an end (righteousness and the beatific vision) fundamentally different from that of an unregenerate person. As a result, the choices of these two types of people will in one sense be very different. On the other hand, both types of people begin with the same psychological tools: a knowledge of goodness and a desire for happiness. As a result, while their internal motivations are different, there is much common ground in their external behavior. Both are pursuing happiness, and there are many things that both agree are good when considered in themselves (such as pleasure and wealth). The regenerate person knows that one's happiness ultimately lies with the greatest of all good things—God—but also knows that God provides lesser good things to be enjoyed as well, within the boundaries God sets. The unregenerate person seeks enjoyment only of the lesser goods, not the greater, and will acknowledge fewer boundaries on how they may be used. Nonetheless, the two types of persons agree that the lesser goods are good and that they can and should be enjoyed.

Aquinas's view therefore provides considerable common ground between the regenerate person and the unregenerate person. A person can know that things like pleasure and wealth are good things without knowing that they are subordinate to God. Hence, between the two types of

---

[14]See *Summa theologica* First Part of the Second Part, question 5, art. 8; and question 18, art. 1.

Church and State in the Middle Ages

Natural-law doctrine teaches that the proper basis of civil authority is the natural law rather than special revelation. But medieval societies had laws forbidding religious offenses such as heresy, blasphemy and apostasy; the civil punishments for these crimes were often severe. It is difficult for us to see how they could maintain such laws if they believed in natural law. If civil authority is only supposed to enforce the natural law, how can it be a civil crime to deny Christ or to hold a false theology? As we will see in some detail in chapter six, natural-law doctrine did eventually arrive at the conclusion that religious freedom is a necessary consequence of the natural-law understanding of government. But why did it take so many centuries to reach this conclusion, which seems so obvious in retrospect?

The purpose of government, according to natural law, is to manage the common concerns of the community for the public good. One of the foremost common concerns of the community is the survival of the community itself. And until the emergence of religious freedom, it was believed that the community could not survive if its majority religion was not maintained, which in turn was thought to require the support of government power. We will look at the reasoning behind this view more closely in chapter six, but the basic idea was that government had to enforce moral rules (such as do not kill, do not steal, etc.) and a shared community religion was necessary to maintain social adherence to these rules. Thus, heresy and other religious offenses were considered not just sins, but also a danger to the survival of the community, because they undermined the public's adherence to the moral rules on which civil law is based. Or to put it another way, the basis of government was the natural law, but only good and pious people could be expected to obey the natural law, and government support for religion was necessary to keep people good and pious.

Interestingly, in his lengthy discussions of heresy and church power, Ockham came to realizations that were well ahead of his time on the subject of religious freedom. A person should not be subject to civil punishment simply for believing in a false theology, he wrote, because such a person does no one else any harm. Ockham made this toleration conditional on a willingness to listen to corrective teaching from the church, and—more important—on the person's never seeking to convert others to his view. An actively proselytizing heretic, Ockham concluded, was indeed a threat to social stability and could be punished. But Ockham still went further than almost any other political thinker in the Middle Ages in allowing some degree of freedom of conscience.

person, there is a large degree of agreement on which things are good. And since the good things that are proper to politics are generally the kinds of things that almost everyone agrees are good—civil peace, justice, prosperity and so forth—all people can cooperate in pursuing them. This cooperation in things that are of common concern to believers and unbelievers is how politics should work.

This common ground is limited, however. Natural law extends only to those moral laws known to all people through reason, such as those concerning murder, theft, lying and so on. It does not include moral laws delivered by special revelation, such as those concerning salvation from sin, the right worship of God, the institution of the church and so on. For Aquinas, this distinction between two different types of divine law arises from two different ways in which human beings can participate in God's knowledge of his own righteousness. All people participate in God's knowledge to a certain extent by nature, insofar as they are thinking beings—because thinking itself would be impossible if God did not think. It follows that all people are responsible for the way they respond to and use the natural knowledge of God that they have as thinking beings. But some people participate in God's knowledge beyond what is available by nature, because they have received special revelation from God's explicit commands and have been brought into fellowship with him. By trusting in God through his revealed Word, believers come to participate in God's knowledge on a new level. In doing so, they become responsible for how they respond to and use this additional knowledge. On the other hand, those who have never received this additional knowledge of God cannot be held responsible for responding to it or using it. Thus, all people are responsible for how they respond to the knowledge of God that is available to them by nature, but not all people are responsible for how they respond to the knowledge of God specially revealed in his Word.

It follows that the moral rules arising from natural knowledge of God can be enforced on all, but not the moral rules arising from specially revealed knowledge of God. In Aquinas's time, the implications of this conclusion were not fully realized: everyone who was raised in a Christian society was considered responsible for knowing both the natural and special rules, and so it was considered acceptable to let the state enforce the natural rules on all people while the church enforced

William of Ockham (ca. 1288–ca. 1348)

William of Ockham's career can be divided fairly neatly into two periods. During the early period, lasting until his rupture with the pope and flight into German exile in 1328, he wrote extensively on subjects in technical philosophy such as epistemology and metaphysics. During the later period, for obvious reasons, his writing turned toward more practical fields: politics, ethics and ecclesiology (the study of the church).

During his early period, Ockham was one of the foremost critics of idealism, the predominant metaphysical philosophy of the day. *Idealism,* which originated with Plato, holds that abstract ideas have real existence—that ideas like "one" and "red" and "man" actually exist on their own, on a higher plane of existence beyond the physical world, and these independently existing ideas form the basis of our thoughts. Idealists believe this view is the only sufficient explanation for the occurrence of abstract ideas in the human mind.

Ockham championed an alternative view, which has come to be called *nominalism.* This view holds that abstract ideas do not have independent existence, and more generally that complex metaphysical explanations of phenomena should be avoided. In the next few centuries, nominalism gained ever-greater influence, and its rise eventually contributed to the eclipse of scholasticism (since so much scholastic thought had been idealist).

It was in the course of this fight over idealism that Ockham developed the principle of thought now known as Ockham's razor. This principle is widely misunderstood; contrary to popular opinion, it does not hold that the simplest explanation of a phenomenon is the most likely to be true. Rather, it holds that one should not believe in the existence of something unless the known facts cannot be explained any other way. Thus, for example, you can safely believe that the author of this book exists (or at least that he did at one point), because you know that this book itself exists, and the existence of the book is inexplicable without the author. But Ockham's razor would forbid you to believe that there is an invisible man reading the book along with you right now, because none of the available facts requires this view. So Ockham's razor concerns not the complexity of an explanation, but the number of entities whose existence it proposes. This principle was a major step forward in epistemology.

During his later period, Ockham produced a number of works discussing our moral obligations in a variety of practical areas, the most important of which was the *Dialogue on the Power of the Emperor and the Pope.* Ockham's chief concern in his practical writings, not surprisingly, is the question of heresy and the church. His views on the need for limits on power were mainly developed in his consideration of the church's power to condemn heresy and the status of the pope within the church. However, having developed these views in the context of the church, he went on to apply them to the state as well.

the special rules on all people (see sidebar "Church and State in the Middle Ages"). However, as we will see in more detail in chapter six, later generations of natural-law thinkers arrived at the conclusion that the natural rules are the only ones that should be enforced on all people, while enforcement of the special rules should be limited to those who voluntarily accept them.

Like all natural-law thinkers, Aquinas places limits on what government can legitimately do. For Aquinas, the limit on government authority is "the common good," by which he primarily means the establishment of justice and civil peace, as well as managing all the other common concerns of the community that pertain to life in the present world.[15] Aquinas further states that it would be irrational for human law to demand perfection of people, even in worldly matters, because such perfection is unattainable; government should only forbid actions that pose a serious threat to the community.[16] He writes that human law is only just if it does not violate God's law, if it serves the common good, if it is within the legitimate authority of the lawgiver who made it, and if it treats people equitably (with fairness).[17]

However, for Aquinas these limits are not developed into a system of what we would call "limited government." Aquinas is concerned to show governments what limits they should acknowledge for their use of power, but not to show subjects effective ways to keep governments within those limits. The initiative lies on the government's side to obey God, not on the subject to keep the government obedient.

Aquinas does say that in extreme cases, resistance to a tyrannical government may be acceptable.[18] But he is adamant that this remedy is available only in extreme cases. Even nonviolent refusal to obey an unjust order—what we now call "civil disobedience"—should only be used where fidelity to God requires it. Frequent civil disobedience, Aquinas argues, would tempt others to sin and undermine the stability of society; thus from the standpoint of the common good, it would hurt more than it would help.[19] Frequent rebellion would be even worse.

---

[15]See *Summa theologica* First Part of the Second Part, question 95, arts. 2-3.

[16]See *Summa theologica* First Part of the Second Part, question 96, art. 2.

[17]See *Summa theologica* First Part of the Second Part, question 96, art. 4.

[18]See *Summa theologica* Second Part of the Second Part, question 42, art. 2, esp. reply to obj. 3.

[19]See *Summa theologica* First Part of the Second Part, question 96, arts. 4-5.

This reticence about creating institutions that constrain government power, not to mention rebellion against tyrants, was nothing new. It had been the overwhelmingly predominant attitude of Christian political thought since the origins of Christianity, and it would remain so until the seventeenth century. For most of the history of Christianity, a firm belief in limits on legitimate government authority existed side by side with a reluctance to build constraining institutions or to sanction rebellion in any but the worst circumstances. We will see in chapter seven how the predominance of this position came to be challenged much more strongly in the seventeenth century and onward.

OCKHAM'S CONCEPT OF NATURAL LAW

Although Ockham's conception of natural law differs from Aquinas's in important ways and serves as the starting point for a separate school of natural-law thought, it is important to realize that the differences are not radical. Ockham and Aquinas both subscribe to all the common principles of natural-law thought identified above. Ockham also agrees with Aquinas that the content of the natural law is based on God's righteousness, and that eternal fellowship with God is the end for which human beings were made. The two schools are recognizably part of a single intellectual tradition.

One question on which Ockham disagrees with Aquinas is whether sin involves a choice of evil as such over good as such. For Ockham, a choice is not morally meaningful unless the chooser is making a choice between good and evil. Aquinas had held that the choice of a lesser good (e.g., money) over a greater good (e.g., God) may be an evil choice, but it is not a choice of evil as such over good as such. Ockham, to the contrary, says that an evil choice is precisely a choice in favor of evil as such. That, he argues, is what it means to call a choice evil. A related difference between Ockham and Aquinas is the different relationship between God's righteousness and our moral knowledge. Aquinas had written that the source of our moral knowledge is the mind of God: we know right from wrong because God knows his own righteousness and extends some of his knowledge to us. Ockham held that the source of our moral knowledge is God's will rather than God's mind: we know right from wrong because God wills that his righteousness should be a law for us to know and obey.[20] This view places greater emphasis on the status of the natural law as a law—that it is laid down by a legislator who will back it up with rewards and penalties. Aquinas and Ockham agree that the natural law is both morally good and legislated by God, but Aquinas's view places more emphasis on the former, while Ockham's places more emphasis on the latter.

These disagreements may sound like nothing but an argument over semantics and abstractions, but they make a profound difference in how we understand what the natural law is and how it works. Probably the most important difference is that the good things of this world provide less common ground between believers and unbelievers on Ockham's view than on Aquinas's view, and the common ground they do provide is more problematic for Ockham. Aquinas and Ockham agree that choosing to put the good things of this world ahead of God is evil. However, they disagree over exactly what it means to make such a choice: they disagree over what an evil choice essentially is. For Aquinas, the person making such a choice is choosing a good, just the wrong good. For Ockham, the person making such a choice is choosing evil, even though the object he is choosing (money, pleasure, etc.) is in itself good. So while they both hold that the moral psychologies of believers and unbelievers are different, Ockham holds that the difference is more fundamental. Aquinas's view provides grounds for at least some optimism that all people, Christian and non-Christian, will generally desire good things for the community. Ockham provides far less grounds for such optimism and thus offers less reason to think that worldly things in themselves will hold the community together.

This is not to say that Ockham denies any common ground between believers and unbelievers. He is, after all, a natural-law thinker. The basics of community life, the most fundamental principles of justice and civil peace, will generally be agreed upon by all. But Ockham's view does imply a narrower scope of agreement than Aquinas's does. As the basic

---

[20]For a fuller discussion of the differences between Aquinas and Ockham on the foundations of natural law, see Marilyn Adams, "Ockham on Will, Nature, and Morality," in *The Cambridge Companion to Ockham*, ed. Paul Spade (Cambridge: Cambridge University Press, 1999).

principles of justice and civil peace are applied to real-world situations, there will inevitably come a point where believers and unbelievers start to disagree about their application. Ockham's more pessimistic view of the psychology of sin teaches us to expect that point of disagreement to arrive sooner than Aquinas does, and to expect such disagreements to be more intractable.

Ockham also draws much narrower limits on the use of power than does Aquinas. Clearly this stance arose partly because of his clash with the pope. At this time popes were claiming much greater authority in the church than they previously had; some claimed that the pope had what was called "fullness of power," meaning the right to command anything that did not directly contradict God's law. Ockham defended an older and more restrictive view of the pope's authority; he vehemently denounced the claim to "fullness of power."[21] However, Ockham's desire to limit the use of power cannot be attributed solely to his opposition to the pope. He also denied claims that the German emperor possessed "fullness of power," even though the emperor was his only protection from the pope and even though Ockham was a strong proponent of monarchy over other forms of government.[22]

Like Aquinas, Ockham believed that power was only to be used for the common good. Thus Aquinas and Ockham were agreed in opposing any claim to "fullness of power." Kings and popes alike were to use their power only to serve the community.

However, Ockham went further than Aquinas in laying down specific limits to the use of power, limits that he thought were a necessary consequence of the principle that power is only to be used for the common good. He argued that reason and Scripture alike teach that ordinary subjects are not slaves, and that therefore political rule must always preserve their freedom; he laid down a similar limitation on the pope's authority in the church. Aquinas's rule that power is to be used for the common good only limits the purpose for which power can be used; Ockham's additional rule also limits how far power can be used even when it is being used for a

---

[21]See William of Ockham *Dialogue on the Power of the Emperor and the Pope* dialogue 1. For online resources see <www.ivpress.com>.
[22]See William of Ockham *Dialogue on the Power* dialogue 3.

good purpose. At least as a general rule, the freedom of individuals cannot be compromised for the sake of the common good.

Ockham also favored greater scope for resistance to abuses of power. He held that no one is infallible: no individual, not even the pope, and no body of individuals, not even an ecumenical church council. This was a fairly radical position at the time, especially concerning church councils. As a result of this view that no one is infallible, he concluded that all authorities must be held accountable for their use of power. As one team of Ockham scholars puts it, Ockham's view is that "justice must prevail at all costs, and no ruler's authority is sufficiently powerful to evade or subvert this requirement."[23]

Obviously Ockham did not mean that authority could be resisted after any abuse, no matter how trivial; only serious abuses of power justify resistance. And in virtually all cases, Ockham envisions the various authority figures within the government or the church holding each other accountable, rather than ordinary subjects holding the government accountable or laypeople holding the church accountable. If the king abuses power, the nobility should resist him, not the subjects; if the pope abuses power, the bishops should resist him, not the laity. However, in the extreme case where all authority figures abuse power at once, Ockham is willing to countenance popular resistance. No individual or group should ever be totally beyond accountability for misuse of power.

Still another difference between Ockham and Aquinas is that Ockham wanted church and state to be more independent of one another. Although natural-law doctrine had long since drawn a sharp distinction between the source of the state's authority and the source of the church's authority, these two institutions were still held to be interdependent in important ways (see sidebar "Church and State in the Middle Ages"). Ockham thought that if government really arises from one source (natural law) while the church really arises from a different source (special revelation), it must follow that each exercises its authority independently of the other. The most immediate issue for Ockham was the question of whether a civil ruler lost his political authority if the church determined him to be

---

[23]John Kilcullen and George Knysh, "Ockham and the *Dialogus*" (manuscript, British Academy, U.K., 2002). For online resources see <www.ivpress.com>.

a heretic or otherwise unfit to rule. This was the original source of the rivalry between the German emperor and the pope; the pope claimed that the emperor could not rule without his approval, which he refused to give, but the emperor ignored the pope and continued to rule. Obviously Ockham came down on the emperor's side. But this was not merely a self-serving move on Ockham's part. The principle that church authority and state authority should be more independent of one another grows naturally from his broader understanding of what these institutions are for and how power is supposed to be used. For example, he also holds that non-Christians should retain all the same civil rights (such as citizenship or property) as Christians—another somewhat radical view at the time.

Ockham's views were, indeed, too radical for most of his medieval contemporaries; the Thomist school of natural law predominated for most of the remainder of the Middle Ages. But the school following Ockham gained ground in the late Middle Ages with the decline of scholasticism; it was particularly influential in the wake of the Reformation, as Protestants developed their own understandings of natural law, which we will look at in chapter five. It remained ascendant throughout the Enlightenment, particularly during the emergence of the Christian political theories of religious freedom, natural rights and liberal democracy, which we will look at in chapters six and seven. Then, however, as Protestants increasingly turned away from natural law in the twentieth century (for reasons we will look at in chap. 8), the Thomist school once again ascended to fill the void in our time.

5

REGIO VERSUS *RELIGIO*

THE REFORMATION AND THE NATION-STATE

We must obey God
rather than men.

PETER, QUOTED IN ACTS
OF THE APOSTLES

IN 1516, A PREVIOUSLY OBSCURE FRIAR named Johann Tetzel took a new job as an indulgence preacher. He could not possibly have known how fateful that career move would turn out to be: he soon became the most famous traveling salesman in history. The aftermath of his tour through Germany would include the fracturing of Western Christianity, two centuries of some of the cruelest and bloodiest warfare ever waged, the emergence of the nation-state as the fundamental unit of politics in Europe and around the world, and (eventually) the development of an entirely new structure of political ideas centered around the freedom of the individual.

MY CONSCIENCE IS CAPTIVE TO THE WORD OF GOD

Tetzel obtained this position because Pope Leo X had called for a dramatic increase in the distribution of indulgences: special pardons by which the Roman Catholic church claims to release a sinner from the temporal punishment of sin in purgatory. Sinners are required to earn these pardons by acts of penance, and the normal practice at that time was to make a contribution to the church. In other words, indulgences were sold. Leo radically expanded the sale of indulgences in order to fund the construction of an enormous, opulent new papal church, the Basilica of St. Peter.

Tetzel was good at his new job. His preaching was lucrative and his methods were not subtle. He would scare his audiences with vivid depictions of the suffering their dead loved ones were enduring in purgatory—suffering that was also awaiting them as soon as they died. Then he would offer to relieve these sufferings for those who did penance by giving to the church. He even pioneered the use of a rhyming jingle to advertise his services; the traditional English translation of it goes, "When the coin in the coffer rings, a soul from purgatory springs."

In 1517, Tetzel began a barnstorming tour of the German countryside. But he could not preach indulgences in the region of Saxony because the local lord, known as Frederick the Wise, had forbidden it. Frederick had founded a theological university in the town of Wittenberg, the first university in Germany founded without permission from the church. One of its theologians, a protégé of Frederick's, had become a leading critic of indulgences. But Frederick also had more mercenary motives for opposing indulgences: he owned a collection of religious relics that brought him income as people paid to see them, and indulgence campaigns diverted this revenue. In addition, a portion of Tetzel's profits was going to his sponsor, Albert of Mainz, one of Frederick's political rivals.

Undaunted by the ban, Tetzel set up shop in a town just outside Saxony, and many of Frederick's subjects flocked over the border to purchase release from the torment of purgatory for themselves and their loved ones. Witnessing this spectacle caused something to snap in Wittenberg's star theologian. For some time he had harbored doubts, not just about indulgences but also about the larger doctrine of the sacrament of penance: the doctrine by which the Catholic church claims to be the mediator between God and humanity and to dispense God's forgiveness of sins. Raising doubts about the sacrament of penance was a far more radical position than merely opposing indulgences; the Wittenberg theologian was now challenging the entire structure of the church's theology of salvation.

But disgust with Tetzel's exploits broke through his last remaining hesitation about expressing these doubts. He wrote an angry proposal suggesting ninety-five propositions (or theses) about the sacrament of penance for the Wittenberg faculty to debate. On October 31, 1517, he posted it on the door of the city's church, as was the standard practice for university discussions. He also sent a copy of the proposal to the local archbishop— Albert of Mainz, the very man who was sponsoring Tetzel's campaign.

The proposal set the university on fire with its biting, sarcastic attack on indulgences and its ringing declaration that God's forgiveness is freely available to everyone. In the Bible, the proposal argued, Jesus does not connect forgiveness to specific acts of penance. He calls us to make our whole lives an act of penance—or "repentance," as the proposal insisted the word should instead be translated. "Our Lord and Master Jesus Christ, when he said *Poenitentiam agite*, desired that the whole life of believers should be repentance," declared the theses' opening line. "This word cannot be understood to mean sacramental penance, that is, confession and satisfaction, which is administered by the priests."[1]

This was not just a technical dispute over a small point. It implied a far-reaching rejection of the church's whole system of doctrine on how individuals receive salvation, and consequently a rejection of the church's understanding of what the church itself is. After its opening shot, the proposal went on to make much of this implicit rejection explicit. The church cannot dispense forgiveness of sins; it can only declare that God has forgiven sins.[2] The church cannot remove the temporal penalties of sin; it can only pray that God will do so.[3] The proposal stopped short of denying that penance is a sacrament or that purgatory exists; it did not contain the

---

[1]Martin Luther, "Disputation on the Power and Efficacy of Indulgences," theses 1-2. This work is more commonly referred to as "Martin Luther's 95 Theses." I rely on the translation of Adolph Spaeth, L. D. Reed, Henry Eyster Jacobs et al. For online resources see <www.ivpress.com>.

[2]See Luther "Disputation" theses 5-6.

[3]See Luther "Disputation" theses 26-28.

Sources of the Reformation

One of the most important subjects of debate among historians is why the Reformation occurred. There was no one factor that would have been sufficient to bring about the Reformation by itself; a number of important forces had to converge.

One traditional approach has been to explain the Reformation as a reaction against corrupt practices (real and perceived) in the Catholic church. There is some truth to this; practices like bribery and the sale of indulgences certainly were a problem in the medieval church, and the pope's aggressive fundraising for St. Peter's Basilica only made things worse. However, the medieval church was never really as corrupt as we tend to depict it.[a] And if the Reformation had been primarily a reaction to corrupt practices, it would have ended after the church adopted sweeping anticorruption reforms in the second half of the sixteenth century.

Another common approach is to explain the Reformation as the inevitable result of changing political and economic conditions. The princes and feudal lords of Europe had been steadily growing more powerful relative to the church for centuries, and the Reformation was their declaration of independence. Again, there is much truth to this. There can be no doubt that many of the princes who supported the Reformation did so from a selfish desire to be free of church control. And the increased power of the feudal lords explains why the sixteenth-century Reformers were able to thrive where dissenters with similar ideas in previous centuries had always been successfully suppressed by the church. But this, by itself, also fails to explain the Reformation. The Catholic church had accommodated rivals for power many times before, yet without the need for schism. And the Reformation could not have succeeded on the support of the lords alone; it also needed popular support.

As important as these and other factors were, the fundamental cause of the Reformation was theological. Cultural developments like frustration with church corruption and underlying economic and political transformations were necessary conditions of the Reformation's success, but were not sufficient to produce the Reformation by themselves. What drew millions of ordinary people to embrace the Reformation was its teaching that sins are forgiven by grace alone, through faith alone, in Christ alone.

The most important reason this understanding of the gospel emerged in the sixteenth century was the *humanist* intellectual movement. In reaction against the scholastic methods of the Middle Ages, the humanists preferred to study original sources (including the Bible, the early church fathers and the pre-Christian literature of Greece and Rome) rather than the leading scholarly teachers. *Ad fontes*, "back to the sources," was their motto.

The printing press was making those sources widely available for the first time. Over the sixteen years from 1490 to 1506, one publisher produced the first ever scholarly edition of Augustine's works, carefully collected and edited to facilitate serious study. This led to a great revival of interest in Augustine's ideas, which were tremendously influential on Luther and the other Reformers. Even more important, the greatest of the humanists, Desiderius Erasmus, produced an edition of the New Testament in the original Greek in 1516, with his own suggested Latin translation. Erasmus's disagreement with many of the traditional translations in the officially sanctioned Latin texts prompted anxiety over whether the traditional theology of the church as it had developed over the Middle Ages was faithful to the original biblical text. Erasmus's work also provided the foundation for many of Luther's complaints against Rome; Erasmus insisted, for example, that Christ had not said "Do penance," but rather, "Repent."

---

^aThe corruption of the medieval church has been exaggerated by both sides; Protestants have an incentive to exaggerate it because it makes the Catholic church look bad, and Catholics also have an incentive to exaggerate it because it allows them to emphasize medieval church corruption rather than Luther's critique of Catholic theology in explaining the Reformation (on corruption and reform in the church before Luther, see Diarmaid MacCulloch's *The Reformation* [New York: Penguin, 2003], pp. 3-52, 88-105).

slogan that its author and his followers would later make famous, that the forgiveness of sin is by grace alone, in Christ alone, and received through faith alone. But it came somewhat close to articulating that position: "Every true Christian, whether living or dead, has part in all the blessings of Christ and the church; and this is granted him by God, even without letters of pardon," it declared.[4] Only a little more development of these premises would be necessary before the author arrived at a fully developed alternative understanding of salvation, with no more sacrament of penance or purgatory involved.

Soon the proposal was published and widely distributed, and much of Germany was on fire for the 95 Theses. People came to believe that so long as they were faithful and repentant, God had already forgiven their sins. Revenue from indulgence preaching dried up. Heated debates ensued over the sacrament of penance and the vast structure of doctrine that depended on it. Against his will, Wittenberg's theologian was

---

[4]Luther "Disputation" thesis 37.

Theology of the Reformation

The theological disputes of the Reformation ultimately arose from a disagreement over the authority of Scripture. The Reformers believed that Scripture must take precedence over church tradition because Scripture is the Word of God while tradition is not. The Catholic church, on the other hand, believed that Scripture and church tradition were both forms of divine revelation and had to be interpreted cooperatively. This meant that the church's tradition of scriptural interpretation must take authoritative precedence over the individual believer's own understanding of Scripture.

Of all the doctrinal issues on which Rome and the Reformers clashed, the most important was the proper understanding of *justification:* the act by which God declares sinful human beings to be righteous, so that he can take them into eternal communion with himself. Traditional theology treated justification as the culmination of a process: God, acting through the sacraments of the church and responding to the sinner's willingness to cooperate with his will, gradually purifies the sinner from his sin by infusing Christ's righteousness into him. Theologians call this process *sanctification*. At the end of the process, the sinner is pure and righteous, and at the last judgment he receives justification: God declares him just. But the Reformers argued that justification occurs before sanctification, not afterward. God directly and unilaterally *imputes* (attributes or accounts) the righteousness of Christ to the sinner while the sinner is still unrighteous. Gradual sanctification then follows, as the Christian becomes totally conformed to the righteousness received from Christ.

This may sound like quibbling over technicalities, but the difference is crucial. On the Catholic view, sanctification is at the heart of salvation, and justification is simply an outgrowth of sanctification; a person is declared just and taken into eternal communion with God solely because that person has been purified from sin. On the Protestant view, by contrast, justification is at the heart of salvation, and sanctification is simply an outgrowth of justification; a person becomes conformed to the righteousness of Christ solely because that person has received Christ's righteousness through justification. The Reformers considered Rome's view works righteousness, building salvation upon our own merits or good works, especially since Rome teaches that sanctification is a cooperative act in which God responds to the sinner's willingness to be saved. Meanwhile, Rome says the Reformers' view makes justification into a "legal fiction," because the Reformers taught that God declares sinners to be just when they are not.

This difference, if taken seriously, is radically church-dividing. Virtually every aspect of Christian life is changed by the view we take on this fundamental question. The Protestant rule that Scripture must take precedence over tradition may have produced many other disputes, both between the Reformers and Rome and among the Reformers themselves. But the dispute over justification was always the central issue of the Reformation.

In spite of their differences, Protestants united around five mottos known as the five *solas:* God's authoritative word is found only in the Bible ("scripture alone," *sola scriptura*); God saves sinners solely because he loves them, and his love is not a response to any goodness or merit they possess ("by grace alone," *sola gratia*); salvation is mediated only by Christ and is conditioned only on Christ's saving work ("in Christ alone," *solus Christus*); justification is received only through faith and not through sanctification ("through faith alone," *sola fide*); and in all of human life only God is to be glorified ("glory to God alone," *soli Deo gloria*). The key to these mottos is the word *alone:* Rome has always affirmed that salvation is by grace and in Christ, and that justification is received through faith; but it denies that salvation is by grace *alone* or in Christ *alone*, or that justification is received through faith *alone*.

thrust into international fame and quickly found himself opposed and rejected by his own church. Despite the radicalism of his positions, he had never intended to break with Rome. But he would not draw back from affirming what he believed Scripture taught, and he churned out a virtual flood of new books and treatises in which he further developed the implications of his ideas. He now turned his fierce attacks more directly upon the pope and the church hierarchy, denouncing them for teaching that forgiveness of sin comes through the church and its sacrament of penance, rather than directly through faith in Christ. Rome responded by excommunicating him and calling for the German civil authorities to put him to death as a heretic.

On April 16, 1521, Martin Luther stood trial for his life before an Imperial Diet—a formal assembly of the nobles and lords of the empire—in the city of Worms. The prosecution, such as it was, was carried out by central Europe's most prominent theologian, Johann Eck. Eck was Luther's most dangerous intellectual adversary; it was Eck who had shown conclusively, in a public debate with Luther at Leipzig in 1519, that Luther's position could not possibly be reconciled with Catholic teaching. But at Worms there was no debate. Eck confronted Luther with a table full of

Pre-Christian Politics Revived

The same revival of interest in ancient sources that contributed so much to the Reformation also brought about a huge revival of interest in pre-Christian history and literature. So, during the bloodshed of the sixteenth and seventeenth centuries, some people began to echo the ancient Roman critics of Christianity, arguing that Christianity's moral laws were too strict to allow rulers to do what was necessary to preserve the community.

Appalled at the pathetic state of Italian politics, Niccolò Machiavelli became obsessed with studying the politics of ancient Italy (that is, the Roman Empire), hoping to find a model for improving politics in modern Italy. Just a few years before Martin Luther would publish his 95 Theses, Machiavelli wrote a little book based on his research: *The Prince*. The manuscript circulated privately for years and was published only posthumously in 1531. Along with his other works, it gained a wide audience. During the Reformation, much of Europe was becoming as broken and chaotic as Machiavelli's Italy had been, and many people were now as anxious as he was to find a better way to keep order.

Machiavelli's political theory is sometimes described as amoral, but that description is misleading. He did want to scrap the Christian view that justice is the foundation of politics, because he thought a prince must "learn how not to be good"—practicing deceit, betrayal and murder when necessary to preserve order.[a] But he was also disgusted with princes who used their power for their own selfish ends rather than for the good of the community. His fundamental goal, reflecting the worldview of the pre-Christian Romans he studied so diligently, was the glory of the community.

Later another diligent student of ancient politics, Thomas Hobbes, found a similar audience. He wrote during the English Civil War, one of the bloodiest conflicts in an age of especially bloody conflicts. After long study of ancient historians, he constructed a great systematic theory of politics in his 1651 book *Leviathan*.

Hobbes's theory was that people are by nature at war with each other because they all desire power and security, but cannot trust one another. He wrote that "the state of nature" is a "war . . . of every man against every man," in which human life would be "solitary, poor, nasty, brutish and short."[b] He concluded that the imperative to end this conflict was a natural law. However, by "natural law" he meant not a divine law, or even a moral law, but simply the dictates of our nature: he claimed that the strongest human emotion is the fear of violent death. From this he concluded, on the one hand, that submission to government authority must be absolute (or else resistance to government might bring back the war of all against all), and on the other hand that government's only job is to keep peace (and therefore it should involve itself as little as possible in matters like religion and morality).

Both of these thinkers, and the line of later thinkers who were—and are—influenced by them, represent the reintroduction of a particular kind of pre-Christian political theory. The idea that politics should be based not on justice but on the glory of the community or our selfish desire to survive was precisely the view that was originally opposed by Plato, Aristotle, Cicero and the other Greco-Roman philosophers whose ideas have been so influential on Christian thought. The philosophers' arguments for politics based on justice rather than either glory or selfishness had lived on in Christian tradition; in the sixteenth and seventeenth centuries the philosophers' old, long-dormant adversaries returned to challenge them again. These alternatives to politics based on justice have remained influential down to the present day.

[a]Niccolo Machiavelli *The Prince* chap. 15. For online resources see <www.ivpress.com>.
[b]Thomas Hobbes *Leviathan* part 1, chap. 13. For online resources see <www.ivpress.com>.

his writings and asked whether he would recant them. Luther, aware that this was the point of no return, balked. He asked for a day to consider, which was granted to him. The next morning, after an anguished night of prayer, Luther declared:

> Unless I am convinced by Scripture and plain reason—I do not accept the authority of the popes and councils, for they have contradicted each other—my conscience is captive to the Word of God. I cannot and I will not recant anything, for to go against conscience is neither right nor safe. [Here I stand, I cannot do otherwise.] God help me. Amen.[5]

Luther had put the noose around his own neck. However, thanks to a promise of safe conduct that Frederick had extracted from the emperor, Luther was permitted to return home before he would be formally condemned to die. As he was traveling back to Wittenberg, Frederick's men "kidnapped" Luther, and he went into hiding. Luther would spend the rest of his life under the protection of Frederick and other sympathetic princes.

[5]The famous line "Here I stand, I cannot do otherwise" does not appear in contemporary accounts of the trial and probably was not spoken by Luther; the line was added to the story later by Luther's biographer, apparently as an embellishment. See Diarmaid MacCulloch, *The Reformation* (New York: Penguin, 2003), p. 131.

A CRISIS OF AUTHORITY

By this time, there were many cities and towns where the population had embraced Luther's understanding of the gospel. After the trial, the number of such communities continued to grow. Before long, these communities had been formally expelled from the Roman Catholic Church and were maintaining their local churches as independent religious institutions. Western Christendom had been divided.

The conflict quickly turned violent on both sides. Radical Protestant mobs attacked Catholics and ransacked their churches, particularly to destroy the many religious images and artworks that they believed were idolatrous. Meanwhile, Catholic rulers executed Protestants as heretics. Shocking as it was, even this was only the beginning. Over the next two centuries the violence frequently escalated into full-scale warfare, including both international wars and civil wars. The era of the Reformation saw some of the worst violence Europe has ever experienced, because those who fought saw their enemies not merely as unjust but also as satanic. For both sides, the very survival of Christianity was felt to be at stake.

This religious and political upheaval set off a crisis in the development of Christian political thought. Christianity had always held that obedience to God trumped obedience to civil authority when the two came into conflict. As Peter said when the apostles were ordered to stop preaching Christ, "We must obey God rather than men" (Acts 5:29). Following this commandment in the face of government persecution could obviously pose a serious practical challenge, but it had never before posed a serious intellectual challenge. Obedience to God and obedience to government had come into conflict only in those particular instances where a ruler gave a command that violated God's law. Such instances were deemed to be exceptional cases, and the proper course of action for Christian subjects was always clear: simply decline to obey and suffer whatever consequences followed. Now, however, in much of Europe there was a fundamental, systematic and continuing conflict between political and religious authority. This was quite different from dealing with the occasional unlawful command: the entire political system had been thrown into chaos.

What made this crisis so much worse than any that had occurred before was a weak point in natural-law theory that had previously gone unnoticed. One of the bedrock rules of natural-law doctrine was the rule against subjects using force against those in lawful authority over them. Even if a ruler's orders had to be disobeyed for the sake of conscience, this disobedience was to be nonviolent. Anyone who used violence against those in lawful authority, even in response to wrongful behavior by that authority, was no more than a rebel. And rebels had to be put down by force of arms, to protect the safety of society. What had not been sufficiently addressed was the question of exactly who was in lawful authority and who were the rebels. It was taken for granted that normally this would be obvious. Surely there were occasional situations where two or more people claimed to be the rightful ruler and it was not immediately clear whose claim was right. However, these were understood to be unusual cases that could be dealt with individually as they arose. No one felt it to be urgent that Christianity develop a detailed theory of how to distinguish rightful rulers from rebels and usurpers.

During the Reformation, however, disputes over who had a right to exercise authority were no longer rare and exceptional, but the norm. Each side saw the other as rebelling against lawful authority. To Catholics, Protestants were heretics who refused to submit to the teaching of Christ's church; to Protestants, Catholics were usurpers who had set themselves upon Christ's throne. Each side therefore believed it had a duty to oppose the rebellion of the other side by force of arms.

But the problem did not stop there. Because of the way church-state relations were structured under the medieval understanding of natural law, any dispute over who should have authority in the church could not help but create another dispute over who should have authority in the state. As we saw in chapter four, medieval natural-law doctrine called for cooperation between church and state in enforcing religious laws because heresy, blasphemy and other religious crimes were seen as a threat to the survival of the community. So it was the church's job to declare what was heresy, and the state's job was to defend the community by suppressing heretics.

For obvious reasons, on this view a heretic could never rightfully serve as the community's ruler. And now all of Western Europe was divided among Protestants and Catholics, with each side seeing the other side as heretical. Every single ruler in Western Europe faced a challenge to his right to rule: Protestants could not recognize Catholic rulers, and Catholics could not recognize Protestant rulers. This situation threatened nothing less than the destruction of all political order in Western Europe.

The crisis in Christian political thought caused by the Reformation is widely misunderstood. It has become commonplace to say that the Protestant Reformers rejected natural-law doctrine, but the truth is much closer to the opposite. Some leaders of what is called the Radical Reformation—movements that rejected the existing, mainstream clergy and sought radical social transformation, such as the Anabaptists—did reject natural law for a time. However, not all radical Protestants took this position. And none of the leaders of the so-called Magisterial Reformation—a label that applies to Lutherans, Calvinists and other Protestant movements that were led primarily by established clergy and did not seek radical social change—ever rejected natural law. The Magisterial Reformers certainly rejected a great deal of medieval scholastic thinking.[6] But they just as certainly did not reject the idea of natural law.[7] Nor did the intellectual traditions established by the Magisterial Reformers reject natural law; Lutheranism and Calvinism remained firmly committed to natural law for centuries after their founders left the scene. Even the followers of the Radical Reformation dropped their opposition to natural law by the close of the Reformation era.

The issue for political thinkers was how natural-law theory ought to deal with the crisis of authority brought on by the Reformation. A new way of coping with the boundary between church and state had to be found.

The first generation to live through the Reformation found three different ways to cope with the crisis. One approach died out quickly, because it only made the crisis worse. The other two approaches proved to be more helpful and were thus more lasting. However, by themselves even

---

[6]Even here, the Reformers' rejection of medieval scholastic theology was less complete than is often thought: they were deeply indebted to Anselm's theory of imputation, for example.

[7]See Stephen J. Grabill, *Rediscovering the Natural Law in Reformed Theological Ethics* (Grand Rapids: Eerdmans, 2006).

these two approaches were not sufficient to resolve the political crisis. The policy that would bring about a lasting peace did not arrive until the second half of the sixteenth century, and it would take another full century after that for this policy to be formally codified as official policy throughout Europe. Until then, Europeans could only do their best to cope with the slow-motion collapse of the medieval political order.

THE RADICAL APPROACH

The first and most straightforward approach to the crisis was among the followers of the Radical Reformation, who rejected wholesale the previous fifteen hundred years of Christian political philosophy. This meant denying the accumulated body of Christian political thought and starting again from scratch. For the radicals, traditional Christian political thought was a body of doctrine developed by a false church, based on a false understanding of revelation, used to prop up an oppressive political system in which church and state had cooperated to keep people deprived, ignorant and obedient.

Since all existing political institutions rested their claims to legitimacy on traditional Christian doctrine regarding the authority of the state, it was not long before the radicals who rejected traditional doctrine were openly rejecting the legitimacy of all existing political institutions. Kings and feudal lords claimed to have a right to rule because the community had appointed them, which it was authorized to do under the natural law. By contrast, the radicals quickly settled on the view that the state was appointed by God to restrain the evil of unbelievers, and therefore true Christians should have no need of it. Any institution claiming the right to exercise authority over Christians, whether a church or a government, was usurping Christ's place as the one true king of Christians. And obviously any such usurper was in open rebellion against lawful authority and had to be put down by force.

Not all leaders of the Radical Reformation embraced the violent conclusion of this line of thought. While some pursued violent political change, others advocated nonviolent means of bearing witness to their views, or argued that Christians should separate themselves from the affairs of the world entirely. Not all of the radicals were *politically* radical; many were just theologically radical. But not surprisingly, it was the political radicals whose radicalism had immediate political consequences.

In many parts of Germany, radical mobs rose up to remove both church and state, seeking to replace them with a new kind of Christian community that would have no place for any human authority. The first signs of rebellion were visible within a few years of the publication of the 95 Theses. One of Luther's colleagues on the university faculty, Andreas Karlstadt, began stirring up popular resistance movements in Wittenberg while Luther was in hiding after his trial at Worms. Luther himself opposed Karlstadt's radicalism, for reasons we will look at in detail below; Frederick eventually had to bring Luther out of hiding to put a stop to Karlstadt and expel him from Wittenberg.

But in many other parts of central Europe, the radicals were more successful. The message of the radicals—that Christians should bow to no ruler but Christ, and that established authorities were nothing but usurpers—transformed ordinary tensions between the economic classes into religious warfare. There had always been periodic bouts of hostility between the peasants and the nobility. Medieval peasants did not enjoy being peasants any more than anyone else would enjoy it, and when taxes grew too high or the laws became too strict, they were not above sending a message to their rulers. Riots were not unknown. Before the Reformation these disturbances were usually short-lived, and rulers and peasants generally found ways to accommodate each other. In the 1520s, however, peasants following the Radical Reformers were no longer willing to put up with business as usual.

In 1524 rioting broke out in southwestern Germany. Where previous riots had subsided quickly, this one not only continued but also spread. By 1525 most of central and southern Germany was in unrest, an episode known as the Peasants' War. Other uprisings occurred in the rest of central Europe, even as far away as Hungary and northern Poland. The Radical Reformation had become a serious threat to the established order.

The established order responded in kind. The riots had time to spread mainly because the nobility were slow to realize that the situation had changed, that these were not just routine uprisings in which the peasantry would blow off steam and then come to a negotiated settlement. Once they understood what was going on, however, the nobility cracked down with ferocious force. The rebels were shown no mercy and were killed in large numbers.

But radical anarchism did not fail simply because it was crushed by force. It was also discredited by its own failures, most notoriously in the city of Münster. In the early 1530s Münster became a refuge for Anabaptists (lit., "rebaptizers," so called because they rejected infant baptism and permitted multiple baptisms for adults) and other followers of the Radical Reformation who had been driven out of their homes in northern Germany and the Netherlands. One such refugee was the radical preacher Jan Matthijszoon, who proclaimed that the end of the world was arriving and that Münster would be the New Jerusalem. He gained an enormous following, and in 1534 his supporters drove out the local prince and seized control of the city. The expelled prince laid siege to the city, and at one point his forces succeeded in killing Matthijszoon himself. But the city held out against the siege, and for the next seventeen months Matthijszoon's followers built their vision of a purely Christian community within its walls.

All of Europe was horrified by the policies of the Münster radicals. Believers were required to practice communism; private property was forcibly taken from its owners and redistributed. However, many of the more wealthy citizens managed to have themselves exempted from this requirement. The radicals thus gained a reputation both for wealth-destroying extremism and for flagrant hypocrisy. Equally shocking, because there were far more women than men in the city, polygamy was instituted in imitation of Old Testament figures. When the siege tightened and things looked grim, the city's new leader, Jan of Leiden, responded by appointing himself the new messianic king of the world and minting currency with his image on it. Unsurprisingly, this stratagem failed to defeat the siege; the prince was soon back in charge of the city, and the remaining radical leaders were executed.

By the late 1530s, political radicalism had been thoroughly discredited. The Lutheran cities of northern Germany had been so disgusted by the

Münster radicals that they temporarily swallowed their opposition to Rome and threw their support behind the city's Catholic prince. It would not be the last time during the Reformation when Catholics and moderate Protestants would set aside their differences to make common cause against radicalism. Even the radicals themselves gave up on political radicalism in favor of nonviolent withdrawal from the world: virtually all of the radicals renounced the use of force after the 1530s, advocating disengagement from politics instead.[8] The Radical Reformation was no longer a political force. The bloodbath of the Peasants' War and the spectacle of Münster had convinced Europeans of virtually all religious persuasions that nothing was more dangerous, and even anti-Christian, than political radicalism.

EVERY MAN RESPONSIBLE FOR HIS OWN FAITH

It was clear that a wholesale rejection of political institutions was not the solution to the Reformation's political crisis. However, the anarchism of the radicals did have one lasting effect: it provoked dramatic responses from other prominent Reformers, especially the leaders of the Magisterial Reformation. They had to explain why they rejected the anarchism of the radicals. This forced them to work out detailed theories of the basis of political authority and how it fit in with their reformational religious ideas. Naturally these Protestant theories prompted responses from Roman Catholic thinkers, and so the entire Western European world was soon hard at work in developing new political ideas.

Though there were many different approaches to dealing with the crisis, those that did not embrace radicalism generally fell into two distinct categories. One sought to defuse the crisis by saying that a person's religious status (for example, as a heretic) should have as few political consequences as possible. This might be called the "neo-Augustinian approach": it was inspired by Augustine's view that the goal of politics is to maintain civil peace among all inhabitants of both the "City of God" and the "City of Man." Like Augustine, those who took this approach were skeptical about the amount of good that could be accomplished through politics in a fallen

---

[8]See MacCulloch, *Reformation*, pp. 207-10.

world; however dangerous heresy may be, government simply is not competent to stamp it out by the sword.

Luther became the most prominent advocate of this approach during the early years of the crisis, especially in his 1523 treatise *Secular Authority: To What Extent It Should Be Obeyed*. (In this use the word *secular* means "pertaining to this world," in contrast to things that pertain to eternity; to call government authority secular does not imply that it is not under God.) Luther had always been a devoted student of Augustine, and in *Secular Authority* he gives us Augustine with a vengeance. Luther even pushes some of Augustine's principles further than Augustine himself pushed them.

Like Augustine, Luther bases his view of politics on a division of the world into two types of people, those who put God ahead of themselves and those who put themselves ahead of God. Echoing Augustine's terminology, Luther calls these groups the "kingdom of God" and the "kingdom of the world." Luther also agrees with Augustine that we should not expect a very high level of goodness from worldly politics. Luther was even more pessimistic on this point than Augustine had been, writing that political power will virtually always be in the hands of the "kingdom of the world."[9]

Luther concedes one point to the anarchist radicals. Ideally, Christians should not need government:

> If all the world were composed of real Christians, that is, true believers, no prince, king, lord, sword, or law would be needed. For what would be the use of them, since Christians have in their hearts the Holy Spirit, who instructs them and causes them to wrong no one, to love everyone, willingly and cheerfully to suffer injustice and even death from everyone?[10]

However, Luther goes on to indicate that in real life, Christians do not live up to the standard God sets for them: they are still sinners and still need the restraint of government.

More important, though, Luther argues that those who are still in the kingdom of the world rather than the kingdom of God desperately need

---

[9]See Martin Luther *Secular Authority: To What Extent It Should Be Obeyed* part 1, sec. 4; and part 2. I rely on J. J. Schindel's translation. For online resources see <www.ivpress.com>.

[10]Luther *Secular Authority* part 1, sec. 3.

civil government to restrain their sin. Like Augustine, Luther thinks every society is a mixture of the two kingdoms, and the two are not always easy to tell apart. Many people may appear to belong to the kingdom of God when they actually belong to the kingdom of the world. Our fellow citizens may need the restraint of government much more than we realize, because we cannot see how sinful their hearts truly are. Christians who do not support government are doing a terrible disservice to their neighbors, whose sin would be given free rein without it.[11]

Luther, like Augustine, sees the state primarily as a maintainer of civil peace. "Worldly government has laws that extend no further than to life and property and what is external upon the earth. For over the soul God can and will let no one rule but himself."[12] But Luther presses this point further than Augustine himself had pressed it, because his expectations for the state are even lower than Augustine's had been. Luther does not expect the state to be able to do anything more than restrain the most heinous sins, because that is all the power of the sword is able to accomplish.

In particular, Luther does not believe that government has the power to compel people in matters of faith. In *Secular Authority* he opposes all civil punishment of religious crimes such as heresy, blasphemy and apostasy—not a surprising position for Luther to take, given that he himself was under a death sentence for heresy. Luther argues that the limitation of government authority to external matters, not spiritual ones, is inherent in the nature of its power:

> [Rulers] must confess that they have no power over souls. For no human being can kill a soul or make it alive, conduct it to heaven or hell. . . . A court ought to be quite certain and clear about everything, if it is to pass sentence. But the thoughts and intents of the heart can be known to no one but God; therefore it is useless and impossible to command or compel any one by force to believe one thing or another. . . . Furthermore, every man is responsible for his own faith, and he must see to it for himself that he believes rightly. As little as another can go to hell or heaven for me, so little can he believe or disbelieve for me; and as little

---

[11]See Luther *Secular Authority* part 1, sec. 5.
[12]Luther *Secular Authority* part 2.

as he can open or shut heaven or hell for me, so little can he drive me to faith or unbelief.[13]

The sword has no power to produce faith; therefore it has no authority to enforce faith. "Every man is responsible for his own faith."

However, these low expectations for what government can do did not detract from Luther's passionate defense of the legitimacy of civil government. And since he believed in the legitimacy of government, Luther quite naturally saw the anarchist radicals as enemies of society. He encouraged the German princes to treat them as such. His views on the subject were expressed with particular clarity in one treatise, *Against the Murderous and Thieving Hordes of Peasants,* which is every bit as delicate and restrained as its title suggests. Like every other major Christian thinker before or since, Luther considered rebellion against lawful authority a monstrous sin and encouraged government to suppress such rebellion by force.[14]

Luther's political theory relies on a natural-law conception of politics, even more so than that of his Roman Catholic adversaries. Although he does not use the term "natural law," Luther's analysis of the relationship between reason and civil law clearly affirms a natural-law understanding of the basis of politics:

---

[13]Luther *Secular Authority* part 2.

[14]Many historians scratch their heads in wonder that Luther condemned the radicals so harshly, given that the radicals claimed to be following Luther's ideas, and several of them were even former students or colleagues of his. Why did Luther not embrace them as potential allies, even if he needed to correct them about the authority of government? These historians often seek out explanations for Luther's strange behavior. Was he trying to flatter the German rulers and gain their favor? Was he terrified of the radical forces his ideas had unleashed and desperate to be reassured that order could be maintained? Was he simply a volatile and fickle man who was just looking for reasons to condemn people? Did his unhappy relationship with his father play some role? The one explanation that rarely seems to be considered is that Luther, like every other major Christian thinker before or since, really did think that rebellion against a lawful government was an abominable sin that deserved to be unequivocally condemned, and that lawful governments had not just a right but also a duty to suppress rebellion by force. There is nothing surprising about a Christian writer condemning violent rebels and calling for their forcible suppression; what would have called for an explanation would have been Luther not condemning them. Certainly Luther uses stronger language than many Christian writers do, but that is just the way Luther always wrote, no matter what the subject; compare what Luther says about the anarchists in *Against the Murderous and Thieving Hordes* to what he says about the philosopher-theologian Erasmus (a man to whom Luther owed an incalculable intellectual debt, as Luther himself admits) in his greatest theological work, *Bondage of the Will.*

No matter how good and equitable the [written] laws are, they all make exceptions in cases of necessity, in which they cannot be enforced. Therefore
a prince must . . . decide in his own mind when and where the law must be
applied strictly or with moderation, so that reason may always control all
law and be the highest law and rule over all laws.[15]

Saying that something is known by reason is just another way of saying that it is known by general revelation. Moral law known by reason is
just another word for moral law known by general revelation—in other
words, natural law. Thus, to say that in politics reason must "control all
law and be the highest law and rule over all laws" expresses the heart
and soul of natural-law doctrine. For a prince, Luther writes, "a good
and just decision must not and cannot be given out of books, but must
come from a free mind, as though there were not a single book."[16] That
is, written law exists only to point us to the higher law known by reason:
the natural law. Reason has this authority because it is given by God as
a natural form of revelation.[17]

To say that Luther relies on a natural-law conception of politics does
not mean that his political theory is not scripturally based. To the contrary, Luther appeals to Scripture in support of his arguments frequently
and emphatically. But the conception of politics that Luther draws from
Scripture is a natural-law conception.

There is a traditional story that Luther once said he would "rather be
ruled by a wise Turk [a Muslim] than by a foolish Christian." There is no

---

[15]Luther *Secular Authority* part 3, introductory section.

[16]Luther *Secular Authority* part 3, concluding section.

[17]Ironically, Luther is sometimes portrayed as denying natural-law doctrine. One reason for this
perception is that Luther frequently attacked the medieval scholastics, and other theological and
intellectual movements, for having too much confidence in the power of human reason to disentangle complex metaphysical questions and other philosophical subtleties. In the bombastic
rhetoric for which he has become notorious, he sometimes phrased these diatribes as attacks on
"reason." But Luther's arguments never really implied a rejection of reason itself or opposition to
natural law; when he denounced "reason," he was actually denouncing speculative philosophy,
especially that of the scholastics, which he thought was tainted by the influence of Aristotle's
metaphysics. Luther strongly affirmed the importance of human reason, provided that we respect
its inherent limits. He was, after all, a devoted student of Augustine, the man who did more than
any other to solidify the incorporation of Greco-Roman philosophy into Christian tradition. At
his trial, Luther offered to recant his views if they were refuted either by Scripture or by "plain
reason." He thus affirmed that Christians have a duty to believe the truths God has revealed by
reason as well as those revealed in Scripture—a position he never seriously retreated from.

direct record of Luther actually having said this, and Luther definitely did not have a high opinion of Islam.[18] Nonetheless, the story contains a grain of truth. Luther did think that true Christians would rarely, if ever, hold political power, and that the job of a prince was simply to administer justice in the things of this world according to reason. He may not have said that he would rather be ruled by a wise Turk than by a foolish Christian, but that principle is at least suggested by his political ideas.

LIMITED SUCCESS OF THE NEO-AUGUSTINIAN APPROACH

This neo-Augustinian approach was appealing to many Protestants. One reason was that it promised a resolution to the political crisis. Another reason was that Protestants, as targets of the heresy laws in Catholic Europe, were eager for an argument against civil punishment of religious crimes. And a third reason was the extraordinary personal influence that Luther exercised among Protestants; the same ideas would not have found nearly the audience they did if they had been championed by anyone else.

At the same time, many Roman Catholics were also rediscovering the wisdom of Augustine's low-expectations approach to politics. Not all Catholic monarchs chose to persecute Protestants. In particular, the neo-Augustinian approach was already the predominant view in Eastern Europe, because that region had long since been divided between Roman Catholic and Eastern Orthodox populations. Granting roughly equal civil status to Catholics and Orthodox had kept the peace for centuries, so the Eastern monarchs found it only natural to do the same for Protestants. As a result, even the parts of Eastern Europe that had significant numbers of Protestants experienced little to no political trouble.

---

[18]After conquering Greece, the Ottoman Empire invaded Europe in the 1520s and swept across the southeastern European region of Hungary-Bohemia. Its armies arrived outside Vienna, the seat of the German Empire, and laid siege to it in 1529. Although European armies eventually pushed back the Ottoman threat, the prospect that all Europe might be conquered by Islam suggested to many European Christians that God was punishing them for their failure to follow the true faith, and even that the end of the world was near—thoughts that often exacerbated the violence between Protestants and Catholics. Luther was one figure who thought along these lines; he denounced Islam in the same vigorous terms he used to denounce Roman Catholicism, and he argued that God had permitted the Ottomans' military success as a disciplinary measure imposed on Christendom.

Some Catholic rulers in Western Europe eventually switched to this approach as well. France, after suffering nearly half a century of internal warfare between its Catholic majority and a sizeable minority of Protestants, decided to give the neo-Augustinian approach a try. King Henry IV, realizing that he could not successfully stamp out Protestantism in his kingdom, issued a 1598 law known as the Edict of Nantes, granting a large measure of toleration to French Protestants. Henry would have preferred to see Protestantism eliminated, and extended toleration to Protestants only because he couldn't defeat them, but that does not make the Edict of Nantes any less a neo-Augustinian document. The underlying principle of the neo-Augustinian approach was not a benign attitude toward religious differences—Luther certainly did not have a benign attitude toward Rome—but rather a recognition that the state cannot remove those differences.

But while this approach did help to reduce violent conflicts in the parts of Europe where it was tried, by itself it could not produce a lasting solution to the Reformation crisis. There were two main reasons—one theoretical and the other practical.

First, for this approach to resolve the crisis, people would have had to follow Luther's principles all the way to the conclusion that religion should have no effect on a person's civil status whatsoever—implying that heretics could legitimately hold political power so long as they administered justice in the things of this world according to reason. Most people, Luther himself included, were simply not willing to take things all the way to that conclusion. How could the community put its very survival into the hands of a person who, in the community's view, had rejected the true faith? Even where the neo-Augustinian approach had succeeded in keeping a measure of civil peace, suspicion of heretics died hard. Those who would not affirm the majority religion of the community were looked upon as quasi-traitors. In France, for example, Henry's grandson Louis XIV revoked the Edict of Nantes in 1685 and began a severe crackdown that wiped out virtually all French Protestantism.

The problem was exacerbated when two countries of different religions came into conflict. In such cases, religion was often viewed (sometimes rightly, sometimes wrongly) as a proxy form of political loyalty. Thus, when the predominantly Protestant Netherlands had to fight off the Catholic king of Spain's attempts to seize control of their territories, toleration for Catholics in the Netherlands was narrowed considerably. Likewise, toleration for Protestants in Catholic Poland was reduced after Poland was drawn into a series of wars with Sweden, which was Lutheran.[19]

Even laying aside the personal suspicion of those who were judged to be heretics, there was the more general problem of how to hold a political community together without a shared religion. To say that a heretic could rule would be to imply that the community does not need to have a shared belief about what is right and wrong; yet how can government enforce laws without claiming that some things are right and other things are wrong? Luther did not provide a satisfactory answer to that question. (We will look at this problem in more detail when we examine the emergence of religious freedom in chap. 6.)

The second reason Luther's approach did not fully resolve the crisis was that religious authority and political authority were too thoroughly intermingled in sixteenth-century Europe. It was simply not possible to just say that the one would henceforth have nothing to do with the other.

Luther's own example demonstrates this: a few years before he published his treatise *Secular Authority*, he had published another treatise calling on the local feudal lords across Germany to take the lead in reforming their local churches. In his *Appeal to the Ruling Class of Germany*, he explains that he is calling on the princes to act in their capacity as Christians rather than as rulers exercising political power, because the civil government has no authority to interfere in the church. And yet when it comes to making specific recommendations, Luther repeatedly calls on the princes to exercise their political power in order to extract churches from Roman control. As it turned out, the princes ignored Luther's recommendations, but the *Appeal* still proves the limitations of the neo-Augustinian approach. Because church and state had become so interdependent, the separation of religious authority and political authority that Luther envisioned in *Secular Authority* could not have been accomplished in practice unless the state had exercised precisely the kind of interference with the

---

[19]See MacCulloch, *Reformation*, pp. 364, 368.

church that *Secular Authority* forbade it to exercise. And Luther's strict distinction between civil and religious authority would only become more compromised in later years, as he made a series of further concessions to civil authorities in order to gain their support for religious reform.[20] Given the realities on the ground in the sixteenth century, the political vision of *Secular Authority* was not achievable.

A PUBLIC FORM OF RELIGION

While the neo-Augustinians sought to defuse the crisis by reducing civil enforcement of religious laws, others thought the crisis could not be defused. They held that government authority had to arise from the shared religion of the community. This meant civil enforcement of religious laws, since government would have to protect the source of its authority. Those who took this view thought that attempting to hold the community together without enforcing a shared religion was bound to end in failure, bringing on even greater chaos and violence.

Medieval thought had often described this model as the doctrine of "two swords." The state wields the physical sword, and the church wields the spiritual sword.[21] Those who rejected neo-Augustinianism sought to preserve and refine the two-swords approach. Their preferred solution to the crisis was to do a better job of defining and distinguishing the specific roles of church and state.

John Calvin was one of the most famous advocates of this approach—so famous, in fact, that a large number of myths have grown up around his political views and behavior. In the mid-sixteenth century the city of Geneva underwent extensive civil and religious reform under Calvin's intellectual and spiritual leadership (but not directly under his political leadership: Calvin never held political office). Critics of Calvin sometimes depict this period as a reign of terror, as though there were rivers of blood flowing through the streets from all the executions of heretics. While

---

[20]See ibid., pp. 210-11.

[21]The "two swords" were sometimes presented as being allegorically represented in Lk 22:38. The description of "spiritual weapons" in passages such as 2 Cor 10:3-5 and Eph 6:10-20 is another important source.

the historical record of this period is somewhat incomplete, there is no evidence that anything like a reign of terror occurred. On the contrary, the evidence strongly suggests that few of the executions carried out in Geneva during the period of Calvin's influence were for religious crimes as opposed to civil crimes like murder.[22] Calvin did support government enforcement of religious uniformity, and there were some executions of heretics in Geneva—just as there were some executions of heretics in every part of Western Europe during the Reformation crisis. But the balance of the historical evidence provides little reason to think that Geneva under Calvin suffered the same kind of violent convulsions that occurred so often on the blood-soaked battlefields of the Reformation in places like Germany, France and England.

If Calvin's Geneva has been singled out in historical memory as being particularly guilty of religious violence, it is not because Geneva was in fact more guilty than other cities, but because Calvin was one of the period's foremost intellectual defenders of civil enforcement of religious laws.[23] Like Luther, Calvin was forced to develop a detailed theory of civil government in response to the Reformation's political crisis. His definitive work, *Institutes of the Christian Religion*—which in its final form was longer even than Augustine's monumental *The City of God*, running to over 1,300 pages in modern editions—was the main catalyst for the widespread eruption of Protestantism in France and became the cornerstone of a new Protestant tradition to rival Lutheranism. Although the *Institutes*

---

[22]Claims about the number of executions that took place in Geneva during Calvin's tenure are circulated, but these claims do not seem to be based on solid evidence. From the historical documentation we have, it appears that the large majority of executions in Geneva during the period of Calvin's influence belong to a single incident in 1545, in which the city went into a panic after two men were caught allegedly smearing people's doorknobs with plague-infected blood. In the ensuing hysteria, 31 people were executed as alleged conspirators (see Bernard Cottret, *Calvin: A Biography* [Edinburgh: T & T Clark, 2003], pp. 180-81). Calvin was caught up in the madness along with everyone else, but it was a madness directed at murderers, not heretics. Such was the terror of plague throughout Europe that it is not hard to imagine something similar happening almost anywhere.

[23]In many cases, the ignorance and mythologizing that surrounds Calvin's politics also seems to arise from the strong hostility that many people have against Calvin because of his religious ideas. Here, though, the causation probably runs both ways, because Calvin's theology is also the subject of widespread ignorance and mythologizing. It is not clear to what extent Calvin's theology is treated unfairly because of popular hostility to his politics, and to what extent his politics are treated unfairly because of popular hostility to his theology. Either way, the man can't seem to catch a break.

was originally written before Calvin arrived in Geneva or had any public responsibilities, it devotes its final chapter to an account of civil authority. It was the first systematic Protestant statement of belief to incorporate a formal political theory.[24]

Calvin considers the promotion of religious piety, including the punishment of impiety, to be among the most important duties of government, right alongside the maintenance of civil peace. He summarizes the purpose of government as seeing to it "that a public form of religion may exist among Christians, and humanity among men."[25] For Calvin, civil peace and religious orthodoxy are just two different aspects of the "public form of religion" that government exists to maintain. Citing the scriptural passages affirming that government is ordained by God, Calvin argues that if it is God who puts the sword into the rulers' hands, rulers must in turn have the right to enforce obedience to God's authority. Rulers should "exert themselves in asserting and defending the honor of him whose vice-gerents they are, and by whose favor they rule."[26] He also contrasts the Old Testament's praise for kings who enforced correct worship of God with its condemnation of the spiritual anarchy that prevailed both before the Davidic monarchy and during the reign of corrupt kings.

In all this, Calvin's political thought is not very different from medieval natural-law theory. As we have already seen in chapter four, government enforcement of religious laws had always been an integral part of natural-law doctrine; according to medieval natural-law thought, one of the duties imposed on the state by natural law is the duty to enforce religious laws (see sidebar "Church and State in the Middle Ages"). Calvin himself identifies his view as a continuation of Christianity's historic natural-law tradition, and rightly so.[27] In fact, Calvin's support for government enforce-

---

[24]See MacCulloch, *Reformation*, p. 195.
[25]John Calvin *Institutes of the Christian Religion* 4.20.3. I rely on Henry Beveridge's translation. For online resources see <www.ivpress.com>.
[26]Calvin *Institutes* 4.20.9.
[27]He declares that all written laws spring from "the equity on which the enactment [of the law] is founded and rests." This "equity" on which all laws are based is known to all human beings by nature: "Equity, as it is natural, cannot but be the same in all." It can also be called the moral law of God or the natural law: "As it is evident that the law of God which we call moral, is nothing other than the testimony of natural law, and of that conscience which God has engraved on the minds of men, the whole of this equity of which we now speak is prescribed in it" (Calvin *Institutes* 4.20.16; see also 4.20.14).

ment of religious laws is so similar to that of the previous fifteen hundred years of Christian natural-law thought that Calvin seems to have felt that it was somewhat silly that anyone should ask him to defend it. "No man has discoursed on the duty of magistrates, the enacting of laws, and the common weal, without beginning with religion and divine worship. Thus all have confessed that no political community can be successfully established unless piety is its first care." Even the pre-Christian political thinkers of ancient Greece and Rome had made the cultivation of public piety a high governmental priority. "Seeing then that among philosophers religion holds the first place, and that the same thing has always been observed with the universal consent of nations, Christian princes and magistrates may be ashamed of their heartlessness if they do not make it their care."[28]

But Calvin did more than simply repeat what previous natural-law thinkers had said before him. For one thing, Calvin ensured the incorporation of natural law into Protestant tradition by making a scriptural case for it. Characteristically, Calvin prefers to back up his arguments with appeals to Scripture rather than citations of traditional scholarly authorities, which was the preferred method of the medieval scholastics. By defending natural law with Scripture, Calvin helped to ensure that natural-law doctrine would flourish in Protestant traditions as well as in Catholic ones during the centuries following the Reformation.

More important, Calvin insisted on restoring a sharp distinction between the proper roles of church and state. Though he expected the two institutions to work cooperatively, he also insisted that each had its own distinct sphere of authority. Calvin's account of government begins by drawing a distinction between "civil government" and "spiritual government," the former having to do with the body and the things of this life, while the latter has to do with the soul and the things of eternal life. God exercises spiritual government directly, through the Bible, which is proclaimed by the church; this is the Protestant doctrine that the Bible is the only infallible rule of faith. Meanwhile, God delegates the task of civil government to the state rather than exercising it directly.[29] Because God retains direct authority over spiritual government, the church is not

---

[28]Calvin *Institutes* 4.20.9.
[29]See Calvin *Institutes* 4.20.1.

free to impose whatever rules it thinks fit, but must stick to the Bible. On the other hand, because God has delegated authority over civil government to the state, the state is free to make whatever civil laws will best serve to enforce the natural law.[30] Calvin argues that because both kinds of government come from God, they should cooperate and support each others' authority. Thus the church should proclaim the state's right to rule, and the state should enforce obedience to God's Word as proclaimed by the church.[31]

By these principles, the church's only political role is to interpret the Bible. For example, if a person were charged with heresy, the church would judge whether the person's views amounted to heresy. The state is required to defer to the church where interpretation of the Bible is at stake, because the state's sphere of authority is the natural law rather than the Word of God. But most of the day-to-day work of the state—arresting criminals, maintaining the city's defenses, collecting taxes and so forth—does not raise fine questions about the interpretation of Scripture; Scripture's marching orders for the state consist mainly of exhortations to apply the natural law of justice and equity faithfully.[32] Except where some question of scriptural interpretation is raised, the state has authority and the church must defer.

This principle, put into practice in Geneva during Calvin's tenure there, allowed the church a significantly smaller role in political affairs than it had exercised before the Reformation. The church's involvement in politics was mostly confined to judging cases of religious law. These principles also largely protected the church from the intrusion of political influence. In Lutheran territories, political compromises by the Reformers allowed local rulers to acquire a great deal of authority over the church, including the ability to appoint local pastors. In England, the king set himself up as the supreme head of the church. Zurich had gone even further under its great Reformer, Huldrych Zwingli; there, boundaries between church and state were blurred to the point of being erased entirely. In Geneva, however, and in the other regions influenced

---

[30]See Calvin *Institutes* 4.20.1; 4.20.8; 4.20.14-16.
[31]See Calvin *Institutes* 4.20.2.
[32]See Calvin *Institutes* 4.20.16.

by Calvin's approach, the church retained a strong independence from political control.[33]

Limited Success of the Two-Swords Approach

Calvin was far from the only advocate of the two-swords approach to the Reformation crisis, just as Luther was not the only advocate of the neo-Augustinian approach. Countless cities across Western Europe adopted reforms aimed at refining and perfecting the medieval natural-law model of cooperation between church and state. Though their details varied, the purpose of these reforms was not essentially different from that of Calvin's reforms in Geneva. And just like the neo-Augustinian approach, the two swords approach was pursued on both sides of the religious divide. Large numbers of Protestant princes struggled to enforce Protestant uniformity in their domains, and large numbers of Catholic princes struggled to enforce Catholic uniformity in theirs. And although the Catholic version of the two swords approach was obviously not shaped by Calvin's distinctively Protestant understanding of the proper role of the church, it did seek to reduce the extent to which church and state interfered in one another's proper domains (as understood by Catholic teaching). Geneva is remembered as the main place where this sort of reform was carried out not because similar reforms were not made elsewhere, but because Calvin's relentless drive for reform, his mastery of politics and his exceptional administrative skills—combined with the abundant opportunities for change arising from the city's chronic political instability—produced a broader and more comprehensive restructuring of church-state relations than was achieved in most other places.

It would not be long before the Roman Catholic Church as a whole formally adopted reforms following the two-swords approach. By the 1550s, Rome had lost England, most of Germany, large portions of France, and numerous other important territories like Switzerland and much of the Netherlands. Among the major powers of Western Europe, only Spain and Portugal remained unambiguously Catholic. It was clear that Rome could no longer afford to leave the job of stamping out the Protestant

---

[33]See MacCulloch, *Reformation*, pp. 240 and 355.

heresy in the hands of local bishops and princes, where it had primarily rested during the early decades of the crisis. A comprehensive, continent-wide response was needed, one that would not only mobilize resistance to Protestantism but also make needed changes within the Catholic church. Rome undertook a large-scale reform effort of its own, designed to improve the church's institutional functioning, end abusive practices (including the sale of indulgences), tighten up loose moral standards in the church, lay out a detailed theological response to Protestant teaching, and in general put the church on the spiritual equivalent of a war footing. This movement is now known as the Counter-Reformation.

One aspect of the Counter-Reformation was to reform the church's relationship with the state. During the Middle Ages the church had become a typical career path for the nobility and the upper-middle classes of Europe, such that many of its offices and institutions were made to serve the purposes of politics and economics more than those of religion. High offices in the church were often filled by those born to them, or those who could pay to acquire them. It was not uncommon for the same man to serve simultaneously as both the lord and the bishop of a city or territory, combining political and religious authority in a single person.

Ironically, it had been precisely this extensive entanglement of church and state that had provided the occasion for the start of the Reformation. Albert of Mainz, ruler of the Brandenburg region and an elector in the German imperial government, also wanted to serve simultaneously as archbishop of Mainz, archbishop of Magdeburg and a cardinal of the Catholic church. The pope was in the middle of his fundraising push for St. Peter's Basilica, and he was willing to give Albert the church offices he desired in exchange for a sufficiently large sum of money. In order to raise the money, Albert sponsored Tetzel's heavy-handed indulgence campaign—which provoked Martin Luther's 95 Theses.

The Counter-Reformation adopted a wide range of rules, procedures and structural changes designed to return all church institutions to religious rather than political or economic foundations. For example, church officeholders would henceforth be required to undergo serious religious training, so that church offices could no longer simply be used as political and economic assets. However, the purpose of these reforms was not to separate the church from the state; Catholic doctrine continued to hold that the authority of the state must have divine sanction, and therefore church and state should work together to uphold the shared religion of the community and punish religious crimes like heresy and apostasy. Instead, the purpose of these reforms was to clear away corruption and restore a proper relationship between the two institutions, so that each one would be resting on its proper foundation (general revelation for the state, special revelation for the church) and each would maintain control of its own sphere, doing its own job and not the job of the other. In other words, the political theory of the Counter-Reformation was a close parallel to the political theory of Calvin's Geneva.

The two-swords approach, like the neo-Augustinian approach, accomplished a great deal of good. Over the course of the Middle Ages, the church had gradually been co-opted by politics and economics; in both Protestant and Catholic communities, reformers following the two-swords approach restored the church to religious foundations. This not only advanced the church's religious mission; it also curtailed the many corrupt and exploitative practices that had gone along with the political and economic usurpation of the church.

But the two-swords approach, by itself, was no more capable of resolving Europe's political crisis than the neo-Augustinian approach. The main reason was simply that it failed to reach the heart of the problem. By clarifying and refining the rules for church-state cooperation, it managed to reduce the political role of the church and the religious role of the state. This alleviated many of the worst political abuses of religion and religious abuses of politics. But those who followed the two-swords approach still declared that heretics could not rule, and Protestants and Catholics still regarded each other as heretics. The basic political problem remained unchanged.

HE WHO RULES, HIS RELIGION

It was inevitable that the warring factions would eventually figure out a way to end, or at least minimize, the violence arising from the Reformation. Not even in Europe could people go on killing each other forever. The policy that finally brought this about cannot quite be called a resolution of the Reformation crisis; it was a messy political compromise that did not really resolve the underlying conflict over political legitimacy. What it did instead was channel that conflict into a more manageable form, one that was much less prone to break out into actual violence.

The first region to adopt the new policy was Germany. Though the emperor at first tried to put down the Reformation, he found that the cost of doing so was too high: over time, more and more of the German princes and lords were embracing it. After three decades of conflict and with no end in sight, he was ready to try accommodating his princes rather than fighting them. The empire's highly decentralized political system suggested how this could be done without undermining the emperor's authority. At an Imperial Diet in Augsburg in 1555, the empire adopted a policy known as *cuius regio, eius religio:* "he who rules, his religion." Henceforward, each of the local lords across the German countryside would decide whether the churches in his territory would be Lutheran or Catholic (other forms of religion were still forbidden). Residents of Lutheran areas who wished to attend Catholic churches were granted safe conduct to relocate to Catholic regions, and the same for Lutherans living in Catholic areas.

This policy had first been tentatively adopted at the Diet of Speyer in 1526, but then it had been quickly rescinded in favor of official Catholic uniformity throughout Germany. (The term *Protestant* first arose in reference the official "protest" that the Lutheran princes filed when the policy was rescinded.) Now, thirty years later, the time for compromise had come. And over the following century, other parts of Europe gradually gave up their religious wars as well, adopting *cuius regio, eius religio* as a workable alternative to continued bloodshed. In places where Lutheranism was not the predominant form of Protestantism, other traditions such as Calvinism were soon being permitted under the same principle. Political systems in many places were certainly not as decentralized as in Germany, so *cuius regio, eius religio* did not work as well there; in England, where the throne (and thus the whole country) sometimes passed from Protestant to Catholic to Protestant and back again in rapid succession, it was particularly unsuccessful. But none of the feasible alternatives was any better, and in most parts of Europe it was a success. It was finally codified as the policy of all the great powers of Europe in the Treaty of Westphalia in 1648.

The policy borrowed a little from both the neo-Augustinian approach and the two-swords approach. On the one hand, it represented an admission that there was no final victory in sight for either side in the struggle between Catholicism or Protestantism, and thus the two religious systems were going to have to find a way to coexist peacefully. In this it borrowed heavily from the neo-Augustinian emphasis on accepting imperfections and compromises in the fallen world, and on not trying to use the coercive power of the state to produce faith. On the other hand, the policy of *cuius regio, eius religio* also represented a strong reaffirmation of the medieval two-swords view that each local community must have an officially enforced shared religion. Those who dissented from the local religious preference were not offered toleration and acceptance; they were offered the opportunity to pack up and move out of town. That is certainly a lot better than offering them prison, torture and burning at the stake. But the new emphasis on coexistence between Catholics and Protestants did not envision them living peacefully together, among one another; it imagined them living peacefully apart, near one another but not together.

The policy of *cuius regio, eius religio* gave local lords greater authority over the religious life of their communities. This was an important change. However, implementing the new policy did not mean a radical disruption of the status quo in most places. For example, the new policy provided legal confirmation of the Lutheran practice of allowing the local lord to appoint the local priest—but this was what Lutheran lords were already doing anyway. In other words, the expansion of the rulers' authority under *cuius regio, eius religio* needs to be understood in the right context. In theory, the policy gave the lords final authority over religion in their domains. In practice, however, the exercise of this authority was limited by what the local population would tolerate. The people of Europe believed in the feudal system, but as part of that system, they expected their local lords to take care of them and promote their well-being.[34] As

---

[34]In Germany, the local lord was called the *Landesvater*, and this term ascribed to the lord not only the authority of a father but also the duty of a father to take good care of his family; see ibid., p. 51.

we have already noted, if they felt mistreated, they were not above doing a little rioting to provide their superiors with a more healthy perspective. So there was no question of the feudal lords forcing their subjects to convert against their will; few rulers could get away with such heavy-handedness. If Lutheran lords exercised great power in their local churches, this was primarily because their people permitted it—and to some extent even desired it, since the lords provided a powerful check against Roman influence. The shape of religious life in local European communities had always been a subject of struggle between the priests, the lords and the people. While *cuius regio, eius religio* increased the power of the lords, for the most part the lords were still constrained by the limits of what their people were willing to accept.

Political scientists now view the Treaty of Westphalia as the origin of the modern international political system. It was at Westphalia that the *nation-state* emerged as the defining political unit of Europe, and eventually of the whole world. For all of recorded history, political life had involved both *states* (which are tangible institutions that exercise power) and *nations* (which are units of cultural identity that have no concrete, tangible existence). But the two had not consistently gone together, and there was no particular expectation that they should go together. A single nation might contain many states, as in ancient Greece or medieval Italy, where each city was self-governing; or a single state might contain many nations, as in the Roman Empire. After the Treaty of Westphalia, however, nations and states came to be identified closely with each other, and the single nation-state became the basic unit of political life.

Westphalia brought about the predominance of the nation-state primarily because it established the final continent-wide triumph of *cuius regio, eius religio*. This policy fundamentally changed who would control the use of coercive force. Before Westphalia, the state had only incomplete control over the use of coercive force, because the church exercised a certain degree of coercive power: it enforced religious laws and also controlled family law (such as the rules governing marriage). Now, while the church still exercised these functions, it did so only with the state's approval. For the first time, the state had final say over all forms of coercive force exercised within its territory. The modern concept of *sovereignty* arose from this unification of authority over coercion; the nation-state is said to be sovereign because it has a monopoly on the legitimate use of force.

In addition to increasing the authority of the state, *cuius regio, eius religio* encouraged the strengthening of national identities. Before the sixteenth century, people thought of themselves mainly as members of their local communities and only secondarily as members of nations. But developments like the printing press (which greatly increased the use of vernacular languages as opposed to Latin) and the increasing power of political structures relative to the church had been steadily teaching people to think of themselves primarily as Englishmen, Frenchmen and Germans rather than Londoners, Parisians or Berliners. The wars of the Reformation inflamed the new nationalism, since members of different nations were so often pitted against one another. *Cuius regio, eius religio* confirmed, deepened and entrenched these national identities even further, by aligning religious affiliations with political boundaries. Since religion is fundamental to culture, the sorting out of people across territories according to religion (Catholics move here, Lutherans move there, Calvinists over here, etc.) ensured that in many places nationality would come to be closely intertwined with religious affiliation—which only strengthened people's adherence to their nations.

But while *cuius regio, eius religio* was a workable compromise, it was not a complete solution. It held the neo-Augustinian desire for peace and the two-swords desire for religious uniformity in a delicate balance. In the end, the balance proved too delicate to hold forever, and a new policy developed that did a better job of resolving the inherent tension. That policy, which replaced *cuius regio, eius religio*, will be the subject of chapter six.

6

ON THE ROAD TO JERUSALEM

THE EMERGENCE OF RELIGIOUS FREEDOM

Though we walk in the flesh,
we are not waging war according to the flesh.
For the weapons of our warfare are not of the flesh.

PAUL, SECOND EPISTLE
TO THE CORINTHIANS

FOR MOST OF THE SEVENTEENTH CENTURY, the city of Cleves was suspended in political limbo. It was located in northwestern Germany, but due to a quirk in hereditary succession, it was legally part of the eastern Electorate of Brandenburg and ruled by the Duke of Prussia. Such jerry-rigged arrangements were not unheard of, especially in Germany's decentralized political system, and people generally just accommodated them and got on with life. However, in Cleves the daily habit of accommodating differences would turn out to have far-reaching consequences.

In 1665, England sent a diplomatic mission to Cleves. One of the many clerks and other support staffers attached to the mission was a young man who had recently become a teacher of moral philosophy at Oxford.

Among his few accomplishments was a set of treatises he had written defending the absolute authority of government over all matters, especially religion. Mutual distrust and hatred between Protestants and Catholics—and just as much, if not more, between traditional Anglican Protestants and Puritan Protestants—was the defining feature of political life back in England. These seething hatreds had torn English society apart time and again over the previous century, and the country had only just emerged from an especially bloody period of civil war. In his treatises, the young Oxford scholar had drawn the conclusion that religious dissent of any kind was dangerous and threatened to undermine the unity of society. Only national religious uniformity, enforced by law, could prevent the inevitable descent into anarchy.

The young scholar was dumbfounded by what he saw in Cleves. The city's Prussian rulers had instituted wide-ranging religious toleration, allowing churches associated with a variety of different Protestant traditions, and even Roman Catholic churches, to operate side by side. People were free to profess faith and to worship according to whichever of these churches they chose. And there was no descent into anarchy. There was no political conflict over religion at all. *They didn't even hate each other.* "I cannot observe any quarrels or animosities amongst them upon account of religion," he wrote to a correspondent back home. "They quietly permit one another to choose their way to heaven."[1] Calvinists, Lutherans, Catholics and others all mixed freely and easily with each other as fellow citizens. That people could go to separate churches and worship according to profoundly different creeds on Sunday morning, and then, upon stepping out their church doors, show respect and Christian love to people whom they considered to be heretics and schismatics—this was flabbergasting.

Over the next few years, it gradually dawned on the young scholar that religious dissent is not the cause of political conflict over religion. Rather, the outlawing of religious dissent is the cause of political conflict over religion. Before long he was attacking religious persecution on the same grounds on which he had previously attacked religious toleration:

---

[1]See John Higgins-Biddle, "Introduction," in John Locke, *The Reasonableness of Christianity: As Delivered in the Scriptures* (Oxford: Clarendon, 1999), p. lxxxv.

The Enlightenment(s)

The seventeenth and eighteenth centuries saw an explosion of philosophical and scientific activity that has come to be called the Enlightenment. However, there was a great deal of intellectual diversity among the leading figures identified as Enlightenment thinkers. These differences are important enough that some historians speak of two "Enlightenments," or even more than two, occurring side by side simultaneously.

To a large extent the Enlightenment(s) were responding to the intellectual fragmentation brought on by the Reformation. Christianity no longer provided a unified tradition of knowledge, and with the old system of thought thrown into so much doubt, everything else seemed to have been thrown into doubt along with it. Enlightenment philosophy became intensely interested in epistemology, the study of knowledge, hoping to find a way to justify knowledge by reason so that it would be secure from doubt. This struggle of reason against radical doubt was personified in the famous story of how René Descartes sat alone in a room, in anguish, desperately trying to figure out how he could rationally justify believing in his own existence—and finally seizing in triumph upon the argument that his very doubt proved the existence of a doubter: "I think, therefore I am."

All this intense examination of epistemology in the wake of Europe's religious fragmentation led directly to the obvious question: Could belief in Christianity be rationally justified? On this question the leaders of the Enlightenment split most profoundly, which is why some historians now speak of two Enlightenments: one that continued to affirm Christianity, justifying it by appeals to logic and evidence, and another that rejected Christianity as irrational. Even within these two Enlightenments there was tremendous variation: Those who rejected Christianity argued for various forms of deism, pantheism, agnosticism and atheism. Those who affirmed Christianity differed from one another on exactly how to understand the doctrines they were affirming and why they were affirming them. And there was a significant rise in unorthodox forms of Christianity that denied historic Christian doctrines like the incarnation and the atonement.

The emphasis on epistemology in the Enlightment(s) also gave birth to modern science. The need to more rigorously justify our beliefs led to the development of the set of rules and procedures now known as the scientific method, by which an investigator begins with a hypothesis and systematically rules out alternative explanations, particularly by observing how events take place in artificially crafted situations called *experiments*. Many Enlightenment figures became famous both for their philosophy and for their experimental investigation of the natural world.

as a threat to civic order. And as he grew older, he became increasingly religious; he began to denounce persecution not only as a threat to peace, but more important, as a satanic perversion of Christian behavior and an obstacle to the salvation of souls. His name was John Locke, and by the 1690s, just thirty years after his trip to Cleves, his writings had helped set the English-speaking world decisively on the path toward religious freedom—a path the rest of Europe was soon to follow.

RULES OF THE GAME AND RULES OF THE PARK

Religious freedom is a recent development in the history of politics. There have always been societies that tolerated the existence of minority religions, but the sort of toleration they practiced is not the same thing as religious freedom. Before the seventeenth century, religious minorities were often permitted to exist, but only so long as there was no danger that they might evangelize enough people to threaten the dominance of the majority religion. And even where they were tolerated, minority religions did not have the same civil rights enjoyed by the majority. Toleration was practiced because persecuting minority religions was considered more trouble than it was worth, or as a magnanimous gesture of kindness, or because religious pluralism made it easier to assimilate conquered territories into an empire, or because it helped facilitate foreign trade. The one thing it was never considered was a fundamental right: toleration was extended solely because the majority chose to extend it, not because the majority had a duty to extend it.

Even in the time since religious freedom has emerged, it has remained a minority practice among the nations of the world. Far fewer than half of the world's population can worship freely without fear of criminal sanctions or violent reprisals. Most governments do not even pretend to have religious freedom, and many that do claim to have it do not: the police may not punish you for your faith, but they also will not protect you from the violent gangs who will, and that is more or less the same thing.

So from one perspective it might appear that religious freedom, relatively new and relatively uncommon, is not one of the most important topics in the field of political thought. Yet from another perspective it could be considered the most important topic of all.

Locke's Philosophy

Locke is famous not only for his political philosophy but also for his enormous contributions to epistemology and the philosophy of religion. His lengthy *Essay Concerning Human Understanding* was published at about the same time as his chief political works and was at least as widely debated and influential as they were. One prominent scholar of Locke, a critic of his epistemology, attributes "the making of the modern world" to the *Essay*.[a]

There is a great deal of misunderstanding about Locke's epistemology. Locke was not what is now called an *empiricist;* that school of thought did not come into existence until after Locke's death, and it differed from his views in important ways. Locke's statement that the mind is a "blank slate" at birth is also widely misunderstood. Locke did not mean that the only influence on human behavior is experience, implying that there is no such thing as a universal "human nature." To the contrary, Locke believed that human beings are born with very strong intellectual and behavioral predispositions. Rather, Locke's blank-slate comment was meant to oppose the view that the mind's ideas are already fully formed at birth, rather than developing over time.

Locke had two main goals in the *Essay.* The first was to argue that the mind is more limited than we usually prefer to admit. Locke critiqued the epistemologies of both the medieval scholastics and the more enthusiastic Enlightenment rationalists, arguing that both failed to respect the limits of human knowledge. By knocking down these theories of knowledge, which claimed to have already deciphered many of the workings of the physical world, the *Essay* was crucial in preparing the way for the rise of empirical science. In the *Essay*'s introduction, Locke compared himself to a worker clearing rubbish out of the road so that greater minds than himself, such as his friend Isaac Newton, could go on to greater accomplishments.

Locke's other goal in the *Essay* was to show how beliefs, especially religious beliefs, could be rationally justified despite the limits of human knowledge. But he also wanted to show that a certain kind of faith, the kind that leads to violent fanaticism, could *not* be rationally justified. On the one hand, Locke was anxious to prevent the Enlightenment from discrediting religion altogether; he sought to show that logic and evidence could establish the truth of Christianity against all rational challenges. On the other hand, he was equally anxious to refute those who overreacted to the Enlightenment by denigrating reason and instead relying on their religious feelings for knowledge of God. Locke was convinced that reason and faith were not only perfectly compatible, but interdependent; setting up either one without the other was an invitation to disaster. "He that takes away reason to make way for revelation puts out the light of both," he wrote, "and does much . . . the same as if he would persuade a man to put out his eyes, the better to receive the remote light of an invisible star by a telescope."[b] Locke's epistemological resolution of the reason-faith problem, seeking to avoid the twin dangers of reason discrediting faith and faith discrediting reason, was widely influential.

[a]Nicholas Wolterstorff, *John Locke and the Ethics of Belief* (Cambridge: Cambridge University Press, 1996), p. xv.

[b]John Locke, *Essay Concerning Human Understanding*, 2 vols. (Oxford: Clarendon, 1894), 4.19.4. Different editions of the *Essay* have slightly different chapter and section numbers; I cite the Oxford edition. For online resources see <www.ivpress.com>.

In the West, religious freedom is the defining difference between modern and premodern society and has radically altered our understanding of what the state is. Premodern society had a shared religion and thus a shared conception of how the universe works. Although people certainly did not agree about everything, having a shared religion guaranteed at least a fairly broad level of agreement on topics ranging from metaphysics to ethics, amounting to a shared worldview. This shared worldview produced rules of social behavior, and the state was the enforcement mechanism by which society held its members to those rules. Modern society, by contrast, does not have a shared religion, and thus its members often disagree on things like metaphysics and ethics. The state is still an enforcement mechanism by which society holds its members to a set of rules, but those rules no longer grow from a shared worldview.

This makes an enormous difference. To see why, imagine a large outdoor park divided into numerous fields, which people can sign up to use for designated periods. One group signs up for a field and uses it to play baseball; another group signs up for a field and uses it to have a picnic; and so on. Each group will have rules designed to promote whatever activity it is pursuing. The group playing baseball will follow the rules of baseball, plus its own rules governing who is on what team, who provides the equipment, and so on. The group holding a picnic will have rules for who brings what food, who sets up and who cleans up, and various unwritten rules governing social interaction (e.g., do not offer too much beer to cousin Frank). Separately, the park itself will have its own set of rules governing the use of the fields: do not leave a mess after you're done, do not disturb the people on other fields, and so on.

The premodern state is like the rules adopted by each group for use in its own field. These rules all grow out of a single "worldview," so to speak: the purpose for which the group is meeting. The rules will be specifically tailored to promote that purpose. For example, a group of friends playing baseball just for fun will have different rules from a group that is having a serious athletic competition within an organized league. A company picnic will have rules different from those of a family reunion picnic. The modern state, on the other hand, is like the rules of the park itself. The park manager does not care what kind of activity you are engaged in. He only cares whether you damage the common property of the park (for instance, if your fly ball goes through his office window) or bother other park users (if it lands in Aunt Myrtle's potato salad). As long as you keep to yourself, the manager does not care what you do. The only "higher purpose" behind the park rules is to allow each group in the park to pursue its own separate higher purpose, whatever it is, in peace and security.

CHRISTENDOM FRAGMENTED

The crisis of the Reformation set the stage for the emergence of religious freedom. We have already seen how the Reformation forced Catholics and Protestants into a violent confrontation over political authority, until a new relationship between church and state could be found that would manage the conflict more peacefully (see chap. 5). This compromise position, *cuius regio, eius religio*, in which each local territory would practice one religious tradition and allow other territories to practice other traditions, brought an end to the wars of religion that had characterized the sixteenth and seventeenth centuries in Europe. However, it did not end the underlying conflict over political authority that had fueled those wars, so by itself it did not provide a permanent solution to the problem.

Before the Reformation, the peoples of Europe had been able to take for granted at least a certain baseline of religious, intellectual and even cultural unity among Christians. Of course there were tremendous differences across the various nations, languages, cultures and population groups of Europe. But standing over and above these differences was a shared framework that united all of *Christendom* on a higher level. Whatever disagreements existed among Christians were viewed as tragic, but ultimately secondary, disruptions of the norm. Diligent effort—in theological and philosophical study, in political and social relationships, in championing truth against error, in prayer, in every other way—would eventually resolve these conflicts. Unity was the basic reality, and whatever setbacks might occur, over time the unity of Christendom was going to become stronger, not weaker.

This confidence in the underlying unity of Christendom was one of the main reasons the schism between Eastern and Western Christianity in 1054 did not produce a cataclysmic political upheaval. Over the centuries following the schism, peoples loyal to the Eastern and Western churches often found themselves ruled by the same government; but compared to the two-century bloodbath of the Reformation, there was relatively little conflict over the status of political authority. The main thing that divided the Orthodox churches from the Roman church was the issue of papal authority—a very important issue, to be sure, but a relatively narrow one in terms of its implications for theology, philosophy and culture. This was an issue of schism, but not of heresy. Even while they regarded each other, sometimes with bitter hatred, as schismatics, the East and the West did not give up on the concept of a single Christendom to which they both belonged. The schism was church-dividing but not Christendom-dividing, and hence not very divisive politically.

The Reformation smashed this confident intellectual and cultural unity to smithereens. Just the religious conflict over the theological principles of the Reformation would have been enough to do this on its own; however, the policy of *cuius regio, eius religio* and the consequent rise of the nation-state greatly multiplied the disunity caused by the original religious conflict. National and regional cultures came to be closely associated with religion: to a greater or lesser degree, Catholicism became part of what it meant to be French or Spanish; Lutheranism, part of what it meant to be Saxon or Swedish; Calvinism, part of what it meant to be Dutch or Scottish; and Anglicanism, part of what it meant to be English.[2] As a result, all the distinctive traits of local cultures, and even

---

[2]Naturally, some of these national and regional religious identities were much stronger, were formed much faster, and lasted much longer than others. The Dutch were never as solidly Calvinist as the Scots; Spain was solidly Catholic from the start while France became so much later, and Poland even later still. Nonetheless, the general phenomenon was the same everywhere.

national policies arising from political factors having nothing to do with religion or culture, became inseparably fused into Europe's various religious traditions. Lutheranism became not just a distinct theology, but also a distinct intellectual and cultural tradition, and the same for all the other Protestant traditions. Even Roman Catholicism came to have more distinct political and cultural variations: French Catholicism came to be much more different from Spanish or Bavarian Catholicism than it had been before the Reformation.

In the short term, this fragmentation seemed to make the religious identity of each nation more stable: under the policy of *cuius regio, eius religio*, France was Catholic, England was Anglican, Saxony was Lutheran, and that was all there was to it. Over time, however, this fragmentation ironically made national religious identities less secure, not more so. Now that there was this proliferating variety of traditions to choose from, each nation or locality had to face the ever-present possibility of change. Neither rulers nor populations could be counted on to maintain the same religious affiliations forever. The king often had a brother or a cousin or an illegitimate son who was known to belong to, or be sympathetic to, the "wrong" religious tradition and who might inherit the throne, or even seize it. Even if there were no potential heirs who were openly religious dissenters, you never knew whether someone in line for the throne might still favor the "wrong" tradition secretly, quietly biding his time until he could take power. And while the large-scale conversion of broad national populations became rare after the initial throes of the early Reformation, there was always a certain level of religious change in the population that threatened to create instability. For example, while the spread of Calvinism in France never reached a majority, it gained a large enough minority—including a significant number of important nobles and lords—to create a constant source of doubt about the future of French Catholicism.

This instability meant ongoing conflict within each society, as each religious faction found itself constantly struggling with the others—the dominant faction seeking to maintain its dominance by stamping out rivals, and the others seeking to prevent the dominant faction from stamping them out and meanwhile hoping to become dominant themselves. In some places, most notably England, these conflicts prevented *cuius regio, eius religio* from ever establishing much social peace. In some other places, most notably France, they gradually undermined that peace over time, so that *cuius regio, eius religio* turned out to be only a temporary cure for religious violence.

As it happened, these conflicts came to a head in both England and France at the same time, in the 1680s. In England, during the sixteenth century the throne had passed from Protestant to Catholic and back again in rapid succession, producing a series of religious crackdowns and countercrackdowns as the throne changed hands. Then, after the dominance of Protestantism seemed settled, a new front opened up. Traditional Anglicanism, closely associated with the throne, came into conflict with a religious movement known as Puritanism, which was increasingly associated with Parliament.[3] The extremely violent English Civil War erupted between these two factions in 1642, followed by a prolonged period of political chaos. And then, not long after Parliament and the king finally reached a workable settlement in 1660, the old Protestant-Catholic battle was reopened: the king produced no legitimate sons, and his brother, the heir to the throne, was Catholic. In the 1680s a constitutional crisis ensued. Parliament tried to exclude the Catholic brother from the throne, the king retaliated by abolishing Parliament, and a revolutionary resistance movement began trying to depose the king—ultimately succeeding in 1688. In France, meanwhile, the toleration of Protestantism under the 1598 Edict of Nantes was no longer holding. In 1672 an attempt to reconcile Protestant and Catholic factions went disastrously wrong, leading to widespread anti-Protestant rioting in which large numbers of French Protestants were killed. By 1685 the Protestants were weak enough that the king could now finish them off. He revoked the Edict of Nantes and began a campaign of violent suppression that successfully brought an end to Protestantism in France.

---

[3]Puritanism was a movement that cut across denominational lines; some Puritans were Anglicans while others were Presbyterians and still others Independents. What united them was opposition to the theological compromises that defined the traditional Anglican approach to religion, in which disputed points of doctrine were glossed over with strategically ambiguous statements to avoid conflict and division, rather than being clarified and firmly settled. Thus I have described the conflict as between "traditional" Anglicans and "Puritans."

The Limits of Toleration

Religious toleration, like all political principles, has its limits. We naturally cannot extend toleration to any religion that practices murder, theft or other disruptions of the civil order. Toleration is justified precisely on grounds that a person's religious affiliation is not normally relevant to one's obedience to the laws of justice and equity; in cases where it is relevant, the argument for toleration does not apply.

This is why religious toleration is sometimes called "freedom of conscience." The idea is not to make people free to do whatever they want, but to make them free to do what they think is right: to obey their own consciences rather than the conscience of another. The underlying premise is that no one legitimately believes it to be right to break the rules of civil order. All people know, or should know, that murder and theft and so forth are wrong. Thus, "freedom of conscience" cannot protect such activities.

One difficult problem in Locke's time was that membership in some religions was taken to imply a duty of disobedience to some governments. Locke argues in the *Letter Concerning Toleration* that a Muslim living in the West could not be tolerated if his beliefs required him to assist the Ottoman Empire in its continuing war against the nations of Europe; the Ottomans had besieged Vienna in 1683, so when the *Letter* was published in 1689, this was not a hypothetical issue. Another and even more urgent issue was the continuing problem of Catholics in England. The pope had issued a bull in 1570 absolving English subjects from obedience to their government so long as Queen Elizabeth, a Protestant, was on the throne. In 1580, the Vatican declared the bull unenforceable because it could not be formally distributed in England; for practical purposes, the bull was essentially void. But by then it was too late. Even a full century later, many Englishmen continued to view Catholicism as a form of civil treason. Locke declares that situations like these can be legitimate reasons not to tolerate a religion; but he also makes it clear that this is only because of the political conflict, not the religions themselves.

Early champions of religious toleration also excluded atheism from being tolerated, on grounds that atheism undermines all moral law: in a godless universe there could be no basis for thinking that some actions are right and others wrong. Later, however, toleration was extended to atheism. There were many reasons for the change. One was simply the extension of the principle that coercion does not change beliefs; even if atheism is dangerous, making it illegal does not alleviate the problem. Another was the judgment that real atheism, as opposed to mere deism or pantheism, is very rare and not worth the effort of persecuting. Still another was the observation that even though atheism rules out any justification for moral law, many atheists are nonetheless very moral people by social standards: they simply do not live out the intellectual consequences of their position. Finally, from the nineteenth century onward, a new and different set of arguments for religious toleration emerged, championed most famously by John Stuart Mill, emphasizing that the existence of a variety of beliefs is good simply in itself (see chap. 8).

At this point Locke was no longer a young, politically inexperienced academic. Two years after his enlightening excursion to Cleves, he had been hired into the household of a prominent Member of Parliament who was a leader of the parliamentary faction in the Civil War and had been one of the architects of the compromise that finally ended that conflict. Naturally, this brought Locke into a social circle where his earlier enthusiasm for royal authoritarianism was further challenged. Gradually he became a robust advocate of limits on government authority. During the English political crisis of the 1680s, his employer was a leader of the resistance against the king, and Locke wrote his famous book *Two Treatises of Government*, justifying a right to revolution, which we will look at in detail in chapter seven.

Due to his connection with the resistance, Locke had to flee the country after a failed assassination attempt on the king in 1683, and he lived for several years in Amsterdam under an assumed name. Like Cleves in 1665, the Netherlands was then practicing a broad religious toleration. The state church was formally Calvinist, but adherence to Calvinism was not required for membership, and those who wished to worship in other religious traditions were more or less free to do so. This toleration had been established in the Netherlands in large part because Dutch society had long been fractured into so many factions that no one faction could reliably claim the upper hand. But the Dutch had also come to believe that religious toleration was the most Christian policy as well as the most politically effective policy.[4]

---

[4]See Diarmaid MacCulloch, *The Reformation* (New York: Penguin, 2003), pp. 367-74, esp. p. 372.

THE CHRISTIAN DUTY OF TOLERATION

From his hiding place in Amsterdam, Locke wrote a treatise vehemently attacking all forms of civil discrimination and violence on the basis of religion and defending religious toleration. By the time the parliamentary faction was victorious and he was able to emerge from hiding, the treatise was ready to publish; it appeared in 1689 as *A Letter Concerning Toleration*. Since several major powers were having political crises over religion at the same time, the treatise immediately found an audience all across Europe. Locke had written it in Latin so it could be read by educated people in every country (though it was so successful that it was also quickly translated into French, Dutch and English), and he had framed his argument in quite broad terms, not tailoring it to the particular circumstances of any one country. Two centuries of constantly dreading the next flare-up of violence had built up a broad constituency for finding a different way to handle religious differences; the *Letter* catalyzed that constituency in a new way. Locke's arguments were especially influential in England, where there had been few periods of lasting peace in the past 150 years and people were sick of fighting each other to the death over religion every time the throne changed hands. Locke himself secured a position in the new English government, from which he continued lobbying for greater religious toleration.

The *Letter* opens with a heavy-handed attack on religious persecution, asserting that toleration of all peaceful people is "the chief characteristic mark of the true church," while those who punish people for their religious beliefs "have not really embraced the Christian religion in their hearts." Locke invokes the biblical statements that faith works by love and that physical weapons are not used in spiritual warfare (see Gal 5:6 and 2 Cor 10:4). He contrasts those who "persecute, torment, destroy and kill other men . . . deprive them of their estates, maim them with corporal punishments, starve and torment them in noisome prisons, and in the end take away their very lives" with the "charity, meekness and goodwill in general to all mankind" required by Christianity—required "even to those that are not Christians."[5]

---

[5]John Locke *Letter Concerning Toleration* par. 1. Since the *Letter* contains no sections or divisions, I cite paragraph numbers from the Prentice-Hall edition, ed. Patrick Romanell (Englewood Cliffs, N.J.: Prentice Hall, 1950). For online resources see <www.ivpress.com>.

Thus Locke begins by laying down the biblical basis of the case for toleration. One of the strengths of Locke's case is that he shows much more direct support in the New Testament for his position than John Calvin or any of the other advocates of enforced religious uniformity were able to show for theirs. Their arguments had relied heavily on the Old Testament, where good kings instituted true religion and punished religious error. However, the overwhelming majority of Christian thinkers, including Calvin and the other advocates of religious uniformity, agreed that the theocratic political system of the Old Testament had been abolished in the New. Thus, as Locke points out, the Old Testament example is not applicable to the New Testament era.[6] The only support that opponents of toleration had drawn from the New Testament was the statement that government is ordained by God; yet that statement does not directly or explicitly address the issue of toleration. Locke, on the other hand, appeals to the New Testament's insistence on meekness and charity toward all, as well as Paul's explicit statement that "the weapons of our warfare are not of the flesh" (2 Cor 10:4).

But from long years of study and argument on this issue, Locke knows that the philosophical issues involved are more complicated than his opening broadside allows. Those who favor religious uniformity can respond that a shared religion is necessary to maintain the community, and the breakdown of the community would involve much more violence and suffering than is involved in enforcing religious uniformity. Chaos and anarchy would inflict far more pain and consume far more lives than even the prisons and gallows used to enforce religious laws. And even beyond the question of social stability, there is the fate of souls to consider. If criminal sanctions can suppress error, more souls will be saved, and that must be considered a more important goal than earthly peace. Locke is not inclined to think that these arguments justifying persecution are sincere: "Nobody, surely, will ever believe that such a carriage [behavior] can proceed from charity, love, or goodwill."[7] He nonetheless spends the rest of the *Letter* refuting these arguments.

---

[6]See Locke *Letter Concerning Toleration* pars. 55-57.
[7]Locke *Letter Concerning Toleration* par. 3.

Locke's Christianity

Locke's religious beliefs have long been the subject of speculation and misunderstanding: speculation because he remained silent about his beliefs on some important questions, and misunderstanding because the beliefs he did express do not fall easily into any existing theological system. Historians have spent much time arguing over whether Locke was an Arminian, a Calvinist, a Latitudinarian, a Socinian or an adherent of some other school, but in fact he cannot be said to belong to any of them. The only really adequate label for Locke's Christianity is that it was Lockean.

In his Oxford years, his theological views were conventionally Anglican but not much developed. Later, however, he became more and more intensely interested in theology: after his major philosophical works were published in 1689, almost everything else he wrote was on morality and religion. His most important theological work, *The Reasonableness of Christianity as Delivered in the Scriptures*, published in 1695, attempted to deduce from Scripture exactly what was necessary for a person's salvation. He later wrote that he had hoped the book would help Christians to achieve greater clarity on this issue and would also refute deists who said that no revelation was necessary for salvation and that Christianity entailed irrational beliefs.

The *Reasonableness* concludes that only repentance from sin and faith in Christ are necessary to salvation—the standard Protestant view. However,

much more controversially, Locke argued that the only article of doctrine necessary for saving faith is that "Jesus is the Christ," the Messiah. To really believe in this statement, one would also have to believe in all the doctrines it implies; for example, Locke held that to accept Christ's messiahship, we must receive him both as Savior and as Lord. But there are many other doctrines taught in Scripture that are not entailed in the statement "Jesus is the Christ." Locke thought that Christians had a duty to believe all doctrines taught in Scripture, but he thought that only the doctrine that Jesus is the Christ is necessary to salvation; failure to believe in any of the other doctrines taught in the Bible was a sin, but a sin that would be forgiven in all those who trusted in Christ's messiahship.

This view was controversial because it implies that one can be saved without believing in the Trinity or the atonement, two doctrines that were under fierce attack in Locke's time. Locke himself expressed belief in the atonement, but in his later years he remained publicly silent on the Trinity. We cannot know for sure whether he privately rejected the Trinity. One alternative explanation for his silence would be uncertainty as to whether the human mind could ever adequately grapple with the meaning of the doctrine; this is a plausible possibility given Locke's epistemological emphasis on the limits of the human mind (see sidebar "Locke's Philosophy"). Among historians there are reasonable people on both sides of the question regarding whether Locke rejected the Trinity.

Locke's view of the origin of sin is also unusual. He believed that all human beings are sinners and that they are so because of a moral flaw in human nature; his *Two Treatises of Government* relied crucially on this premise to establish the need for government. To this extent, Locke was perfectly orthodox. However, he rejected the idea that Adam's first sin was the cause of all subsequent people's sinfulness; he thought that would undermine our individual responsibility for our own sins. Christianity has historically held this view to be unorthodox. However, given Locke's affirmation of the universal sinfulness of human nature, his unorthodoxy on Adam had no implications for his political philosophy.

Locke argues that the things that count for the survival of the community are the shared rules of social interaction, not religion as such. Society does not require agreement on all moral rules, and in any case it never actually had agreement on all moral rules. What the community needs to survive is agreement on the specific moral rules governing justice and social relations—rules against killing, stealing, promise-breaking and so forth:

> The commonwealth seems to me to be a society of men constituted only for the procuring, preserving, and advancing their own civil interests. Civil interests I call life, liberty, health and indolency of body, and the possession of outward things. . . . If anyone presume to violate the laws of public justice and equity, established for the preservation of these things, his presumption is to be checked by the fear of punishment.[8]

The "laws of public justice and equity" are sufficient to preserve the community. Other moral laws are important—they may even be more important—but they are not political in nature, and it is inappropriate to attempt to enforce them by law:

> It does not belong unto the magistrate to . . . punish everything, indifferently, that he takes to be a sin against God. Covetousness, uncharitableness, idleness and many other things are sins, by the consent of men, which yet no man ever said were to be punished by the magistrate. The reason is

---

[8]Locke *Letter Concerning Toleration* par. 5.

because they are not prejudicial to other men's rights, nor do they break the public peace of societies.[9]

Anyone who thinks that agreement on religion is needed to maintain civil society "jumbles heaven and earth together, the things most remove and opposite."[10]

Adherence to the community's shared rules of justice does not depend on belonging to one religion or another. All the branches of Christianity that were engaged in fighting each other during the Reformation shared broad agreement on the basic rules of justice and social relations. It was theology, not justice, about which they disagreed. Other civilized religions agree on the rules of justice as well. Locke insists that the right of religious toleration belongs to any peaceful person, "whether he be Christian or pagan," adding that "neither pagan nor Mahometan [Muslim] nor Jew ought to be excluded from the civil rights of the commonwealth because of his religion."[11]

Thus, even though belief in moral rules is fundamentally shaped by religion, Locke argues that people do not need a shared religion to have shared belief in the moral rules that govern society. All of the various worldviews present in Europe held to the same moral rules, at least as far as justice and social interactions are concerned. Society could require everyone to follow the same social rules without having to select one worldview to support them; all the available worldviews supported them.

Nor should it be surprising to Christians that all civilized religions and worldviews end up teaching roughly the same rules of justice. As we saw in chapter four, the Bible teaches that those who have not received the law of God from true religion nonetheless "by nature do what the law requires," because for the whole human race "the work of the law is written on their hearts, while their conscience also bears witness" (Rom 2:14-15). The idea of natural law should lead us to expect that all civilized societies will have more or less the same laws of justice and equity, because "by nature" they "do what the law [of God] requires." And for many centuries natural-law proponents have pointed

---

[9]Locke *Letter Concerning Toleration* par. 54.
[10]Locke *Letter Concerning Toleration* par. 33.
[11]Locke *Letter Concerning Toleration* pars. 27 and 77.

out that the facts bear out this expectation. Behind all the details and specifics of local legal systems, there is a core of rules (do not kill, do not steal, keep your promises, etc.) that are enforced within all civilizations. Each individual society may have particular weaknesses—one society may be partial to breaking one of these rules in a certain way, while another may keep that rule well but have a problem with another rule—but the various legal and social systems of world history are not simply a vast, meaningless jumble. There is a clearly observable pattern, and it is this pattern of shared rules that makes religious toleration possible.

However, Locke acknowledges that the saving of souls is another matter. While adherence to society's rules does not depend on belonging to a particular religion, one's salvation does depend on one's religion, and many people want to use government to try to save souls. Against this, Locke argues first that neither the Bible nor natural law indicates that God has given government—or anyone else—the authority to use force in matters of faith. "It appears not that God has ever given any such authority to one man over another, as to compel anyone to his religion."[12] Second, he argues that even if government had authority over souls, it could not effectively use it. Government's only tool is coercion, and no amount of coercion can produce faith:

> The care of souls cannot belong to the civil magistrate because his power consists only in outward force, but true and saving religion consists in the inward persuasion of the mind, without which nothing can be acceptable to God. And such is the nature of the understanding that it cannot be compelled to the belief of anything by outward force. Confiscation of estate, imprisonment, torments, nothing of that nature can have any such efficacy as to make men change the inward judgment that they have framed of things.[13]

What is more, we could not be saved by conforming to the religious dictates of government even if we wanted to, because God expects us to worship him in spirit and in truth, not just as a formal exercise of political conformity:

[12]Locke *Letter Concerning Toleration*, par. 9.
[13]Locke *Letter Concerning Toleration* par. 10.

All the life and power of true religion consist in the inward and full persuasion of the mind, and faith is not faith without believing. . . . I may grow rich by an art that I take not delight in, I may be cured of some disease by remedies that I have not faith in, but I cannot be saved by a religion that I distrust and by a worship that I abhor. It is in vain for an unbeliever to take up the outward show of another man's religion. . . . In this manner, instead of expiating other sins by the exercise of religion, I say, in offering thus unto God Almighty such a worship as we deem to be displeasing unto him, we add unto the number of our other sins those also of hypocrisy and contempt for his divine majesty.[14]

Only sincere faith can be saving faith, and faith adopted in obedience to government rather than out of conviction is insincere.

The observation that faith cannot be coerced was already a very old one when Locke made it. Augustine had famously declared that "no one is . . . to be compelled to embrace the faith against his will" all the way back at the turn of the fifth century.[15] In the intervening centuries, this position had then been echoed by numerous thinkers, such as Aquinas and Ockham in the Middle Ages, and Luther during the Reformation. What was new was Locke's thorough and unflinching application of this principle. The same Augustine who said, "No one is . . . to be compelled to embrace the faith against his will," also found excuses for using coercive power to maintain orthodox Christianity against heresy, schism, apostasy and other religious offenses. Virtually all of his successors did the same. As we saw in chapter five, even Luther, who had been willing to follow this principle to its logical conclusion when writing his 1523 treatise on government authority, at other times endorsed some use of coercion in religion. Locke forcefully made the case that if we really believe that "no one is to be compelled to embrace the faith against his will," we must unflinchingly accept the consequence: the power of government should not be used at all in matters of faith.

Locke adds the final observation that even if government had both the authority and the means to save souls, most governments would use that

---

[14]Locke *Letter Concerning Toleration* pars. 9 and 40.
[15]Augustine *Against the Book of Petilian the Donatist* 2.84. I rely on J. R. King's translation, as revised by Chester Hartranft. For online resources see <www.ivpress.com>.

power in support of the wrong religion—as is obvious from the mere fact that the many rulers of the world hold a great variety of religious opinions. All people would be required to believe "the religion which either ignorance, ambition, or superstition had chanced to establish in the countries where they were born," and "one country alone would be in the right, and all the rest of the world put under an obligation of following their princes in the ways that lead to destruction."[16]

At one point, Locke compares life in this fallen world to a pilgrimage toward Jerusalem, in which we have to figure out which of the many available roads is the one that will lead us to the holy city. He asserts that the ruler is no more likely than anyone else to know which is the right road: "The one only narrow way which leads to heaven is not better known to the magistrate than to private persons, and therefore I cannot safely take him for my guide who may probably be as ignorant of the way as myself, and who certainly is less concerned for my salvation than I myself am."[17]

FROM TOLERATION TO FREEDOM

The primary agenda of the *Letter* is to argue for religious toleration: allowing all peaceful people to practice their religions without interference. However, Locke also suggests that if he had his way, he might prefer to go even further. In addition to supporting toleration, Locke's principles imply that government should not sponsor a specific church as the nation's official church, or even name one religion as its official religion without sponsoring any particular church. In other words, Locke's principles imply opposition to what is called *establishment* of churches and religions.

This subject brings us to the difficult question of how to distinguish between *religious toleration* and *religious freedom*. Different people use these terms with different meanings. Sometimes the distinction between toleration and freedom is based on the reasoning behind the policy: a system that allows people to worship as they please on grounds that government has no rightful authority in religion is called religious freedom; a system that allows people to worship as they please for some other, more selfish

---

[16]Locke *Letter Concerning Toleration* par. 12.
[17]Locke *Letter Concerning Toleration* par. 38.

reason (for example, because suppressing minority religions is considered more trouble than it is worth) is called religious toleration. When the terms are used in this way, it is possible to have religious freedom and still maintain an established church or an established religion. On the other hand, the distinction is sometimes directly based on the presence or absence of religious establishment: a country that lets people worship as they please but has an established church or religion is said to practice religious toleration, while a country that has no established church or religion is said to practice religious freedom. Obviously, when the terms are used this way, a country with a religious establishment cannot be said to have religious freedom.

Both definitions have their legitimate functions. The first one emphasizes the political ideology of individual liberty in religion, as distinct from political ideas not based on individual liberty. It would be wrong to imply, for example, that the state of religious freedom in England has not changed much since the sixteenth century simply because England still has an established church. The key difference between modern and premodern states in the West is the kind of rules they are governed by. To return to our earlier metaphor, modern England is ruled much more like a park, with many fields being used for many purposes, than it is like a field, where everyone has the same purpose. We should not lose sight of that simply because the archbishop of Canterbury is a government appointee.

However, it is the other definition, the one based on the presence or absence of religious establishment, that is more relevant to our purposes at the moment. This definition emphasizes the question of whether religious establishment can still be maintained consistent with the principles of individual liberty in religion. Now that we have traced the reasoning behind the rise of religious freedom as an ideology, it remains to trace the reasoning behind the rise of religious freedom in the institutional sense.

The key to the argument is that people who do not belong to the established church or the established religion are, at least implicitly, second-class citizens. Even if they are not obviously treated any differently, they bear a different relationship to their government. They are, on some level, governed by a religion in which they do not believe. In the case of an established church, the injury that establishment inflicts on those outside that church is clear enough; their tax revenue is used to fund a church to which they do not belong. However, there is a more important sense in which any establishment, of a church or simply of a religion, reduces some people to a different civil status. If religious establishment means anything, it means that government policy should be guided by the established religion, at least sometimes, on some level. Why else would the government establish a religion? But this means that people of other faiths are, to some extent, forced to submit to policies originating from a faith that is foreign to them. They are not being allowed to practice their religion fully, because to whatever extent government policy is influenced by the established religion, they are constrained to follow that religion rather than their own.

Locke's implicit argument against establishment arises from the principle that no peaceful member of the community should have a different civil status because of his religion. He argues that this principle is required by the very same rules of public justice and equity that are the basis of society. If two people are different from each other with respect to the civil rules governing the political community—for example, if one is a criminal or a foreigner and the other is not—then they may have different civil statuses. But if two people are the same with regard to the civil rules, then the civil rules require government to accord them the same civil status.

Locke begins by observing that treating people differently in civil matters because of their religion implies that the civil rules of justice and equity do not apply equally to everyone. During the previous two centuries of religious conflict, people often justified their actions by saying that promises need not be kept to heretics, civil obedience was not owed to heretical rulers, and so forth. Locke boils these claims down to their essence: that we only need to treat members of our own religious group fairly; the rules of fair play only apply to us, not to you:

> We cannot find any sect that teaches, expressly and openly, that men are not obliged to keep their promise, that princes may be dethroned by those that differ from them in religion, or that the dominion of all things belongs only to themselves. . . . But, nevertheless, we find those that say the same things in other words. What else do they mean who teach that faith is not to be kept with heretics? Their meaning, forsooth, is that the privilege of breaking faith

belongs unto themselves, for they declare all that are not of their communion to be heretics, or at least may declare them so whensoever they think fit.[18]

The whole point of the civil rules of justice and equity is that they apply to everyone equally. That is what it means to call them rules of justice and equity. Those who claim that the civil rules apply only to true believers are really saying that the rules of justice and fairness apply only to themselves—which is manifestly unjust and unfair.

In this part of the argument, Locke goes beyond the position that belief in the rules of justice and equity is distinct from belief in a particular religion, such that uniformity in religion is not needed to produce uniformity in the rules of justice. Now he is arguing that the rules of justice and equity actually require that religion have *nothing* to do with people's civil status. If government plays favorites among religions in any way, it undermines the moral laws on which government itself is based, because those laws require the impartial administration of justice to all people.

Locke stops short of saying explicitly that he opposes establishment of religion, but he comes close to that. In one passage, comparing the theocracy of the Old Testament with the Christian liberty of the New Testament, he flatly declares, "There is absolutely no such thing under the gospel as a Christian commonwealth."[19] It is possible to interpret this passage as nothing more than an argument against continuing the Old Testament practice of theocracy in the New Testament era, but the passage is at least suggestive of more than that.

At any rate, whatever Locke may have really thought about religious establishment, his argument in the *Letter* provided the foundation on which the argument against establishment was built. It was not long before some of Locke's successors developed his argument that government must not play favorites among religions into an argument against religious establishment. In particular, it was precisely Locke's arguments about the proper relationship between religion and politics that were used to oppose religious establishment in the United States. Both Thomas Jefferson and James Madison advanced Lockean arguments against establishment that

---

[18]Locke *Letter Concerning Toleration* par. 69.
[19]Locke *Letter Concerning Toleration* par. 56.

were profoundly influential. Madison, the chief architect of the Constitution, was a particularly active opponent of establishment. He seems to have been greatly affected by a 1771 incident near his home, in which a Baptist minister was flogged—during a worship service, in front of his own congregation—for preaching without a license.[20] Madison published a famous treatise against establishment, called the *Memorial and Remonstrance Against Religious Assessments,* and became involved in the drafting of the First Amendment in order to push for the elimination of established churches in the states.[21] The final text of the First Amendment did not abolish state establishments, as Madison had hoped. But his victory was not long delayed; the last of the state establishments was abolished by the 1830s—within living memory of the adoption of the Bill of Rights.

THE PROBLEM OF PUBLIC VIRTUE

Religious freedom offered a full resolution of the Reformation crisis of authority. Rather than just trying to control the problem of social conflict over religion, like the *cuius regio, eius religio* compromise that preceded it, religious freedom laid out permanent terms of coexistence for the conflicting groups. It aspired to be a peace treaty rather than just a truce.

However, that peace came at a cost. Like all great political ideas, religious freedom creates problems for the political communities that try to practice it—problems for which we have not yet figured out adequate solutions even now, three centuries after Locke's time. Even those who love religious freedom would be foolish not to admit that there are real difficulties associated with it.

We can sketch these difficulties most easily by returning to the parallel drawn earlier between the rules of society and the rules of a park. The analogy between a society and a park is inadequate in at least three ways. First of all, a society (unlike a park) has to be concerned with character formation. The park manager does not have to worry about how to incul-

---

[20]Not long afterward, Madison came into conflict with Patrick Henry over Virginia's establishment of religion; when Henry subsequently arranged for Madison's district to be redrawn, support from Virginia Baptists who remembered with gratitude Madison's opposition to establishment helped him narrowly save his political career. See Michael Novak, *On Two Wings* (San Francisco: Encounter Books, 2002), pp. 52-53.

[21]Ibid., pp. 54-61.

cate the virtues of honesty and fairness into people so that they will obey the park rules. A society, however, cannot survive if its members do not possess enough personal virtue to keep them obeying the rules at least most of the time.[22] Second, in a society (unlike in a park) there are some private behaviors that have a major impact on others and on society as a whole, but whose effects are not immediately and directly felt. A society in which childbearing does not generally take place within marriage will be a different kind of society from a society in which it does. Thus, some of the activities that take place "inside the fields," so to speak, are nonetheless of legitimate concern to the "park" as a whole. And third, it takes a lot more rules to govern a society than it does to govern a park, and as a result there is much more disagreement over what rules should be adopted. A park manager needs only a few simple rules to keep park users out of each others' hair, but to keep a whole society running requires a much greater level of social cooperation—and hence much more effort toward resolving disagreements over what the rules should be.

The original advocates of religious freedom never intended to interfere with government's legitimate concern for character formation and for the impact of private behavior on society as a whole, or to undermine public support for the broad array of rules that keep societies together. When they turned their thoughts to these subjects, they affirmed that society has a legitimate interest in shaping the character and behavior of its members, and that government must have the authority to settle disagreements over the wide variety of rules that are necessary to keep society together.

---

[22]C. S. Lewis compared moral rules to the rules for sailing a fleet of ships, distinguishing between three types of rules. Social rules of morality (do not hurt other people, etc.) are like the rules for steering the ships so they do not crash into each other; rules of good character are like the rules that govern the internal workings of each ship in the fleet; and our understanding of the purpose of human life is like the whole fleet's map to its destination. Lewis observed that "modern people" often want society to be concerned only with the social rules, but that this does not work in practice because the social rules and the rules of character are interdependent: "What is the good of telling the ships how to steer so as to avoid collisions if, in fact, they are such crazy old tubs that they cannot be steered at all? What is the good of drawing up, on paper, rules for social behavior, if we know that, in fact, our greed, cowardice, ill-temper, and self-conceit are going to prevent us from keeping them?" See *Mere Christianity*, rev. ed. (London: G. Bles, 1952), book 3, chap. 1. Lewis also observes that a certain amount of agreement on the ultimate purpose of human life is socially necessary.

However, they did not actually turn their thoughts to these subjects very often. Locke in particular never seems to have considered it a serious possibility that a society without a shared religion would have difficulty justifying public concern for character formation and the social impact of private behavior, or justifying government's authority to settle social disputes when they concern matters of public justice and law. In his comments on these issues, he appears to take it for granted that governmental authority in these areas would never become problematic.[23]

Nonetheless, religious freedom has in fact made these issues much more problematic. Government's ability to take action in all three of these areas (character formation, private behaviors and social cooperation) is constrained because it can no longer appeal to a shared social worldview for justification. A society with religious freedom has to solve these problems with much less help from the power of government.

As these problems became more clear, later generations of Christian political thinkers have argued that institutions other than government—meaning primarily churches and families, but also other social structures—must do the job of cultivating virtue and restraining private behavior that would have negative social consequences. The most famous of these was Alexis de Tocqueville, whose two-volume work *Democracy in America*, published in 1835 and 1840, is widely considered the greatest analysis of American political culture and behavior ever written. Tocqueville sympathized with American democracy in many ways, but at the same time he expressed a deep anxiety that the leveling spirit of democracy might already be well on the way to producing an egalitarian tyranny in which anyone who disagreed with majority opinion was viewed as a public enemy. It was *Democracy in America* that popularized the phrase "tyranny of the majority." Tocqueville's hope was that the moral foundations of American democracy could be maintained by community associations, strong families, and above all by Christianity. "By their practice Americans show that they feel the urgent necessity to instill morality into

---

[23]Consider, for example, how sanguine he is about the continuing enforcement of "those moral rules which are necessary to the preservation of civil society" even under a regime of religious toleration; religious intolerance is the only threat he seems to see to the preservation of social consensus on these rules. See Locke *Letter Concerning Toleration* par. 68; see also pars. 69-71.

democracy by means of religion. What they think of themselves in this respect enshrines a truth that should permeate deep into the consciousness of every democratic nation."[24]

However, Tocqueville warns that this approach to the problem carries with it new dangers of its own. Associations, families and churches are themselves vulnerable to the leveling spirit of democracy. Rather than these social forces transforming democratic society, it might be that democratic society will instead transform these social forces—and not necessarily for the better, since all of them depend crucially on hierarchical principles. One of the worst effects of democracy on religion that Tocqueville discusses is the troubling tendency of American ministers to preach a selfish Christianity. They emphasize the great benefits and advantages of being a believer. Believing will make you happy and earn you rich rewards from God, they are constantly reminding us. Tocqueville concedes that a person who really believes in God will certainly want to get to heaven and be happy there. But if we only engage in religion from a selfish desire to be happy, and not from a selfless love of God, we are deceiving ourselves and are not really coming to God at all.[25]

The worst danger is that when society relies on churches to maintain the moral foundations of the political order, and thus call upon them to play a semipolitical role, it creates a fierce temptation to make "social conservatism" the main purpose of the church, rather than the gospel of Christ. Tocqueville observes the tendency of American ministers to preach a form of Christianity that is less a religion than a political ideology:

> Priests in the Middle Ages spoke of nothing but the other life; they hardly took any trouble to prove that a sincere Christian might be happy here below. But preachers in America are continually coming down to earth. Indeed they find it difficult to take their eyes off it. . . . They are forever pointing out how religious beliefs favor freedom and public order, and it is often difficult to be sure, when listening to them, whether the main object of religion is to procure eternal felicity in the next world or prosperity in this.[26]

---

[24]Alexis de Tocqueville, *Democracy in America,* vol. 2 (New York: Bantam, 2000), part 2, chap. 15. I rely on George Lawrence's translation (New York: HarperCollins, 2000). For online resources see <www.ivpress.com>.
[25]See Alexis de Tocqueville, *Democracy in America* vol. 2, part 2, chap. 9.
[26]*Democracy in America* vol. 2, part 2, chap. 9.

The very hope that religion will solve the problem of virtue in democratic society brings with it an even greater danger. Because society is counting on religion to play this crucial role in supporting freedom, religion can become a tool of political ideology. Christian ministers treat God as though he were the fourth branch of government.

Both these forms of religious corruption use God as a means to one's own ends, rather than worshiping him as the only being who is an end in himself. From the authors of the New Testament onward, Christians have always regarded the subversion of religion to serve oneself as the very worst form of pride. Moreover, it almost goes without saying that when religion lacks real submission to God, it will eventually cease to be effective in teaching people to be virtuous and self-restrained. Thus democratic society's dependence on religion to provide public virtue can not only make Christianity un-Christian; it can also make it unable to do what democratic society relies on it to do.

THE ALTERNATIVE TO VIOLENCE

Given these problems, it is no surprise that religious freedom has been so late in coming and so little practiced in the world. And we have not even mentioned yet any of the other obstacles to adopting it—such as fear that God (or the gods) will punish us for allowing false worship. It begins to look as though the real question is not why most societies have not had religious freedom, but why any societies at all have had it.

It was not because the idea had never been proposed before. Locke was far from the first person to argue for religious freedom. As we have noted, the policy was already popular in the Netherlands, where Locke lived as he wrote the *Letter*. The idea had been expressed by previous generations in England as well; the philosopher and scientist Francis Bacon famously praised Queen Elizabeth for not seeking to "make windows into men's souls." Going even further back, as we saw in chapter five, Luther made an argument quite similar to Locke's, at least in its basic outlines, in his treatise *On Secular Authority*. And Luther in turn could have pointed to others still earlier than himself, who had proposed the idea in the Middle Ages.

Also, in the first century of the Reformation, much of Eastern Europe had embraced the idea. Poland, which at that time encompassed most of the whole northern half of Eastern Europe, had kept the peace for centuries between its Catholic and Orthodox populations by applying a live-and-let-live policy. When the Reformation arrived, Poland just extended the same policy to Protestants. Johann Eck, Luther's great theological rival, wrote to King Sigismund demanding that he suppress the Reformation in Poland; Sigismund replied: "Permit me, sir, to be the king of both the sheep and the goats." His son, Sigismund II, continued the policy, proclaiming himself to be "king of the people, but not of their consciences."[27] Sigismund II died without an heir in 1572, the same year as the anti-Protestant massacre in France; while they negotiated the succession of the throne, the Polish nobility met in Warsaw in order to codify the policy of religious toleration "for ourselves and our successors forever."[28] Similarly, the southeastern kingdom of Transylvania, also long accustomed to managing Catholic-Orthodox tensions, declared in 1568 that "ministers should everywhere preach and proclaim [the gospel] according to their understanding of it. . . . No one is permitted to threaten to imprison or banish anyone because of his teaching, because faith is a gift from God."[29]

However, it was not until the late seventeenth century that the scales of history tipped decisively toward religious freedom. Locke formulated the argument at greater length and in greater detail than his predecessors, and it was in his time that the right political forces aligned to carry his argument to lasting and widespread political success.

It is not hard to explain why the decisive change occurred in the time and place that it did. The conflict over religion lasted longer and caused more suffering in England than anywhere else; because the problem was more urgent and more difficult to solve there, it was there that the philosophy of religious freedom reached its greatest heights, and ultimately it was there that the policy was most completely embraced. This explains why toleration was lasting in England, whereas Eastern Europe abandoned it (contrary to the Polish nobility's proclaiming toleration "for our successors forever"). And it helps explain why it was in an English colony

---

[27]MacCulloch, *Reformation*, p. 192.
[28]Ibid., p. 343.
[29]Ibid., p. 262.

that the policy of religious freedom was implemented to the greatest extent, with the abolition of religious establishments.

The historical relationship between the extreme violence of the sixteenth- and seventeenth-century wars of religion and the emergence of religious freedom also helps answer another question. Given the problems associated with religious freedom, which we have noted above, why has it been so enthusiastically embraced by Western societies? Even as we struggle with the challenges that religious freedom poses for issues like character formation, private behavior that has public consequences, and lack of consensus over the rules of society, few people seriously propose that we return to the premodern system of religious uniformity. Why? The answer lies in the wars of religion that followed the Reformation. Religious uniformity is no longer a live option. After the shattering of the old religious, intellectual and cultural consensus, the alternative to religious freedom is not religious uniformity but religious violence.

Thus the religious violence of the sixteenth and seventeenth centuries can be said to have produced the modern world more than any other single event. And religious freedom was not the only modernizing political idea that came out of that violence. In chapter seven we turn to a second revolution in thought that grew from the wars of religion—this one even more deserving of that term than the previous one, having been not only a revolution in thought but also in deed.

7

AN APPEAL TO HEAVEN

REVOLUTION AND LIBERAL DEMOCRACY

You do me wrong by making war on me.
The LORD, the judge, decide this day between the
people of Israel and the people of Ammon.

JEPHTHAH, QUOTED IN JUDGES

TENSIONS WERE RUNNING HIGH IN BOSTON in March 1770. Popular resistance to English rule had been growing in the American colonies and had frequently been marked by acts of public disorder and occasional violence. For two years, Boston had been garrisoned by British troops, an act intended to pacify the city, but which had the effect of inflaming it further. On March 5 a church bell rang, and suddenly a British soldier on guard duty found himself surrounded by a jeering mob of several hundred people, many with sticks and clubs. He was soon reinforced by eight comrades, who fixed their bayonets and raised their muskets at the crowd. The crowd howled, daring the soldiers to fire. Rocks and ice were thrown at the soldiers. One of them was knocked down with a club.

The British captain allegedly ordered his men not to fire. This order, if given, may or may not have been audible over the crowd, which by then was screeching, "Kill them! Kill them!" Some of the soldiers did open fire, and from there, everything went exactly as one would expect. Five colonists were killed.

The next day, the soldiers were charged with murder. Only one lawyer in Boston was willing to take their case and brave the anger of the city, which was already being inflamed to white-hot intensity by propaganda dishonestly portraying the event as a massacre of peaceful and innocent protestors. Ironically, that lawyer was John Adams, a leading opponent of the British occupation. His cousin Samuel Adams was one of the main people using the "Boston Massacre" for colonial propaganda.

Defending the soldiers was a costly decision for Adams. He was an ambitious man and had become a prominent attorney in Boston, but his career prospects were limited by his open sympathy for the colonial cause. Now, having already alienated the British government by supporting the colonists, he was alienating the colonial enthusiasts by defending the British soldiers. Perhaps even worse was the public hatred he would now have to endure; besides ambition, the other vice to which he was especially prone was vanity. Rumors began to circulate that he had been bribed to take the case. He even began to fear for the safety of his wife, Abigail, who was then pregnant.

The trials (one for the captain, one for the other soldiers) were postponed until the fall, so that emotions could cool. It was an exhausting year for Adams, but when the trials came, he turned in an outstanding performance. Whatever his flaws, Adams was not only a formidable intellect, but also a man of great conscience who was willing to give his all in the service of a just cause. "Facts are stubborn things," he admonished the jury in his two-day closing statement at the second trial, "and whatever may be our wishes, our inclinations, or the dictums of our passions, they cannot alter the state of the facts and evidence." And the fact was that there had not been a noble band of peaceful protesters in the streets of Boston on March 5; there had been a violent mob that attacked innocent people without provocation:

We have entertained a great variety of phrases to avoid calling this sort of people a mob. . . . Why should we scruple to call such a people a mob, I cannot conceive, unless the name is too respectable for them. The sun is not about to stand still or go out, nor the rivers to dry up, because there was a mob in Boston on the fifth of March that attacked a party of soldiers.[1]

The captain and most of the soldiers were acquitted. Two soldiers were found guilty of manslaughter; their thumbs were branded, but they were then released without further punishment.

Adams, to his own and everyone else's surprise, had not sacrificed his career after all. He was catapulted to national fame: such was the public admiration for his courage and eloquence in the defense of justice that he became more successful than ever. Even John's rabble-rousing cousin Samuel, to his credit, appears never to have blamed John for defending the soldiers. John's place in the colonial cause also was not endangered, because he had shrewdly worked an attack on the British government into his defense of the British soldiers. These soldiers, he said, should not be blamed for the government's despicable policy of garrisoning the city, which was the real grievance that had brought the mob into the streets. Far from alienating the colonial patriots, he was soon one of their most important national leaders; six years later, at Philadelphia, Adams's skill and political savvy were the main force behind the Continental Congress's adoption of the Declaration of Independence. And if, in later years, Adams allowed his vanity to draw him to speak too often and too proudly of his decision to defend the soldiers in Boston, few would presume to sit in judgment.

The outcome of the Boston Massacre case is important for much more than the role it played in bringing John Adams to Philadelphia in 1776. It indicates a dramatic change that occurred in world history in the seventeenth and eighteenth centuries. The American Revolution, when it came, would not be the work of street rabble lashing out in spite and envy, as in so many prior revolutions. It would be disciplined by the leadership of gifted natural-law philosophers and carried out in obedience to carefully articulated doctrines of justice and natural rights. A new system of

---

[1]Quoted in David McCullough, *John Adams* (New York: Simon & Schuster, 2001), pp. 67-68; I have relied on McCullough for my account of the Boston Massacre and of Adams's role in the case.

thought about the relationship between the individual and the state had emerged. And when the revolution was complete, the same team of natural-law philosophers would be in a position to craft a government based on this new understanding of politics. The result was the bizarre, exhilarating experiment that political theorists call liberal democracy.

A REVOLUTION IN REVOLUTIONARY THINKING

In sharp contrast to what we saw about religious freedom in chapter six, political revolutions are not a particularly recent phenomenon, nor are they mostly confined to one part of the world. For as long as there have been governments, there have been revolutions. The reason is simple: wherever there is power, there is an incentive to seize it. This incentive is certainly counterbalanced by the enormous costs associated with any war, and in particular by the imbalance of power between those who have control of the government and those who do not. But every now and then some popular movement manages to line up all the right factors—public discontent, government incompetence, foreign support and so on—to pull off a revolution.

What was new was revolution conducted in the name of a highly developed ideology of natural rights. All revolutions are instigated by grievances like class resentment, outrage at barbaric government acts or the desire to remove a usurper who has seized power illegitimately. But revolutions before the seventeenth century did not connect those grievances to a larger philosophical system of revolutionary ideas. To be sure, some revolutions were more intellectual than others. Slave revolts generally had little ideology beyond "We do not want to be slaves anymore." On the other hand, revolutions that resulted from constitutional crises (disputes over who has the authority to do what in a given political system) could involve very intricate legal reasoning. However, none of these revolutions proceeded from a general theory of a right to revolution.

Probably the closest thing to what we might call revolutionary ideology before the seventeenth century would be the occasional instances of religious rebellion. The uprisings associated with the Radical Reformation (see chap. 5) fall into this category. Movements such as these typically did develop theological justifications for revolution. However, this is not the

Divine Right

In addition to making the case for a right to rebellion within the framework of natural law, Locke also had to confront a growing rejection of natural-law doctrine in favor of a radical new theory called divine right. This theory held that God had instituted absolute monarchy as the sole legitimate form of government. It was enjoying a particular boom since the posthumous publication of the book by Patriarcha Robert Filmer in 1680.

Since it rejected natural law, the divine-right theory based its arguments directly on interpretation of scriptural passages. Its most important line of argument was that governmental authority is rooted in the authority of fathers over their families. Society is a sort of extension of the family, like a very large clan, and the king is the father figure of the national family.

In his *Two Treatises of Government,* Locke devotes the first treatise to an excruciatingly detailed critique of Filmer's reading of the Bible. One of his most frequent lines of attack is to show that Filmer twists the meaning of the scriptural passages he cites. Locke was a trained scholar of both Hebrew and Greek, and in some cases his arguments come down to fine points of grammar such as the tenses and declensions of individual words. He makes an extensive case that the Bible does not portray any necessary continuity, or even analogy, between the family and the state; nor does it back up any of Filmer's other claims.

Locke also shows the many inconsistencies and contradictions that are inherent in divine-right theory. For example, if Filmer is right that Adam was sole monarch of the whole world, surely his heir, Seth, would also be sole monarch of the whole world, and then Seth's heir and so on. So the only sort of government truly endorsed by divine-right theory is world monarchy by Adam's heir—but we do not know who could rightfully claim that title today. Or on the other hand, if Adam's worldwide kingdom could legitimately be divided up into smaller domains, why stop at national boundaries? If political authority is just an extension of fatherly authority, why not make every father the political ruler of his household? What right does the king have to usurp the authority of actual fathers?

Most important, however, Locke shows that parental and political authority are inherently different because they serve different purposes under God's law, and all authority is shaped—and limited—by the purpose for which God appoints it. Political authority necessarily includes the power of life and death over those who are ruled because that power is necessary to fulfill government's purpose of keeping the peace and enforcing justice; but parental authority does not include the power of life and death over children because that would be contrary to its purpose of nurturing the children to adulthood. On the other hand, parents have certain powers over children that are necessary to child-rearing but that governments do not have over their subjects because those powers are not necessary to their purpose.

Locke's *First Treatise* is widely neglected today, because divine-right theory is no longer with us. However, a great deal of the analysis in *First Treatise* has wider application than just a refutation of divine right. Locke opposes not only divine right, but also all attempts to base political authority on the Bible; he argues that the Bible itself rules out any such attempt and leaves political authority in the hands of the community under God's natural law.

same as a general philosophy of a natural right to revolution; under these systems of thought, only true believers, not oppressed people simply as such, are authorized to rebel. This confines the influence of the revolutionary ideology to a single religious group and in general makes religious revolutionism a different kind of thing from revolutionary philosophy. At any rate, these uprisings were usually ephemeral. Typically they were either suppressed (as in the Peasants' War) or they collapsed from the instability of their own fanaticism (as in the Münster episode). Few religious uprisings can be said to have had a lasting historical effect, except insofar as they solidified opinion against the idea of rebellion.

This is not to say that there was no concept of morally legitimate revolution before the seventeenth century. Down through the ages most (but not all) political philosophers had argued that revolutions were sometimes justified. Cicero was one of the most prominent supporters of the idea in the ancient world. As we have already seen, he argued that a tyrannical government is no government at all—a position on which Augustine relied in his defense of the Christianizing of the Roman Empire (see chap. 3). Augustine's thinking on this subject has led to a robust (though not universal) tradition of support for rebellion against tyrants in subsequent Christian political thought; we have seen how both Thomas Aquinas and William of Ockham, the founders of the two great medieval schools of natural law, thought that revolutions were sometimes justified (see chap. 4).

However, before the seventeenth century this was, for most thinkers, a relatively unimportant philosophical question. Few philosophers bothered to articulate details such as under what circumstances people could legitimately rebel. More importantly, actual revolutions were not significantly shaped by such ideas. The philosophers' position that revolution was sometimes justified was no doubt a help to revolutionary movements, but it was by and large the only contribution the philosophers made. Revolutions were primarily justified by arguments that were specific to their particular situations, rather than by a general philosophy.

All that has changed, especially in the wake of the Revolutionary War in America and the unprecedented success of the political system that resulted from it. The change was a long time in coming; the first real eruption of revolutionary philosophy came a full century before the American Revolution. However, since 1776 there has been not just an eruption but a worldwide epidemic of revolutions. We have had no end of revolutions guided by new revolutionary philosophies. Philosophies of radical popular democracy have inspired many revolutions and smaller popular uprisings around the world since their debut in the French Revolution of 1789-1799. Marxist and fascist revolutionary philosophies also enjoyed flourishing worldwide careers in the nineteenth and twentieth centuries, particularly in the twentieth.

But the philosophy of a right to revolution under natural law, which emerged from England's Glorious Revolution of 1688 (see below) and guided the American Revolutionary War of 1776-1783, has proved to be the most successful in the long run. It was the decisive victor in the epic ideological warfare of the twentieth century, and it is the only revolutionary philosophy whose influence is clearly still expanding rather than diminishing. It has achieved this sustained and growing influence mainly because it is the only revolutionary philosophy that has succeeded in creating governments less oppressive than the ones it overthrew. Radical populism, fascism and communism "liberated" the people from corrupt monarchies and other dysfunctional governments only to deliver them into the hands of murderous, totalitarian revolutionary regimes. The results of Anglo-American philosophy have included many flaws and inadequacies, but unlike the results of other revolutionary philosophies, they have also included real and lasting liberation.

"Glorious" Revolution

The idea of *natural rights* originally grew out of the Christian doctrine of natural law. The basic concept is that moral rules governing relationships between people can be understood from two perspectives: obligation and entitlement. These two perspectives will perfectly mirror one another:

every obligation perfectly corresponds to an entitlement, and vice versa. Thus, since natural law creates obligations, it also creates entitlements. If John has an obligation not to steal Frank's money, then Frank is entitled not to have his money stolen by John. Similarly, if government is obligated to enforce justice among citizens, then citizens are entitled to have justice enforced. Over the course of the late Middle Ages and the early modern period, especially in the seventeenth century, the entitlements created by natural law came to be called natural rights.[2] To say, "I have a natural right to freedom of speech" is just an alternative way of saying, "Other people have a natural obligation to permit me to speak freely."

In chapter six we first met John Locke as the foremost champion of religious freedom during the period when that policy first emerged and began to create what we now know as the modern state. As it happens, the same John Locke was destined to serve as the foremost champion of the right to revolution when that idea began to shape the modern understanding of the relationship between the state and the individual. Furthermore, as we will see, Locke's account of natural rights provided the crucial starting point for the emergence of liberal democracy a century later. If we add to this his contributions to epistemology and the philosophy of religion (see chap. 6, sidebar "Locke's Philosophy"), Locke can stake a fairly strong claim to be the most influential philosopher since Aquinas, if not since Augustine.

Locke had taken an interest in the idea of natural rights early in his career. As a young scholar at Oxford, he wrote a series of essays on natural law. As we have noted, he began as a firm believer in authoritarianism, arguing that unlimited government authority over all areas of life was the only way to end disputes and maintain society in one piece. But when he was hired away from Oxford in 1667, he had already begun to abandon this line of thinking. His new employer was Lord Anthony Ashley Cooper, a prominent member of Parliament who a few years later would be dubbed Earl of Shaftesbury. Shaftesbury further challenged Locke's authoritarian assumptions. Shaftesbury's career had embodied the need for balance between resisting the king when necessary and making peace when necessary. He had been a leader of the parliamen-

---

[2]For a detailed account of the emergence of the idea of natural rights from medieval natural-law theory, see Brian Tierney, *The Idea of Natural Rights* (Grand Rapids: Eerdmans, 1997).

tary faction against the king during the English Civil War (1642-1648), and had also helped broker the 1660 political compromise that restored the monarchy and ended the period of conflict that followed the Civil War. He and his circle of political allies had a profound influence on Locke's thinking. Locke had been hired to serve Shaftesbury as a medical doctor: medicine was one of Locke's original fields of training, and he ended up saving Shaftesbury's life by overseeing a daring surgical operation. But Locke increasingly found himself writing political tracts for Shaftesbury's faction in support of religious toleration and the rights of Parliament against the king.

During the 1670s, the truce between the king and Parliament began to unravel, and once again it was religion that threatened to throw England back into violence and chaos. Ever mindful of the fragility of the political truce, Shaftesbury maintained a network of contacts and spies to keep tabs on the king, Charles II. At some point, probably in 1673, his spies discovered that Charles, in order to gain France's aid in a war over trade with the Netherlands, had secretly promised to convert to Catholicism and return England to Catholic religious control.[3] There was no specific date attached to the promise, and it was probably unlikely that Charles ever intended to fulfill it. However, the deep distrust between Parliament and the king did not incline anyone to give Charles the benefit of the doubt, especially when it came to maintaining England's independence from Rome. In addition, Charles produced no legitimate sons, and his brother James, the heir to the throne, was Catholic. As the years rolled on, it looked more and more likely that one way or another, England was going to face the prospect of a Catholic king returning to the throne— meaning yet another battle to the death over religion. And awful as that would be, they also feared even worse consequences. Protestantism was already on the way to being eliminated in France; they worried that the conversion of England might well tip the scales of power in Europe far enough to ensure the eventual death of Protestantism itself.[4]

---

[3]See Richard Ashcraft, *Revolutionary Politics and Locke's "Two Treatises of Government"* (Princeton, N.J.: Princeton University Press, 1986), pp. 17-20, 115-16.

[4]See John Marshall, *John Locke: Resistance, Religion and Responsibility* (Cambridge: Cambridge University Press, 1994), p. 357.

In 1681, Parliament tried to meet to vote for a law that would exclude Catholics from the throne. Charles prevented this by dissolving Parliament for new elections—and then not holding any elections. Parliament could not meet. Charles had set himself up as the sole ruler of England.

Shaftesbury and his circle were quickly radicalized. They no longer had any legal way to resist the king within the system. Only two options were available. One was to submit to sole rule by the king, including not only sole rule by Charles, but also sole rule by a Catholic successor who could reasonably be expected to impose his religious preference on the nation, just as all previous monarchs had done since Henry VIII about 150 years earlier. The other option was violent resistance: assassinate or overthrow the king as an enemy of the English constitution. Shaftesbury's circle chose the latter.

In 1682, Shaftesbury was arrested for his involvement in a failed assassination attempt. The jury, however, was stacked with parliamentary supporters and acquitted him; he fled to exile in the Netherlands and died soon afterward. Another assassination attempt failed in 1683, and this time it was Locke's turn to flee into hiding in the Netherlands. While living there under an assumed name, he did a lot of writing: one of his projects was revising the manuscript of a book he had written defending the use of violence by the resistance movement.

Charles II died in 1685, and James II successfully put down a military uprising conducted by the parliamentary faction on behalf of Charles's illegitimate, but Protestant, son. However, James would not sit on the throne for long. In 1688, the parliamentary faction finally succeeded in overthrowing the king and installing a Protestant, Parliament-friendly monarchy consisting of James's Protestant daughter Mary and her husband, the Dutch prince William of Orange. Parliament quickly passed, and William and Mary quickly signed, an act declaring the limits of the monarchy's power. The act was called the Bill of Rights and later served as the inspiration for the American constitutional provisions of the same name. The parliamentarians' victory was dubbed the Glorious Revolution.

The following year, in 1689, Locke returned to England and was finally able to publish his *Two Treatises of Government*. His decision to publish the book even after the success of the Glorious Revolution highlights an important point: though the immediate issue of control of the monarchy had been settled, the larger political and philosophical implications of the Glorious Revolution were still uncertain. Many people saw it simply as a last-ditch defense of the English constitution against a usurping king—a defense, ultimately, of English political traditions. Locke published the *Two Treatises* to persuade people to see it as the vindication of a certain philosophy of natural rights, and most important, the right of revolution against any government that violates the natural law in certain specific ways.

Violence and Moral Judgment

To make the case for a general, natural right to revolution, Locke in his *Two Treatises* must overcome the standard arguments that are made against such an idea. One of the most important of these is that the Bible commands us to obey government, and the command would be meaningless if we could decide to obey some rulers and not others. John Calvin, for example, argues that "if we have respect to the Word of God," we must obey "all princes, by whatever means they have so become," even if "there is nothing they less perform than the duty of princes."[5] As we have seen in chapter two (see esp. sidebar "The Authority of Government"), several passages of the New Testament command obedience to government. These passages explicitly attribute the authority of government to God's ordinance, and for good measure they specifically rule out rebellion against the rulers of first-century Rome. In light of these passages, the prima facie case against a Christian theory of a right to rebellion is formidable. Any such theory must make it a top priority to reconcile its views with these passages.

Another key argument against a Christian theory of a right to rebellion is that the whole point of having a government is to exercise control over people, to take out of their hands the ultimate decisions about matters of life and death. If people in general could be trusted to decide for themselves when violence was necessary, what would be the point of government? We

---

[5]John Calvin *Institutes of the Christian Religion* 4.20.25.

have government precisely because people cannot be trusted with control over the use of force. Without the restraint of the laws, people murder and fight and steal and cheat. And if people cannot be trusted with the use of force under ordinary circumstances, what will happen if we tell them that they have a right to rebel? Why would we expect them to use their right to rebel against government properly, when the very reason government exists is because they do not normally make that kind of decision properly? The end result of a right to rebel will be a right to anarchy.

Locke's analysis begins with the argument that the natural law, being God's law, can never be moot. It is the very nature of the natural law that it is universally applicable; that is what distinguishes it from "positive" or human laws. Therefore, in all situations, there must be somebody who has the authority to enforce the natural law, punishing those who break it. "For the law of nature would . . . be in vain, if there were nobody that . . . had a power to execute that law, and thereby preserve the innocent and restrain offenders."[6] If the natural law were ever unenforceable, God's sovereignty over humanity would be compromised.

It follows, Locke argues, that resistance to government must be legitimate in at least some situations. To say that resistance is never permissible is the same as saying that we must obey anyone who succeeds in seizing power, no matter how that person got it or how that person uses it. And if we took that position, what would happen? "There would be no distinction between pirates and lawful princes, he that has force is without more ado to be obeyed, and crowns and scepters would become the inheritance only of violence and rapine."[7] Under such circumstances, the natural law that God gave us to govern politics would be moot.

Another way of thinking about this problem is to ask: Who ought to have power? "The great question which in all ages has disturbed mankind, and brought on them the greatest part of those mischiefs which have ruined cities, depopulated countries, and disordered the peace of the world, has been, not whether there be power in the world, nor whence it came, but who

---

[6]John Locke *Two Treatises* treatise 2, sec. 7. Different editions of the *Two Treatises* have slightly different section numbers; I cite the Everyman edition: ed. Mark Goldie, 3rd ed. (London: Everyman, 1994). For online resources see <www.ivpress.com>.
[7]Locke *Two Treatises* treatise 1, sec. 81.

should have it."[8] If we say that resistance to government is never legitimate, then we are really saying that whoever has power, ought to have it—because we have ruled out any grounds for taking power away from that person. This destroys the distinction between rightful and wrongful possession of power, and hence it destroys any possibility of politics founded on justice rather than simply on brute force. Might would make right. Resistance must sometimes be legitimate, if only because it is the only way to maintain the distinction between rightful and wrongful possession of power.

How, then, are we to judge who ought to have power? To address this question, Locke introduces the concept of the state of nature. The state of nature is a traditional concept that some natural-law theorists have used to illustrate aspects of the natural law. Ockham, for example, distinguishes three different senses in which the term "natural law" can be used; one of them is "that which ought to be kept by those who use natural equity alone, without any human custom or statute, which is natural because it is not contrary to the original state of nature."[9] Locke uses the concept of the state of nature to mean the same thing as Ockham: any situation in which people are morally obligated only to obey the natural law, not any human law or custom, is a state of nature.[10]

The state of nature is not a thought experiment, a hypothetical philosophical speculation. Nor does it refer to a primordial time in the early history of humanity.[11] According to Locke, states of nature occur all the time. All nations, he writes, are always in a state of nature relative to one another; they are not under a common system of government, and when they interact with one another, they are obliged only by the natural law. People living in different nations are likewise in a state of nature relative

---

[8]Locke *Two Treatises* treatise 1, sec. 106.

[9]William of Ockham *Dialogue on the Power of the Emperor and the Pope* dialogue 3; I rely on Ewart Lewis, *Medieval Political Ideas* (New York: Alfred A. Knopf, 1954), pp. 79-85.

[10]Locke's understanding of natural law grows out of the tradition following Ockham; see Francis Oakley, "Locke, Natural Law, and God—Again," *History of Political Thought* 18 (1997): 624-51.

[11]Locke's real accounts of early human history come in his discussion of Adam in the *First Treatise* and his description of early human society in chap. 8 of the *Second Treatise*, neither of which has anything to do with the state of nature. His famous comment that the natives of the newly discovered continent America seem to live in a state of nature arises not from any assumption that they are closer to humanity's primordial state, but simply from the claims made by European travelers that the American natives lived without any government (see Locke *Two Treatises* treatise 2, sec. 102).

to one another.[12] Anyone who wants to be in a state of nature relative to all the rest of humanity can easily do so by renouncing all citizenship, getting into a boat and sailing out into international waters.[13] Such a person could still come into conflict with others, and in some cases the outcome of that conflict might look quite similar to the enforcement of human laws. If our hypothetical oceangoing hermit started practicing piracy, for example, such a pirate might be captured and subjected to punishment. But on the Lockean understanding, the moral basis of this punishment would not be that this person owed rightful allegiance to the laws of any human government. It would be that this person violated the universal laws of justice: the natural law.

To find out who should have the authority to enforce the natural law, Locke begins by asking who has that authority in the state of nature: when we strip away human laws and conventions, where does the authority ultimately reside? Locke argues that in the state of nature, no one person has any more authority than any other person. In the absence of human laws and conventions to distinguish one person's legal status from that of another, everyone would have equal legal status because everyone is equally God's creation and equally obligated by the natural law.[14] But we know that somebody must have the authority to enforce the natural law, or else God's law would be moot. Locke takes these premises and makes a bold deduction: if someone must have the authority to enforce the natural law, but in the state of nature no one has any more authority than anyone else, then in the state of nature the authority to enforce the natural law must belong to everyone equally. "The execution of the law of nature is in that state [of nature] put into every man's hands, whereby everyone has a right to punish the transgressors of that law."[15] If there is no established government to punish wrongdoers, then when anyone does wrong, everyone is entitled to punish him.

There is a major problem with this system, however. People do not naturally do a good job of enforcing the natural law, because human nature

---

[12]Locke *Two Treatises* treatise 2, sec. 145.

[13]This example assumes that citizens are legally permitted to renounce their citizenship; Locke thinks it is legitimate for governments not to permit renunciation of citizenship once it has been voluntarily embraced (see Locke *Two Treatises* treatise 2, sec. 121).

[14]See Locke *Two Treatises* treatise 2, secs. 4-6.

[15]Locke *Two Treatises* treatise 2, sec. 7.

is morally flawed. Although people accept the law of nature in general, when it comes down to their own specific circumstances, they often find excuses for not applying it to themselves. They are "biased by their interest" in their own favor. "Though the law of nature be plain and intelligible to all rational creatures, yet men . . . are not apt to follow it as a law binding to them in the application of it to their particular cases."[16] People are very good at inventing (and believing in) excuses for their own behavior. They will readily acknowledge the general rule against stealing, but they are reluctant to acknowledge (in many cases even to themselves) that any particular act they have committed was an act of theft. And the victims of crime are just as biased by their self-interest as the offenders, which makes the issue of punishment doubly problematic. "Men being partial to themselves, passion and revenge is very apt to carry them too far, and with too much heat, in their own cases."[17] The offended party has "no absolute or arbitrary power, to use a criminal when he has got him in his hands, according to the passionate heats or boundless extravangancy of his own will, but only to retribute him so far as calm reason and conscience dictates."[18] But the wronged party cannot be counted on to restrain himself to "calm reason and conscience."[19]

The heart of the problem is moral judgment. It is not simply that people enjoy doing wrong to others but do not enjoy having wrong done to them. The problem is that people's self-interest biases their opinions about whether any particular act is right or wrong. After we engage in a business transaction, I may sincerely come to the conclusion that you cheated me while you equally sincerely come to the conclusion that it was a fair deal. In the state of nature, every situation where this happens will end in conflict—often violent conflict, since the person who thinks he has been wronged will exercise his right to punish the wrongdoer, while the other party thinks himself innocent and will exercise his right to self-defense.

The problem of moral judgment is especially clear in a biblical example that Locke uses to illustrate his point. In the Old Testament book of

---

[16]Locke *Two Treatises* treatise 2, sec. 124.

[17]Locke *Two Treatises* treatise 2, sec. 125.

[18]Locke *Two Treatises* treatise 2, sec. 8.

[19]Locke also briefly mentions a third reason: in the state of nature, those who wish to punish the offender often lack sufficient power to do so (see Locke *Two Treatises* treatise 2, sec. 126).

Judges, the Israelites are threatened by an invasion from the Ammonites, who claim that the Israelites have stolen their land. The Israelites ask Jephthah to lead them against the Ammonites. Jephthah writes a letter to the Ammonites, laying out the facts and explaining that the land was not stolen. The Israelites had tried to travel in the land peacefully, but its rulers attacked them without provocation; they ended up in possession of the land as the result of a just war. God had confirmed their claim to the land by special revelation. And at any rate, it was not the Ammonites from whom the Israelites had taken the land, so what claim did the Ammonites have to it? They never possessed it. They never even made any claim to it before the Israelites had it. "I therefore have not sinned against you, and you do me wrong by making war on me," the letter concludes. "The LORD, the Judge, decide this day between the people of Israel and the people of Ammon" (Judg 11:27). This last sentence is Jephthah's characterization of the armed conflict that is to come: since the Ammonites will not listen to reason, the only way the Israelites can stand up for their rights is by war, and Jephthah appeals to God to give them victory.

Pointing to Jephthah's example, Locke argues that wherever there is a state of war, it is because the parties have failed to resolve their differences by peaceful discussion, and thus they have no option left but to "appeal to heaven" as Jephthah did.[20] In using violence, each party is rejecting the moral judgment of the other party, appealing instead to God's judgment. Even if they do not explicitly say this is what they are doing, it is implied by their actions. Over the course of the *Two Treatises*, Locke repeatedly refers to Jephthah, arguing that where there is no common authority on earth to settle disputes, the parties must appeal to the one common authority over all humanity—God—and the only way they can do so (assuming that peaceful means have failed) is to "appeal to heaven" by violence.[21]

AUTHORITY AS A TRUST

Because differences of moral judgment arising from people's self-interested bias are prone to end in violence, the community needs a better way to resolve conflicts. The only solution is to create a neutral judge who can settle

---

[20]Locke *Two Treatises* treatise 2, sec. 21.
[21]See Locke *Two Treatises* treatise 2, secs. 21, 168, 176, 241-42.

questions of moral judgment without a self-interested bias, and then treat its judgments as authoritative; this means that people must voluntarily set aside their own moral judgments and instead obey government's judgments. A person leaves the state of nature and becomes a member of a civil society when "he authorizes the society . . . to make laws for him as the public good of the society shall require, to the execution whereof his own assistance (as to his own decrees) is due."[22] This is the origin of government.

Locke argues that government exists by the consent of the members of the community. "Where any number of men have so consented to make one community or government, they are thereby presently incorporated, and make one body politic, wherein the majority have a right to act and conclude the rest."[23] This idea, like the state of nature, has deep roots in traditional natural-law philosophy: Ockham writes that "no one should be set over a body of mortals except by their choice and consent."[24] Aquinas writes that a tyrant may be resisted if he "has violently seized power against the will of his subjects, or has forced them to consent."[25] Locke argues that there are only two ways people can be made to cooperate: by their consent or by force.[26] Government cannot be created by force, because the key difference between the state of nature and civil society is social cooperation in moral judgment. Rule by force would not produce this social cooperation; people ruled by force do not "authorize" government to make laws for them that they will help execute as though they were their "own decrees." If people obeyed only because they were forced to do so, they would not be members of a political community, but would be slaves.[27] Since the

---

[22]Locke *Two Treatises* treatise 2, sec. 89.

[23]Locke *Two Treatises* treatise 2, sec. 95.

[24]Ockham *Dialogue on the Power of the Emperor and the Pope* dialogue 3. I rely on Lewis, *Medieval Political Ideas*, pp. 79-85. For online resources see <www.ivpress.com>.

[25]Thomas Aquinas *Commentary on the Sentences of Peter Lombard*. I rely on *St. Thomas Aquinas on Politics and Ethics*, trans. Paul Sigmund (New York: W. W. Norton, 1987), pp.65-66, n. 8. For online resources see <www.ivpress.com>.

[26]The contrast between consent and force as the only two modes of social cooperation dominates the *Two Treatises*; on this point, see Greg Forster, *John Locke's Politics of Moral Consensus* (Cambridge: Cambridge University Press, 2005), pp. 225-30.

[27]The first word of the *Two Treatises* is "slavery": "Slavery is so vile and miserable an estate of man, and so directly opposite to the generous temper and courage of our nation, that it is hardly to be conceived that an Englishman, much less a gentleman, should plead for it" (Locke *Two Treatises* treatise 1, sec. 1). Throughout the *Two Treatises*, the denial of a right to rebellion is equated with

political community does not exist by force, we must conclude that it exists by consent.

Rule by consent is not the same thing as democracy. The community can give its consent to any form of government. To those who say that government cannot originate by consent because primitive governments were tribal patriarchies in which power was held by heads of families and clans, Locke responds that members of primitive societies consented to be ruled by tribal patriarchy. Could the head of the clan really force the whole clan to obey him if it did not want to? Locke adds that consenting to tribal patriarchy was a rational decision on their part, because it was "best suited to their present state and condition."[28] While Locke clearly does prefer democracy for his own society, his consent theory is not a defense of democracy as such.

Locke further argues that government authority, rather than being absolute, is held in trust on behalf of the community. All forms of power, if they are to be legitimate, must be understood as being held in trust. Power can be rightly exercised only for the good of those over whom it is exercised, not for the good of the one exercising it; this is simply because all power is under God's law, which commands that we preserve others rather than exploiting them for our own preservation. Locke defines "tyranny" as "making use of the power anyone has in his hands, not for the good of those who are under it, but for his own private separate advantage."[29] Thus all forms of authority are limited in scope. Parental authority is rightly exercised only for the good of the children, and thus is held in trust by parents on the children's behalf, and extends only to acts that promote their good.[30] Similarly, the authority of governments is rightly exercised only for the good of their subjects; thus it is held in trust on their subjects' behalf and extends only to acts that promote their good:

---

slavery. Locke is not referring to the actual practice of African slavery, but to slavery as a general concept; on the use of slavery in the *Two Treatises*, and on Locke's historical connection to African slavery, see James Farr, "'So Vile and Miserable an Estate': The Problem of Slavery in Locke's *Two Treatises*," *Political Theory* 14 (1986): 263-89.

[28]Locke *Two Treatises* treatise 2, sec. 107.

[29]Locke *Two Treatises* treatise 2, sec. 199.

[30]Locke *Two Treatises* treatise 2, secs. 57-74.

> Their power, in the utmost bounds of it, is limited to the public good of
> society. It is a power that has no other end but preservation, and therefore
> can never have a right to destroy, enslave, or designedly [intentionally] to
> impoverish the subjects. The obligations of the law of nature cease not in
> society. . . . Thus the law of nature stands as an eternal rule to all men, leg-
> islators as well as others. The rules they make for other men's actions must
> . . . be conformable to the law of nature, i.e., to the will of God . . . and the
> fundamental law of nature being the preservation of mankind, no human
> sanction can be good or valid against it.[31]

Locke insists that the ruler is the "trustee or deputy" of "the people" and
must act "according to the trust reposed in him."[32]

When government uses power for its own good rather than the public
good, it violates its trust. But there are two different ways this can happen, and the distinction is crucial to Locke's theory of revolution. There
will always be a certain amount of misuse of power in any government;
this can be chalked up to the normal imperfections that will happen
in any human endeavor. People are sinful, and the things they do will
always reflect that to some degree. In some situations the level of "ordinary misuse of power," if we may call it that, may even get fairly high
while still being attributable to ordinary human imperfection. This sort
of misuse of power should be reformed wherever possible, but it does not
justify a violent response.

However, some abuses of power are so persistent and flagrant that they
can only mean that government is intentionally violating its trust: the rulers are no longer even trying to rule, but have set themselves up on purpose
to do nothing with their power but exploit the people for their own profit.
The people will tolerate "great mistakes . . . many wrong and inconvenient
laws, and all the slips of human frailty." However, "a long train of abuses,
prevarications and artifices, all tending the same way," will "make the
design [of tyranny] visible to the people."[33] It is not the mere severity of
the abuse that marks the difference between ordinary misuse of power
and real tyranny; nor does it make much difference what particular type

---

[31]Locke *Two Treatises* treatise 2, sec. 135.
[32]Locke *Two Treatises* treatise 2, sec. 240.
[33]Locke *Two Treatises* treatise 2, sec. 225.

of abuse is taking place (e.g., religious persecution, military aggression, theft of property, etc.) The key difference is the "design" of tyranny: it is one thing for government to execute its trust poorly; it is another thing for government to intentionally abandon that trust and give up even trying to be a government, and engage in exploitation instead.[34]

Like Augustine, Locke adopts Cicero's argument that a tyrannical government ceases to be a government at all. "Governments are dissolved . . . when the legislative or the prince, either of them, act contrary to their trust."[35] When government intentionally abuses its trust, that trust is forfeited; since government exists solely as the depository of that trust, when the trust is gone the government goes with it. It is an essential element of any kind of trust that it is forfeited if it is intentionally abused. "All power given with trust for the attaining [of] an end being limited by that end, whenever that end is manifestly neglected or opposed, the trust must necessarily be forfeited."[36] Once an abusive government gives up even the intention of doing the job of a government, it is no longer a government in any meaningful sense. It is instead just a very large criminal organization. In such cases, the authority that the community gave to government in trust returns to the community. "Thus the community perpetually retains a supreme power of saving themselves from the attempts and designs of anybody, even of their legislators whenever they shall be so foolish or so wicked as to lay and carry on designs against the liberties and properties of the subject."[37]

---

[34]This point is one of the essential differences between Locke's theory of revolution and the theory of radical populism that fueled the French Revolution; Locke thinks that revolution is only justified where there is clearly intentional abuse of power, while the theory of radical populism gives the people the right to change their government at any time, for any reason—and to overthrow it if it refuses to be changed.

[35]Locke *Two Treatises* treatise 2, sec. 221. Cicero was one of Locke's favorite philosophers throughout his career, and his whole analysis of moral law is heavily indebted to Cicero's thought (see Marshall, *Resistance, Religion and Responsibility*, pp. 229-326). As Augustine had done before him, Locke adjusted Cicero's thought to bring it into line with Christianity (see Forster, *John Locke's Politics*, pp. 215-17), though Locke had a different set of concerns: for Augustine at the turn of the fifth century, the main problem was Christianity's continuing struggle with dualistic rationalism (see chap. 2); for Locke at the turn of the eighteenth century, the problem was reconciling Ciceronian ethics with Christian efforts, during the Enlightenment, to develop a more detailed account of moral psychology (see chap. 6 sidebar "The Enlightenment[s]").

[36]Locke *Two Treatises* treatise 2, sec. 149.

[37]Locke *Two Treatises* treatise 2, sec. 149.

Furthermore, by abusing their power, the rulers have created a state of war between themselves and the community. "Using force upon the people without authority, and contrary to the trust put in him, [the ruler] that does so, is [in] a state of war with the people." Given that the rulers started the war between themselves and the people, there can be no question that the people have the right to fight in their own self-defense. "In all states and conditions the true remedy of force without authority is to oppose force to it."[38] If the rulers abuse their trust and refuse to change their ways, "the appeal then lies nowhere but to heaven. Force . . . which permits no appeal to any judge on earth," is "properly a state of war, wherein the appeal lies only to heaven."[39] It is the abusive rulers, not the people, who are the real rebels, because they rebelled against the very lawful authority that was entrusted to them by the community.[40]

This is how Locke's theory of a right to rebellion against tyrants can be squared with biblical passages like Romans 13 and 2 Peter 2 (see chap. 2, esp. sidebar "The Authority of Government"). These passages command obedience to government. However, on Locke's view, a government that becomes tyrannical ceases to be a government and hence forfeits its entitlement to obedience under the apostolic command.[41]

This is not a semantic trick; it goes to the heart of what the apostles were really commanding. As we have seen, Locke argues that without this distinction between legitimate governments and tyrants (who are not really rulers but merely very powerful criminals), the command to obey government would obliterate all distinction between rightful and wrongful possession of power: might would make right, and citizenship would be just another word for slavery. Since the Bible clearly does not permit us to say that might makes right or that all citizens are slaves, and since each individual passage of the Bible must be interpreted in light of the whole, there is at least a difficult problem in these passages. Locke's theory is not a cheap play on words but a serious effort to work out that problem.

---

[38]Locke *Two Treatises* treatise 2, sec. 155.
[39]Locke *Two Treatises* treatise 2, sec. 242.
[40]See Locke *Two Treatises* treatise 2, sec. 226.
[41]See also Locke's commentary on Rom 13:1-7 in his *Paraphrase and Notes upon the Epistles of St. Paul.* For online resources see <www.ivpress.com>.

Locke's view implies that the government of ancient Rome was not a tyranny when the apostles commanded obedience to it, but the government of England in the 1680s was a tyranny when Locke rebelled against it. This is certainly an odd claim at first glance; after all, ancient Rome routinely practiced abuses and cruelties not known, or paralleled, in 1680s England. But Locke argues that what really distinguishes the abuses of power against which he rebelled is not their severity but their purpose. Though Locke does not say so, he may be relying on an implicit assumption that historical changes in social standards are relevant to this judgment. To a great extent, the rulers of ancient Rome were only doing what most people at the time thought it was normal for rulers to do. England in the 1680s had much higher standards of government rectitude, in large part due to the historical influence of Christianity. This consideration lends more plausibility to Locke's claim that the rulers of ancient Rome, or at least the particular rulers who held power at the time when the apostles wrote, might have committed worse abuses than the rulers of 1680s England while being less "tyrannical" in the particular sense that determines whether rebellion is justified.

As for the possibility that the people will use their right to rebellion wrongly, Locke cannot absolutely rule that out. Thus, his philosophy does not completely resolve the problem of flawed moral judgment. Locke does list a number of reasons why it is much safer to leave this one ultimate moral judgment in the hands of the people rather than the government, even when all other moral judgments are left to the government. Some of these include the enormous power of government, which will deter people from rebelling unless they absolutely have to, and the fear that a wrongful rebellion will earn them God's severe displeasure. "He that appeals to heaven must be sure he has right on his side, and a right too that is worth the trouble and cost of the appeal, as he will answer at a tribunal that cannot be deceived and will surely retribute to everyone according to the mischiefs he has created."[42]

But his ultimate answer is that the very nature of moral judgment prevents this ultimate decision from ever being taken out of the peo-

---

[42]Locke *Two Treatises* treatise 2, sec. 176.

Charles Montesquieu (1689-1755)

Charles-Louis de Secondat, Baron de Montesquieu—remembered in history, for obvious reasons, by the simpler name Charles Montesquieu—was born into one of France's most prominent families. He owned a great deal of land and served in a series of public offices, but his real vocation was the study of law and politics, primarily through historical reading and travel. His 1748 masterpiece, *The Spirit of the Laws,* condensed a full twenty years of study into a work that was quite weighty in both the philosophical and the physical sense (over 700 pages in modern editions). "I swear that this book nearly killed me; I am going to rest now," he wrote upon its publication.[a]

Montesquieu's observations were widely influential and were often treated as authoritative. Both supporters and critics of the U.S. Constitution appealed to his authority, quoting his works to prove that the Constitution either did or did not live up to the wisdom of the greatest political sage of the era.

It is mainly due to Montesquieu's influence that the American founders' generation held the separation of powers to be essential to liberty. The chief threat to liberty, he writes, is people's desire to have power over others. Government's job is to protect liberty by providing each person with security against others: "Political liberty . . . is that tranquility of spirit which comes from the opinion each one has of his security, and in order for him to have this liberty the government must be such that one citizen cannot fear another citizen." But private citizens need security not only from their power-desiring neighbors, but also (especially) against their power-desiring rulers. This is what the separation of powers provides: "When legislative power is united with executive power in a single person or in a single body of the magistracy, there is no liberty, because one can fear that the same monarch or senate that makes tyrannical laws will execute them tyrannically. Nor is there liberty if the power of judging is not separate from legislative power and from executive power."[b] But where power is held separately, the tyrannical aspirations of one branch will be checked by the others.

Montesquieu was also the main proponent of the conventional wisdom that republics could only work in small rural communities. He argued that to succeed, each type of government—monarchy, republic or tyranny—needed the support of a particular "spirit" among the people—honor, virtue or fear respectively. Monarchies did not need virtue because the spirit of honor (willing obedience to superiors) helped to contain factions, but republics did not have that advantage and had to rely on the virtue of a small homogeneous community instead. Opponents of the Constitution particularly cited Montesquieu on this point, favoring continued reliance on local government.

Montesquieu particularly praised England's institutional mechanisms, like the separation of powers, for their success in controlling factions. He had also popularized many of the political reforms adopted by the founders—but he had promoted them for monarchies, since republics (being small and virtuous and therefore factionless) had no need of such reforms. The founders' innovation was to build a republic on the prin-

ciples that Montesquieu had laid out for monarchies.

---

[a]Quoted in Anne Cohler, "Introduction," in Charles Montesquieu, *The Spirit of the Laws* (Cambridge: Cambridge University Press, 1989), p. xi.

[b]Montesquieu, *Spirit of the Laws*, book 11, chap. 6. I rely on the translation of Anne Cohler, Basia Carolyn Miller and Harold Samuel Stone (Cambridge University Press, 1989). For online resources see <www.ivpress.com>.

ple's hands. God requires every person to obey his own conscience, so the submission of one's moral judgment to government can never be absolute and total. "No man or society of men having a power to deliver up their preservation . . . to the absolute will and arbitrary dominion of another, whenever anyone shall go about to bring them into such a slavish condition, they will always have a right to preserve what they have not a power to part with."[43] The problem of moral judgment does not permit a full solution as long as we live in a world where each person is responsible for his own behavior and imperfect in his ability to judge right from wrong.

LOCKE AND THE AMERICAN "APPEAL TO HEAVEN"

Locke's philosophy was especially influential in colonial America and profoundly shaped the American Revolution. Other influences certainly operated on the American founders as well, but in many cases these other influences had in turn been influenced by Locke, or they promoted ideas quite similar to his. For example, it would be artificial to draw a hard and fast distinction between Lockean political ideas and Calvinist or Puritan political ideas in late eighteenth-century America, because Lockean ideas were widely influential among American Calvinists of that period.[44] Sim-

---

[43]Locke *Two Treatises* treatise 2, sec. 149; see also sec. 241.
[44]Consider, e.g., the influence of Calvinist theologian John Witherspoon on the political thought

ilarly, if the American founders often invested their cause with deep religious significance and drew heavily on Scripture to justify their cause and motivate their troops, this also does not mean they were any less Lockean; Locke's political theory is a Christian natural-law theory.[45]

The Declaration of Independence shows how thoroughly they were, at heart, sons of Locke:

> We hold these truths to be self-evident, that all men are created equal, that they are endowed by their Creator with certain unalienable rights, that among these are life, liberty and the pursuit of happiness; that to secure these rights, governments are instituted among men, deriving their just powers from the consent of the governed; that whenever any form of government becomes destructive of these ends, it is the right of the people to alter or to abolish it, and to institute new government, laying its foundation on such principles and organizing its powers in such form, as to them shall seem most likely to effect their safety and happiness. Prudence, indeed, will dictate that governments long established should not be changed for light and transient causes; and accordingly all experience hath shown that mankind are more disposed to suffer, while evils are sufferable, than to right themselves by abolishing the forms to which they are accustomed. But when a long train of abuses and usurpations, pursuing invariably the same object, evinces a design to reduce them under absolute despotism, it is their right, it is their duty, to throw off such government, and to provide new guards for their future security.

It has long been observed that the line about "self-evident" rights to "life, liberty and the pursuit of happiness" bears the heavy stamp of Locke's influence. But in fact this entire passage is drawn directly from the principles of the *Two Treatises*. Governments are instituted by consent,

---

of the founding; see Michael Novak, *On Two Wings* (San Francisco: Encounter Books, 2002), pp. 14-18, 52-53, 151-52. Locke himself had been preceded by Calvinist theologian Samuel Rutherford, whose 1644 book, *Lex Rex*, anticipates important elements of Locke's argument. Rutherford and Locke both influenced later Calvinists, and their political ideas are similar enough that Locke's influence and Rutherford's influence should not be treated as totally distinct.

[45]If some partisans of the American cause thought that America had been singled out for a special destiny by divine providence, this is obviously not something they found in Locke's works, but there is also nothing in such a belief that contradicts those works. The important question is how the Americans explained the justice of their cause, and on that subject they were Lockean.

to secure natural rights; when government becomes destructive of those rights, the people may alter or abolish it; people will suffer great evils rather than rebel; but when it is clear that the abuses are intentional, they will and should rebel.

In particular, the most important distinguishing feature of a revolutionary philosophy is its understanding of what, exactly, must happen before a rebellion is authorized. On this point, compare the founders' criterion, "when a long train of abuses and usurpations, pursuing invariably the same object, evinces a design to reduce them under absolute despotism," with Locke's "if a long train of abuses, prevarications and artifices, all tending the same way, make the design [of tyranny] visible to the people." The overwhelming bulk of the Declaration is devoted to reciting a list of grievances against the king. The purpose of this list, as the Declaration itself states, is not simply to show the wrongs done to the colonists but to establish "a history of repeated injuries and usurpations all having in direct object the establishment of an absolute tyranny over these states." The founders' deviations from Locke—such as Thomas Jefferson's substitution of the romantic phrase "pursuit of happiness" for Locke's more down-to-earth term *properly*—pale in comparison to their utter dependence on him in the fundamentals of their revolutionary creed.

Locke's influence on the Revolutionary War is visible elsewhere as well. During the siege of Boston in the winter of 1775-1776, warships commissioned by George Washington bore flags that declared, in large black letters on a white background, "AN APPEAL TO HEAVEN." The flag was adopted by the Massachusetts Navy in April 1776.[46]

LIBERAL DEMOCRACY AND THE SCIENCE OF POLITICS

After they won the War for Independence, the founders faced the equally daunting task of designing a government that would not repeat the errors of the one they had just thrown off. They set out to redesign government in order to bring it into compliance with the natural law more effectively and consistently. These leaders built on the foundation of Lockean philosophy and drew on many insights from the explosion of political philosophy dur-

---

[46]See Edward Richardson, *Standards and Colors of the American Revolution* (Philadelphia: University of Pennsylvania Press, 1982). For online resources see <www.ivpress.com>.

ing the Enlightenment, especially the thought of the French philosopher Charles Montesquieu (see sidebar). The combination of Lockean moral principles and Enlightenment ideas about constitutional design gave birth to the political system now known as liberal democracy.

A series of newspaper essays published in 1787 and 1788 defending the new U.S. Constitution, which has come to be called the *Federalist Papers*, provides a window into the thinking of its major architects. Naturally, not all the American founders agreed with everything in the *Federalist Papers*. Moreover, the state and local political systems of the time did not always reflect the broadly Lockean and liberal-democratic approach to politics favored by the founders as they crafted the national government. However, the *Federalist Papers* do lay out the fundamental philosophical commitments of liberal democracy better than any other source we could turn to.

In the opening of the first essay, Alexander Hamilton expresses the founders' sense that they stood at a great crossroads in the history of political philosophy:

> It has frequently been remarked that it seems to have been reserved to the people of this country, by their conduct and example, to decide the important question, whether societies of men are really capable or not of establishing good government from reflection and choice, or whether they are forever destined to depend for their political constitutions on accident and force. If there be any truth in the remark, the crisis at which we are arrived may with propriety be regarded as the era in which that decision is to be made; and a wrong election of the part we shall act may, in this view, deserve to be considered as the general misfortune of mankind.[47]

The contrast of "reflection and choice" with "accident and force" is yet another Lockean imprint on the founders. What is new is the intention to design a whole system of politics based on reflection and choice. For Locke, the existing English constitution was taken for granted; it may not have been designed by a process of reflection and choice, but that was not an issue because the people consented to be ruled by it regardless. The founders had the opportunity—and the

---

[47]Alexander Hamilton, James Madison and John Jay, *Federalist Papers* no. 1. For online resources see <www.ivpress.com>.

burden—of designing a new constitution that would be put to an up-or-down vote.

The founders defied the conventional wisdom of Europe by preferring a republic to a monarchy. Hamilton admits that republican constitutions had performed poorly both in the ancient Greco-Roman world and in the few places where they appeared in medieval Europe. But things have changed, he argues:

> The science of politics . . . like most other sciences, has received great improvement. The efficacy of various principles is now well understood, which were either not known at all, or imperfectly known, to the ancients. The regular distribution of power into distinct departments, the introduction of legislative balances and checks, the institution of courts composed of judges holding their offices during good behavior, the representation of the people in the legislature by deputies of their own election; these are wholly new discoveries, or have made their principal progress towards perfection in modern times. They are means, and powerful means, by which the excellencies of republican government may be retained, and its imperfections lessened or avoided.[48]

Of all the scientific advancements made during the Enlightenment, the advances in the "science of politics" would turn out to be the most important. Of all the inventions produced in that period, the most extraordinary would be a republic that actually worked.

The essential problem the founders were trying to solve was the problem of power. Government must have enough power to govern, but not so much that it becomes oppressive. When government is strong, rulers will be constantly tempted to abuse power. When government is weak, it is susceptible to a host of equally dangerous problems: manipulation by selfish factions seeking to promote their own good over the public good; domination by stronger foreign powers, in the form of overt military bullying or covert subversion by bribery and infiltration; and ultimately, collapse at the hands of domestic uprisings or foreign conquest.

The founders had vivid examples of both problems before them as they crafted the Constitution. Pennsylvania's constitution, adopted in the

---

[48]*Federalist Papers* no. 9.

Adam Smith (1723-1790)

Adam Smith, a Scottish professor of moral philosophy, led an unremarkable life and by all accounts was a dull person to be around. His most famous work, *An Inquiry into the Nature and Causes of the Wealth of Nations*, is mostly devoted to lengthy analyses of late eighteenth-century British economic policies that are of little interest today; they also were of little interest even in the late eighteenth century except to those who took a serious interest in the details of economic policy. Yet contained in that long, dry book is a philosophy of economics that was so explosive and revolutionary, and so important to the full development of liberal democracy, that it well deserved to be published (as it was) in the fateful year of 1776.

Smith's main argument for free markets was that they produced more prosperity for everyone, but his argument also had a moral dimension. Just as Madison encouraged people to stop trying to make men into angels and instead seek to produce public good out of private selfishness, Smith encouraged people to take a similar attitude toward economic selfishness. If government simply maintained a free market and otherwise left people more or less alone, natural incentives would do a better job of mitigating the economic effects of human selfishness than any artificial constraints government could adopt for that purpose.

Human life, he argued, is naturally structured so that each person's pursuit of wealth works for the benefit of society. People seeking to make more money have an incentive to work more diligently and efficiently. These natural incentives are an "invisible hand" guiding selfish people to behavior that benefits society, since increased national wealth alleviates the many painful effects of poverty. Artificial interference with free labor and exchange hurts rather than helps the public good; it does not alleviate man's natural selfishness, and it impoverishes the nation by interfering with healthy natural incentives.

Smith was far from a libertarian; he affirmed that a great deal of government activity was necessary to maintain the social conditions that made free labor and exchange possible, including public virtue. Commercial societies, he wrote, are particularly vulnerable to the loss of virtue; education and religion are the necessary antidotes. Once again the solution here was freedom; in a free market, schools and churches face healthy natural incentives, because if they must gather voluntary support to survive, they have incentives to work hard, to be virtuous and even to teach truth—since anyone teaching error is liable to refutation by his competitors. Religious establishments or excessive government subsidies for education (beyond what was needed to educate the poor) undermine these healthy incentives.

heady days of 1776, created a radically democratic government in which popular passions were constantly overriding justice and individual rights. The independence of the judiciary and even the right to a jury trial were subverted in order to vindicate popular causes and ensure that unpopular defendants would be convicted. Quakers, those who had opposed the Revolutionary War, and others were disenfranchised and subjected to other forms of persecution. On the other hand, the constitution of Massachusetts had adopted so many cumbersome limits on government power that it could not effectively govern. The state could not raise funds to pay its war debts, particularly the pay that had been promised to Revolutionary War soldiers. In 1787, unpaid ex-soldiers revolted, an uprising known as Shays' Rebellion after its leader, decorated war veteran Daniel Shays. The state was unable to raise funds for troops, and the uprising ultimately had to be put down by a privately funded militia—a deeply troubling precedent on many levels. These alarming events in Pennsylvania and Massachusetts galvanized support for drafting a new constitution.[49]

AMBITION COUNTERACTS AMBITION

The founders did not think the solution lay in simply making the weaker governments stronger across the board, and stronger governments weaker across the board. They did not want government to be "strong" as such or "weak" as such; they knew that it had to be strong when fulfilling its rightful functions, but that its strength had to be limited when it tried to go beyond those rightful functions.[50] Their approach was to design a series of mechanisms that would have a general tendency to strengthen government when it was acting rightly, but weaken it when it was acting wrongly.[51]

---

[49]See James Wilson, *American Government: Brief Version*, 5th ed. (Boston: Houghton Mifflin, 2000), pp. 11-13.

[50]See esp. *Federalist Papers* no. 70.

[51]I think one of the main reasons we now tend to speak only of making government simply "stronger" or simply "weaker" is our tendency to frame the relationship between the individual and the state in terms of a direct trade-off between liberty and security. The founders generally do not frame the problem this way, and the *Federalist Papers* explicitly reject this conception of the problem. The authors acknowledge that to create a government, people must give up some of the rights they had in the state of nature (see *Federalist Papers* no. 2). However, once government has been created, the greatest danger to liberty is not security but insecurity; as Hamilton shrewdly observes, it is only after government has failed to provide security that people begin to speak of

To understand their solution to the problem of power, we must understand what they thought was the underlying cause of that problem: the selfishness of human nature. The founders were animated by a keen appreciation of sin and the imperfections of worldly politics. Describing the mechanisms to be used to restrain the abuse of power, James Madison famously writes:

> It may be a reflection on human nature that such devices should be necessary to control the abuses of government. But what is government itself but the greatest of all reflections on human nature? If men were angels, no government would be necessary. If angels were to govern men, neither external nor internal controls on government would be necessary.[52]

Madison frames the political aspect of human selfishness in terms of "factions," by which he means any group of people seeking to put its own good ahead of the public good. Writing of "the violence of faction," he says that "the friend of popular governments never finds himself so much alarmed for their character and fate as when he contemplates their propensity to this dangerous vice." In a centralized monarchy, the king can suppress factions—unless of course he himself acts as a faction, which is the main problem with centralized monarchies. The main problem with republics, by contrast, is that they lack any means to suppress factions at all. Historically, the most important reason for the failure of republics had been their susceptibility to takeover by factions. And the new American government would have even less hope of suppressing factions than the older republics, since it was so robustly devoted to individual liberty. "Liberty is to faction what air is to fire," Madison writes, observing that every form of freedom is an invitation to faction. Thus freedom of religion creates a diversity of religious groups, which will often seek to dominate each other; economic freedom creates a diversity of economic interests, which will seek to enrich themselves at the expense of others by pursuing government favor.[53]

---

the need to circumscribe their liberties (see *Federalist Papers* no. 8). Liberty and security are interdependent and mutually reinforcing; a well-designed government provides both, and a poorly designed government provides neither.

[52] *Federalist Papers* no. 51.

[53] *Federalist Papers* no. 10.

The solution to the problem is not to try to remove the selfishness of human nature. The corruption of sin runs too deep for that. The solution is to contain the consequences of selfishness. Fortunately, every society troubled by the problem of factions also contains a very strong force capable of restraining those factions: the factions themselves. Each faction acts as an opposing force to its rivals. By cultivating a large number of factions, the founders ensured that no one faction would have enough strength to impose its will on the country very often. Where there are only a few factions, one faction may defeat the others and run amok, perhaps even taking over the system permanently. But where there are hundreds of factions, no one of them will ever score too great a victory. In fact, they will never achieve any victories at all except by forming coalitions that draw many factions together—and that means compromise. Compromise means no faction gets all of what it wants, so no faction gets too much of its own selfish desires. And the inherent selfishness of the factions guarantees that coalitions among them will neither be very strong nor live very long.

This does not mean that the founders saw factions as good. They did not endorse selfishness any more than Augustine endorsed sinfulness when he insisted that the world would remain sinful no matter how hard Christians worked to reform it. The authors of the *Federalist Papers* especially are clearly disgusted with factions, and their revulsion is shared to a greater or lesser degree by all the founders. It means instead that they thought the selfishness of factions, though bad in itself, was socially useful. Like Augustine, the founders thought that if evil could not be eradicated, its consequences could nonetheless be turned to good.

To ensure that each faction would keep the others under control, government must contain what Hamilton, in the passage quoted above, referred to as "balances and checks." When power is divided into many hands, each person in the system having some ability to block or constrain the actions of others, the natural selfishness of each person will put them all into competition. "Ambition must be made to counteract ambition," Madison writes.[54] Each of these power centers in the government acts as a sort of self-contained faction.

---

[54]*Federalist Papers* no. 51.

There was a great deal of precedent in the history of philosophy for
the idea of dividing government power in order to prevent any one person from becoming too powerful. Aristotle mentions it in his book about
politics, and philosophers following him had repeated the idea in the centuries since.[55] Calvin, though he was not otherwise inclined to agree with
Aristotle very much, picked up the idea as well.[56] Indeed, the presbyterian
system of church government practiced among most Calvinists, with its
elected representatives and federal structure, was an important influence
on the American founders.[57] But it was not until the eighteenth century
that political philosophers developed this idea to the point where it could
serve as the basis of a political system.

The first of the two major mechanisms that produce balances and checks
in the U.S. Constitution is the *separation of powers*, dividing political authority among legislative, executive and judicial branches. These branches each
have a self-interested incentive to watch over the conduct of the others. Madison calls the separation of powers an "essential precaution in favor of liberty.
. . . No political truth is certainly of greater intrinsic value, or is stamped with
the authority of more enlightened patrons of liberty." He even goes so far as
to say that the separation of powers is necessary to free government: "The
accumulation of all powers, legislative, executive, and judiciary, in the same
hands . . . may justly be pronounced the very definition of tyranny."[58]

Some of the Constitution's "more respectable adversaries," as Madison called them, objected that it did not have an adequate separation
of powers because it gave each of the three branches a certain degree
of control over the actions of the others.[59] Madison argues that giving
each branch partial control of the others is actually necessary to have
a true separation of powers, because it is the only effective way to give
each branch some power to keep the other branches in check. "It will
not be denied that power is of an encroaching nature and that it ought

[55]See Aristotle *Politics* books 4-5, esp. 4.11-12. For online resources see <www.ivpress.com>.
[56]"Owing, therefore, to the vices or defects of men, it is safer and more tolerable when several bear
rule, that they may thus mutually assist, instruct, and admonish each other, and should any one
be disposed to go too far, the others are censors and masters to curb his excess" (Calvin *Institutes*
4.20.8; see also 4.20.31).
[57]See Diarmaid MacCulloch, *The Reformation* (New York: Penguin, 2003), p. 176.
[58]*Federalist Papers* no. 47.
[59]*Federalist Papers* no. 47.

to be effectually restrained from passing the limits assigned to it."[60] This problem can be addressed "by so contriving the interior structure of the government as that its several constituent parts may, by their mutual relations, be the means of keeping each other in their proper places."[61] The insight that separation of powers requires each branch to be able to interfere in the business of the others was one of the founders' most important political innovations.

The second major mechanism producing balances and checks is *federalism,* the division of government into local, state and national branches. Today, we mostly think of federalism as an alternative to power concentrated in the national government; at the time, however, it was an alternative to power concentrated in local government. The national government created by the Articles of Confederation, the precursor to the Constitution, had little authority and even less practical power.

Madison observed that there are far fewer factions in any given locality than there are in the nation as a whole. This makes local government much more susceptible to subversion by a strong faction than national government, since there are fewer factions competing for power. "Extend the sphere and you take in a greater variety of parties and interests; you make it less probable that a majority of the whole will have a common motive to invade the rights of other citizens; or if such a common motive exists, it will be more difficult for all who feel it to discover their own strength and act in unison with each other."[62] No one faction is strong enough to dominate the whole nation, but one faction may be able to dominate a town or sometimes even a state.

The founders adopted many other mechanisms designed to improve the functioning of republican government. *Representative democracy*—rule not by the people directly, nor by an aristocracy, but by representatives elected by the people—blended accountability to the people with the maintenance of a certain distance from dangerous popular passions. "The people are the only legitimate fountain of power," Madison writes. But direct democracy, or even the overly frequent election of representatives, introduces "the dan-

---

[60] *Federalist Papers* no. 48.
[61] *Federalist Papers* no. 51.
[62] *Federalist Papers* no. 10.

ger of disturbing the public tranquility by interesting too strongly the public passions."[63] The people tend to be irrational in the short term but rational over the long term.[64] If elections were too frequent, "the passions . . . not the reason, of the public would sit in judgment."[65] Madison also worries that if elections were too frequent, the people would tend to favor more power for the legislature and not enough for the executive.

Another important innovation was *judicial independence.* Subversion of the judiciary has been one of the most common sources of oppression in human history. Hamilton writes that appointing judges for life is "one of the most valuable of the modern improvements in the practice of government" and is "the citadel of public justice and the public security." The founders disagreed over the precise extent of judicial authority, especially in the question of what is now called *judicial review,* the court's authority to rule that a law is unconstitutional. Hamilton favors judicial review, but he argues that wherever one comes down on the question, judicial independence can be no threat to liberty if the legislative and executive branches are watchful. "The judicial department is beyond comparison the weakest of the three departments of power. . . . It can never attack with success either of the other two." It "has no influence over either the sword or the purse," which are controlled by the executive and legislative branches respectively.[66] The only way judges could take too much power would be if the other branches stood by and allowed them to do so. Here as elsewhere, the founders' "science of politics" counts on the ambition of each branch to check the others.

THE PROBLEM OF PUBLIC VIRTUE (AGAIN)

Madison's approach to the problem of power turned conventional wisdom on its head. The dominant theory had been that republics could only function if there was a very high degree of homogeneity and civic virtue in the population. In the absence of a strong king who could suppress selfish factions, the only thing to do was to prevent such factions from forming

---

[63] *Federalist Papers* no. 49.
[64] See *Federalist Papers* no. 50.
[65] *Federalist Papers* no. 49.
[66] *Federalist Papers* no. 78.

in the first place. This could be done by stamping out all forms of social difference, such as religious dissent or economic stratification, and culti-vating extreme discipline and selflessness in the citizenry. Thus, republics could realistically be expected to work only in small rural communities.

Madison insisted that if republics were large and diverse instead of small and homogeneous, they required no more public virtue than any other form of government. We do not have to shoot for some pie-in-the-sky standard of perfect moral purity; men need not become angels, nor do we need to find angels to govern them. Sinful humanity could still live in freedom, if only it adopted the right constitution.

This is not to say that Madison or any of the other founders thought that virtue was not necessary to politics. Running throughout the *Federal-ist Papers,* and the writings of the founders generally, is the argument (or at least the assumption) that a certain baseline of public virtue is necessary to liberty. This is both because the people must ultimately serve as the fi-nal authority over government and because the more immoral people are, the more government must exercise control over them.[67] Their point was not that virtue did not matter, but that republican government did not re-quire extraordinary levels of virtue, and hence did not have to be confined to small, homogenous societies.

The founders disagreed profoundly over the right way to maintain this baseline of virtue. Some placed high hopes on the inculcation of virtue through education, while others were more skeptical of such hopes. Some wanted to keep power concentrated in local governments as much as pos-sible, on the theory that local communities were far more homogeneous than the nation as a whole and could thus maintain a higher degree of virtue; this was an attempt to hedge Madison's bet, maintaining to some extent the old, pre-Madisonian view that republics needed to be small and homogeneous. Others thought that localism had been tried under the Articles of Confederation and found wanting; thus they claimed that a strong national government and, perhaps just as important, a strong sense of national identity among the American people were needed to put an

---

[67]Examples of this thinking among the American founders are far too numerous for any one selec-tion to adequately represent them. There are many books that provide a concise review of the evidence on this point; see, e.g., Novak, *On Two Wings,* esp. pp. 52-73.

end to the problems of localism that had led the nation to scrap the Articles in the first place.

Most of the founders also thought that religion was an indispensable support for public virtue. But here again there was profound disagreement over what, if anything, government could legitimately do to encourage religion. On this subject the founders ran the gamut from supporting established churches and a certain degree of religious compulsion (at least at the state level) to opposing any government involvement with religion as a dangerous entanglement of spiritual and worldly affairs, with numerous positions between these extremes.

These disagreements over the problem of public virtue did not prove to be temporary. In a liberal democracy, government is not supposed to play favorites among religions, and its power to do so is limited by the balances and checks embedded in the system. Thus the problem of maintaining public virtue is inherent in the system, as we have already seen in chapter six. Eventually, starting in the early twentieth century, the growing frustration over this long-unsolved problem led to a new crisis in Christian thought; we are still living through that crisis, and its end result is still uncertain. That crisis is the subject of our final chapter.

8

THE FIERY TRIAL

CHRISTIAN RESPONSES TO TOTALITARIANISM

Beloved, do not be surprised
at the fiery trial when it comes upon you to test you,
as though something strange were happening to you.

PETER, FIRST EPISTLE OF PETER

IN THE SOVIET UNION, the existence of dictatorship and poverty in the "worker's paradise" was officially explained as a necessary transition phase between the bad old days of capitalism and the perfect communist utopia that was right around the corner and would arrive any day now. A popular joke had a boy asking his father what things would be like after the transition from capitalism to communism was complete.

"After the revolution," says the father, "everyone will have strawberries and cream."

"But I don't like strawberries and cream," objects the boy.

"After the revolution," responds the father, "you will like strawberries and cream."

The joke reflected the alarming new reality of totalitarianism. Humanity's advancing technological abilities had produced countless benefits, but
they had also armed evil regimes with powerful weapons and tools of
surveillance and propaganda such as no rulers had ever possessed before.
The leaders of these regimes were confident that with these new tools
they would be able to keep hold of absolute power forever—in particular,
by using their total control of the environment to program people to think
what the regime wanted them to think. If you did not like strawberries
and cream, you could be made to like strawberries and cream. Many opponents of totalitarianism feared that the dictators might be right and
that a victory for totalitarianism would prove to be irreversible. The great
international conflicts of the last century were more than ordinary wars;
the whole future of the human race was felt to be at stake.

As if to make the ordeal of the twentieth century as excruciating as
possible, just at the moment when these unprecedented external threats
were arising, liberal democracy's long-running internal difficulties also
escalated into a full-blown crisis. A series of powerful critiques of liberal democracy had undermined many people's confidence in it. And even
among those who believed in liberal democracy, its historical roots in natural-law doctrine were coming under fire from new religious and philosophical movements. Some of these were Christian movements arguing
that natural-law doctrine was wrong because it compromised Christianity; others were non-Christian movements arguing that natural-law doctrine was wrong because it was Christian. While some of these theories
had appeared in the eighteenth and nineteenth centuries, it was in the
already tumultuous early twentieth century that they produced a philosophical crisis.

This crisis struck at the heart of liberal democracy's ability to face its
external enemies, because the struggle with totalitarianism was primarily
a struggle of ideas. It is a common observation that the twentieth century
was a period of completely unprecedented phenomena: world wars, totalitarianism, weapons capable of destroying all humanity. But one of the
most important new phenomena is often overlooked: the overwhelming
power of political ideas in shaping political events. The two great struggles that dominated the twentieth century were more purely ideological

in nature than any had been before. Three great political philosophies—fascism, communism and liberal democracy—were contesting for nothing less than the fate of the world. And right at that moment, liberal democracy was suddenly no longer sure what it believed in.

As the consensus in favor of natural law has broken down, Christian political thought in the last century has been characterized by such discord that there is no way to adequately cover it all. This chapter will review three Christian responses to the political crisis of the twentieth century, representing three major approaches to the problem. These three positions do not even begin to cover the full spectrum of Christian responses to the crisis, but they at least provide an outline that shows the real breadth of those responses.

All three of the figures covered here are responding to the threat of totalitarianism, explaining how and why Christians should fight it. Additionally, in their different analyses of the crisis, these thinkers also demonstrate three distinct Christian positions regarding the natural-law doctrine that had historically produced liberal democracy. The first, Karl Barth, rejects natural-law doctrine wholesale on grounds that it invites compromise with worldly evils: he argues that Christians should scrap it in favor of a thoroughly Bible-centered political theory that would put Christian love into political action against totalitarian hatred. The second, Reinhold Niebuhr, rejects much of the historic natural-law tradition as being tainted by the prejudices and self-interests of those who produced it, yet he would still prefer to keep many of its core philosophical elements, holding that an approach to politics grounded only in the Bible is not feasible in a fallen world. The third, C. S. Lewis, defends the historic natural-law tradition: he argues that for moral law to be meaningful at all, it must have a basis in the divine image God has planted in human nature.

THE WAR FOR HUMAN NATURE

The titanic confrontations of the twentieth century were all driven by the prospect—a thrilling hope for some, an unimaginable horror for others—that the advance of technology would put humanity in a position to change human nature. Or to put it more accurately, by the prospect that technology would put some people in a position to change the human

Jean-Jacques Rousseau (1712-1778)

Jean-Jacques Rousseau was a Swiss expatriate whose writings in the mid-eighteenth century formed the basis of the Romantic movement. Romanticism was a religious movement at heart; indeed, it was essentially a new religion. The Romantic experience of God is often described as a form of deism. This is true as far as it goes, since the Romantics believed, like the earlier Enlightenment deists, that God made the universe but does not interfere miraculously in its workings. But the deism of Rousseau and his followers was not a mere abstract position of technical philosophy. Romanticism was a full-bodied religious movement. People dedicated their whole lives to living out Rousseau's contemplations of the divine presence; nobody ever devoted a whole life to Thomas Hobbes's recitation of the "first mover" proof.

Romanticism was a religion of moral feelings. Rather than knowing God's will through the study of revelation and natural law, Rousseau and his followers believed that we knew it through the emotions of love, pity and compassion for others. God had placed these emotions in us to show us the way to right behavior and to reveal to us, within our own psychology, as much of the divine mind as we are able to know.

This moral psychology is a crucial element of Rousseau's political philosophy. He holds that people are neither naturally good nor naturally bad; they become good or bad over time, based on how they respond to their moral feelings on the one hand and their lower appetites on the other. Virtue does not come easily, he argued, but is only acquired by extraordinary effort—and in particular with the proper training. As part of that training, the nature of the political community is essential to the learning of virtue. A virtuous political community will produce virtuous people. A political community based on vice will produce vice-ridden people.[a]

Here we come to the central political difficulty. Rousseau argues that government was originally invented to protect and nurture greed. Primitive human beings would have had no need for an elaborate scheme of property rights, and hence no need for government; government would have arisen when people decided that they wanted to accumulate ever-greater amounts of property in order to have the satisfaction of owning more than their neighbors. "The first man who, after enclosing a piece of ground, took it into his head to say, 'This is mine,' and found people simple enough to believe him, was the real founder of civil society."[b] Rousseau writes that most societies continue to function on this basis.

However, he reserved his special scorn for the new politics that was emerging from the Enlightenment, with its lowered expectations for human virtue and its management of people's selfishness for socially useful purposes. Vice is already nearly impossible to counteract, he argued; if society treats vice as inevitable and socially useful rather than as a threat to be resisted, all hope of stopping its expansion is lost.

In a liberal democracy, everyone learns how to be selfish and greedy, so that the political system will have plenty of selfishness to harness for social benefit. Or if things are not quite that bad, at the very least the liberal-democratic system is incapable of teaching virtue; and since rigorous training is necessary to virtue, individuals in such a society will not possess it.[c]

[a]Rousseau writes: "He who dares to undertake the establishment of a people should feel that he is, so to speak, in a position to change human nature"; in Jean-Jacques Rousseau *On the Social Contract* book 2, chap. 7. I rely on Henry Tozer's translation in *The Social Contract and Discourse on the Origin of Inequality* (New York: Wash-

ington Square Press, 1967). For online resources see <www.ivpress.com>.

[b]Rousseau *Discourse on the Origin and Foundation of Inequality Among Men* part 2. I rely on Lester Crocker's translation in *The Social Contract and Discourse*. For online resources see <www.ivpress.com>.

[c]Of the citizen in a liberal democracy, he writes: "Always in contradiction with himself, always floating between his inclinations and his duties, he will never be either man or citizen. He will be good neither for himself nor for others. He will be one of these men of our days: a Frenchman, an Englishman, a bourgeois. He will be nothing"; in Jean-Jacques Rousseau *Émile, or, On Education* book 1. I rely on Allan Bloom's translation (New York: Basic Books, 1979). For online resources see <www.ivpress.com>.

nature of other people. The ability to change human nature would mean the ability to reshape human politics on a completely new level.

Technological changes had always reshaped the use of power, so the idea that changing technology would change politics was nothing new.[1] What was new in the twentieth century was the prospect that technology could reshape not just the use of power, but also human nature itself. Any political or social system whatsoever could potentially be brought into existence and maintained forever simply by creating people whose nature was designed to fit that system. Did the regime want to remake society from top to bottom so that all of life was driven by furious racial hatred?

---

[1]In the nineteenth century, Karl Marx and his followers had founded communism on the idea that economic progress, driven in large part by technological improvement, was the underlying cause of political change. The century before that, Adam Smith wrote extensively on the political impact of economic changes arising from technological improvement. Before that, it was the invention of the printing press, which played a major role in facilitating the Reformation and its accompanying political crisis. Before that it was gunpowder, which changed the balance of military power—a subject that Machiavelli covers in *The Prince*. Before gunpowder it was longbows. The Roman Empire was made possible largely by technological innovations ranging from better weapons to roads and aqueducts. Egypt was built on irrigation technology. For all we know, whatever primordial geniuses invented spears, hammers, fireplaces and wheels—or even more likely, writing—may have caused political cataclysms we can only dream of.

Or abolish private property so that all use of resources, and hence every aspect of human life, would be under the control of a central bureaucracy? No problem. Propaganda techniques, applied from birth onward, would ensure that everyone wanted nothing more than to live under the political and social system their controllers had chosen for them. If a few resisted the process, modern surveillance and weapons technologies would ensure that they were found and made to vanish. And it would not be long, many people felt sure, before technology would allow human nature to be re-shaped even more fundamentally—on the biological level.

Technology thus promised, or threatened, to provide a form of abso-lute power that could never be resisted. Once the initial opposition to the new regime was defeated, there could be no hope that any new resistance would ever arise. What hope was there for any kind of political opposition to succeed under a tyranny that exercised total control over its people? Once this night had fallen, there could be no dawn. Or, for those who saw things from a different perspective, once this day had dawned, there could be no nightfall.

In the twentieth century, totalitarianism only had one major enemy: liberal democracy. All the hopes of humanity lay in the hands of this one champion. But just as the danger of totalitarianism was arising, the societ-ies in which liberal democracy had flourished underwent a radical break-down of social consensus about political philosophy—an internal crisis to match the external crisis of the totalitarian threat.

The timing of the two crises is not entirely coincidental. The break-down of consensus over political philosophy in liberal-democratic societ-ies was partly a result of the rise of totalitarianism. In their early responses to totalitarianism in the 1920s and 1930s, the world's liberal democracies did not exactly cover themselves with glory. If some people lost confidence in liberal democracy, or in the traditional philosophies that stood behind it, that was partly because the people whose job it was to preserve liberal democracy often gave them good reasons for doing so.

It was, notoriously, under the auspices of a liberal-democratic consti-tutional order that the Nazis were able to seize power in Germany. This point can be pushed too far: the Nazis never won an election, and they seized power by breaking the rules of the democratic system, not by following them. Nevertheless, the weaknesses of German democracy under the Weimar constitution were an important contributing factor that gave the Nazis their golden opportunity; the phrase "Weimar Republic" has rightly become a byword for the danger of naive overconfidence in the power of liberal democracy to tame all evils and alleviate all dangers.

Germany was only the worst case of a more general problem. There was a disturbing level of sympathy for totalitarian movements among significant portions of the population in many liberal-democratic societies. Marxists and fascists won important political victories in a number of European countries. Even where Marxism and fascism never became important factors in the mainstream political system, there were still enough people who seemed to be sympathetic to them—or who were at least a little too willing to ignore or excuse their crimes—to raise questions about how solidly liberal-democratic societies really were committed to liberal democracy.[2]

Perhaps even more important was the weakness of the initial response to totalitarianism among those who really did seek to oppose it. The 1920s and 1930s were characterized by an astonishing belief in the power of reason and dialogue to defuse conflicts and settle disputes. In 1928 the world's major powers signed the Kellogg-Briand Pact, in which they agreed that henceforth they would have no more wars, and all international disputes would be resolved peacefully.[3] A total of sixty-two nations eventually signed the treaty. Even as late as 1938, Europe's liberal democracies agreed to let Nazi Germany annex a substantial portion of Czechoslovakia, including most of that nation's border defenses. Democratic leaders thought that bad as he might be, Hitler could be reasoned with, and Germany would be pacified if its neighbors would only address its grievances.

---

[2]Just as a starting point, consider that millions of Western European voters cast their ballots for the Communist Party in parliamentary elections throughout the Cold War.

[3]Article 1 of the treaty states, in its entirety: "The High Contracting Parties solemnly declare in the names of their respective peoples that they condemn recourse to war for the solution of international controversies, and renounce it, as an instrument of national policy in their relations with one another." The signatories did not mean that they were giving up their right of self-defense (as the U.S. Senate noted when it approved the treaty). However, the pact did reflect a general reluctance on the part of the world's great powers to confront aggressors forcefully, as the Munich agreement (1938) shows all too clearly.

The weak response of the liberal democracies to totalitarianism was abetted by the influence of *pietism* among many Christians. Pietism is the belief that society, and especially government, are always under the control of evil. On this view, Christians should not try to reform society and government but should withdraw from them and focus on cultivating their own piety apart from wider social influence. Thus, just at the moment when a robust Christian counterattack against the evils of the world was needed, much of its strength had been withdrawn.

As the early period of confrontation with totalitarianism revealed these weaknesses in liberal-democratic societies, confidence in their governing philosophy was shaken. Critics of liberal democracy, and of the natural-law ideas that had defined what liberal democracy meant, were further emboldened. By the 1940s, the major question of the day for political thinkers was whether to maintain liberal democracy, and if so, whether to maintain it on the basis of its traditional grounding in natural law, or on some other basis.

ILLIBERAL CRITIQUES OF LIBERAL DEMOCRACY

From another perspective, however, the breakdown of philosophical consensus around liberal democracy had been a long time in coming. While criticisms of traditional liberal-democratic ideals were strengthened by the events of the early twentieth century, those criticisms have a much longer history. They must be understood not as products of twentieth-century events, but as long-growing movements that crested in the twentieth century.

The first great attack on liberal democracy had been Romanticism. The founder of Romanticism, Jean-Jacques Rousseau, wrote that people were neither naturally good nor naturally bad, but became good or bad depending on the environment in which they were raised (see sidebar). Rigorous training in childhood and encouragements to self-discipline throughout life were necessary to achieve the higher state of emotional purity on which the Romantics thought moral goodness depended. Liberal democracy was thus the chief danger to human virtue, because liberal-democratic society was based on a low expectation of human virtue. A society that sees human selfishness as an inevitable fact that society should seek to manage rather than eliminate simply could not provide the social environment that the Romantics insisted was necessary to moral virtue; liberal democracy would inevitably produce corrupt citizens and was thus inevitably a corrupt system.

Romanticism provided the fundamental basis for many subsequent critiques of liberal democracy. Two of its major elements—its religion of feelings and its reaction against social greed—served, separately, as the starting points of the two most important movements attacking liberal democracy even after Romanticism itself passed out of favor.

Marxism, the next great challenge to emerge, differed from Romanticism in many ways. It was rationalistic and atheistic, and it aimed at a different final goal: violent revolution culminating in a technologically advanced industrial communitarian utopia, as opposed to Rousseau's desire for retreat into tiny agrarian city-state republics. But Marxism's attack on liberal democracy was built on an account of political origins remarkably similar to Rousseau's: primitive humanity had no system of property rights; government was founded for the purpose of helping people satisfy acquisitive desires and continues to serve this purpose; liberal democracy represents the logical outworking of this system. For those of a more rationalistic bent who could not stomach the moral, emotional and religious elements of Romanticism, Marxism provided an alternative form of Rousseau's attack on the role of social greed in liberal democracy.

Meanwhile, Rousseau's subjectivism was developing in a new direction. In Romanticism's religion of feelings, the focus gradually moved more and more toward the feelings, and the religion became less and less noticeable. The contemplation of the divine presence as experienced through one's feelings eventually gave way to the contemplation of one's feelings simply for their own sake. Among those influenced by this element of Romanticism, subjective experience became disconnected from anything outside itself that could give it objective meaning or a larger significance: one's experience was its own meaning and its own significance.

Thus emerged the movement that is sometimes called *relativism*, although that label is problematic. Another term, *subjectivism*, is a more precise description of what was really at stake in this movement. The key element is the belief that there is no objective truth: there is only my truth (as

Edmund Burke (ca. 1729-1797)

Edmund Burke was an Irishman who served a long career in the British Parliament. He is most famous for his 1790 book *Reflections on the Revolution in France*, written in his twilight years during the early days of the French Revolution (1789-1799). He attacked the radicalism of the revolutionaries and predicted that it would end up creating an extreme democratic tyranny—which it did, just a few years later. The *Reflections* is now looked on as the founding document of conservatism as a coherent ideology.

Burke's critique highlighted the problematic relationship between reason and tradition. The revolutionaries insisted that each generation has the right to remake social institutions according to its own rational analysis: the dead should not rule the living. Burke thought that reason could only reach fulfillment when informed by tradition, since tradition preserves the accumulated reasoning of many generations. A tradition, he wrote, is much more rational than the most intelligent individual.

Burke thought the "prejudices" that people adopt unthinkingly from their traditions are, as a whole, healthy and promote good behavior. Society, he argued, is not like a machine that can be improved by taking it apart and putting it back together. It is like a plant, which grows according to its nature and which simply dies if you try to take it apart. Removing old prejudices does not result in rationality but in new, untested, far more dangerous prejudices.

He also opposed the atheism and radical egalitarianism of the French Revolution, arguing that religion is the basis of civilization and that social classes are necessary so that some people will have the leisure and education to become good leaders.

Burke opposed natural-law doctrine because of what he saw as its overreliance on abstract principles. Context was too important for abstract principles to serve as a reliable guide. Liberty, for example, is good only in the right circumstances; liberty for criminals is bad, not good. Tradition, which is sensitive to context, should be our final guide rather than any philosophy as such.

He nonetheless supported liberal democracy, arguing that it had grown out of English tradition and should be highly prized and carefully preserved as the product of England's long centuries of wisdom. Though he is famous as a champion of traditionalism and is thus in one sense conservative, Burke was actually a member of the Whig party and a leading champion of various reform movements, including prison reform and better treatment of colonial subjects. English tradition demanded high moral standards such as justice and humanitarianism, and there was always room for reforms to bring the actual practices of law and government more into conformity with the principles of English tradition. Burke was simultaneously a conservative traditionalist and a forward-thinking liberal reformer.

I subjectively experience it) and your truth (as you subjectively experience it). According to this view, it is a mistake to think that my understanding of truth refers to some "real truth" outside itself; for me, my understanding is the real truth, and yours is for you.

After gradually developing for more than a century, this movement suddenly burst into its full strength in the thought of Friedrich Nietzsche, who had an explosive impact on philosophy and culture at the end of the nineteenth century. In Nietzsche the breach between the emotional element of Romanticism and its religious element becomes total; for Nietzsche, all morality and all religion that aims at God is precisely the enemy of liberated emotional and impulsive experience, which is the only thing that can make the meaninglessness of human life bearable. He argues that morality is at bottom a colossal swindle: the weak made it up in order to trick the strong into treating them as equals. The history of the rise of Christianity is really the history of the triumph of this swindle. Its end result is the repulsive creature called "the last man": proud of his weakness and contemptuous toward any idea of glorious and masterful action, and yet, paradoxically, also egotistical and self-satisfied. Nietzsche anticipated that the dead religion of morality and Christianity would soon give way to a new lifestyle that would reject morality and embrace the ecstasy of unrestrained obedience to the impulses of our nature.

Significantly, all three of these major movements are either explicitly religious (Romanticism) or quasi-religious (Marxism and Nietzscheism). This is not an accident. The most important problem of liberal democracy, as has already been suggested (see chaps. 6-7) is public virtue. In the absence of a formally shared community religion, liberal democracy has struggled to provide its citizens with a positive moral vision to stand behind its rules of behavior. Its original founders hoped that the moral principles that were shared among all civilized religions would provide a sufficient common ground on which to build the political community. This hope cannot be said to have decisively failed; liberal democracy did win the struggles of the twentieth century, after all, and it is not dead yet. Those who are inclined to support liberal democracy can reasonably hope that it will do a better job of providing a positive moral vision in the next century than it did in the previous

John Stuart Mill (1806-1873)

John Stuart Mill's 1859 book, *On Liberty*, laid out a case for liberal democracy based on the need for happiness and social progress, a case whose principles remain widely influential. Mill's thought grows out of the nineteenth-century movement known as utilitarianism, which held that actions are right if they maximize human happiness. The early form of utilitarianism never found a lasting audience; people were not willing to accept that any action, possibly even murder and theft, would be morally good if it made people happy. Mill himself was the son of a prominent utilitarian and was subjected to a brutally strict educational regimen designed to increase his future happiness even at the expense of an abjectly miserable childhood.

Mill's brand of utilitarianism proved to be much more appealing. Mill argued that we secure the greatest happiness for the most people by having universal rules against actions like murder and theft, so there is really no conflict between utilitarianism and ordinary morality. He thought that ordinary morality really was utilitarian morality if its underlying principles were understood.

If we are interested in the happiness of the greatest number, he argued, we should care most about future generations. Thus we should seek above all to promote the long-term improvement of society: "the permanent interests of man as a progressive being."[a] He believed that humanity was gradually making moral progress.

Politics in every era, he argues, is defined by the struggle between liberty and authority. For Mill, liberty is not simply freedom to obey one's own conscience, as natural-law thinkers defined it (see chap. 6, sidebar, "Limits of Toleration"), but rather the freedom to do whatever one wants. Authority is the need to limit people's behavior in order to protect the weak from oppression. It includes not just the law, but all forms of social control. Mill greatly admired Tocqueville's *Democracy in America;* like Tocqueville, he thought shame and ostracism could be even more oppressive than criminal punishment and political tyranny.

Mill proposed that neither government nor public opinion should constrain liberty for any reason except to prevent harm. He defined *harm* very broadly, including not just physical harm but also things like loss of social esteem. His main concern was not to enforce justice, which would imply a narrower definition of harm. He wanted instead to maximize happiness and promote progress, so he defined *harm* broadly in order to secure as much liberty as possible, social as well as legal.

He argued that as wide a variety of opinions as possible should be tolerated, not just in the law but also in social esteem. It is impossible, he wrote, to ever be really sure whether we are right about our opinions. But even if we are right, society benefits from the presence of beliefs that are wrong or disturbing; it prevents us from getting intellectually lazy and thus promotes progress. Both these arguments represent important differences between Mill and the older natural-law argument for toleration.

Mill's theory of liberty is not fundamentally a theory of limited government. His system requires a far-reaching regulation of private behavior. Government power must often be used to suppress the desires of the majority in order to ensure that dissenting views are not exposed to social harm. Not even all opinions can be tolerated: those who wish to express disapproval of others' opinions are not allowed to say or do anything that might harm them by reducing their social esteem.

ªJohn Stuart Mill *On Liberty* chap. 1.

century. But it is undeniable that since the removal of Christianity as the official community religion, many people have shown that they do not think liberal democracy can have any moral basis at all. The rise of these illiberal religious and quasi-religious movements shows that the desire for politics based on a shared community belief system is still a potent force.

In turn, these critiques of liberal democracy were an important factor contributing to sympathy for totalitarianism in liberal-democratic societies. One of these movements, Marxism, was itself a totalitarian movement. Another, subjectivism, is not totalitarian in itself, but by undermining belief in objective morality, it removes the only grounds on which totalitarianism can be criticized and opposed. Nietzsche was not a fascist, but his influence cleared away obstacles that might otherwise have checked the rise of fascism. The original Romanticism was, in itself, decent and respectable by worldly standards and does not deserve to be classified with either of the other two movements considered here. Nonetheless, even in Romanticism there was an element that provided aid and comfort to totalitarianism. Rousseau's extreme stress on the importance of virtue, which could only be cultivated by intense social training, had a tendency to leave the individual completely at the mercy of the collective—a tendency that Rousseau himself acknowledged and embraced.[4] Again, Rousseau would not have approved of the French Revolution, with its bloodthirsty Reign of Terror (1793-1794), but his influence helped knock down obstacles that might otherwise have stood in its path.

So liberal democracy is faced with a sort of vicious circle. Its difficulty in providing a positive moral vision invites the rise of illiberal religious and quasi-religious movements in reaction against it. These movements knock down obstacles to the rise of totalitarianism. The rise of totalitarianism makes liberal democracy look weak. This in turn further strengthens the reactions against it, which helps further remove the obstacles to totalitarianism, and so on.

NEW THEORIES OF LIBERAL DEMOCRACY

Meanwhile, over the same few centuries when these critiques drew many Westerners away from liberal democracy, the very concept of liberal democracy had been changing. It was being gradually separated from the deeper political philosophy that had originally produced it.

Liberal democracy had historically been a byproduct of Christian belief in natural law. It emerged primarily from the confluence of three intellectual movements: (1) the settling of the Reformation political crisis by the policy of religious freedom; (2) the development of a general ideology of natural rights and revolution against tyranny; and (3) the constitutional reforms arising from the new "science of politics," with its robustly Augustinian appreciation of sin's intractability in a fallen world. The predominant philosophy behind all three of these movements was Christian natural-law doctrine. This is not to say that there were no important contributions to liberal democracy from non-Christians, or from Christians who did not believe in natural law. Nevertheless, at first liberal democracy was predominantly the work of Christians who believed that the proper basis of politics was the moral law revealed by God to all humanity as part of human nature.

The key words in that last sentence, however, are "at first." Almost as soon as it emerged, other intellectual movements began to stake claims to

---

[4]As he famously said, when an individual is forced to obey the virtuous "general will" of the community, he is not losing any freedom, but rather gaining it: "This means merely that he will be forced to be free"; in Jean-Jacques Rousseau *On the Social Contract* book 1, chap. 7.

liberal democracy independently of the intellectual movements that originally produced it. Numerous competing philosophies of liberal democracy emerged, and eventually large numbers of people believed in liberal democracy without believing in the natural-law philosophy from which it originally grew. By the early twentieth century, the point was reached where it was no longer clear whether natural-law doctrine would remain the central animating philosophy of liberal democracy.

Perhaps the earliest alternative philosophy of liberal democracy was *traditionalism,* which received its first distinctive formulation in the writings of Edmund Burke (see sidebar). Burke thought natural-law philosophy suffered from an excessive confidence in the ability of human reasoning to express moral principles in abstract terms and then use them to logically deduce the proper course of action. Burke was not an opponent of reason as such, but he thought that reason reached its highest fulfillment in tradition, which preserved the accumulated wisdom of many people over time. Thus he supported liberal democracy on grounds that it had grown organically, so to speak, out of English tradition.

Another liberal democratic rival to natural law, this one on the political left, grew out of the nineteenth-century movement known as *utilitarianism.* This movement held that actions are right if they maximize human happiness. John Stuart Mill's 1859 book, *On Liberty,* laid out a case for liberal democracy based on the need for happiness and social progress. While strict utilitarianism is no longer popular, Mill's argument for liberty helped form the basis of modern "progressive" politics. Mill argued that the rules of liberal democracy secure the greatest happiness for the most people. Moreover, if we are interested in the happiness of the greatest number, we should care most about future generations. We should seek most to promote the long-term improvement of society: "the permanent interests of man as a progressive being."[5] He believed that humanity was gradually progressing toward ever-better societies; that liberal democracy was the latest product of humanity's progress; and that society, including government, should seek to promote ever more progress.

---

[5]John Stuart Mill *On Liberty* chap. 1. For online resources see <www.ivpress.com>.

Naturally, when people change the supporting philosophy behind a political system, they change the system itself. Those who adhere to these new justifications for liberal democracy have a different understanding of what liberal democracy really is. For the traditionalist Burke, liberal democracy is not a reflection of God's moral design in human nature; instead, it is the English way of doing things. It still does have a powerful moral and religious element for Burke, but he explains that element not in terms of natural law but in terms of the English religious tradition. For Mill, progressive and liberal democracy is the latest phase in the historical outworking of social progress. Where traditional natural-law philosophy locates the system's moral grounding in the timeless eternity of God's attributes, and Burke locates it in a society's shared past, Mill locates it in the future: we should uphold liberal democracy because of our duty to promote social progress for the sake of our posterity.

These differences have policy consequences. Under the idea of natural law, individual rights are held to be grounded in nature; the individual who wishes to claim a right must show that it arises from the moral law as revealed in human nature. By contrast, in a traditionalist liberal democracy, individual rights are defined by the boundaries of social tradition; in a progressive liberal democracy, they are defined by the needs of progress. For example, as compared to natural-law philosophy, Mill's theory of liberty would greatly expand the boundaries of freedom of speech for some people while radically constricting such freedom for others. To express disagreement with someone else's opinion in ways that expose others to shame or ostracism does harm. In such cases, government must restrict the self-expression of the majority in order to ensure that dissenting views are not exposed to harm from social disapproval. People with strange and disturbing opinions are not only entitled to hold their opinions; they are also entitled not to be publicly shamed for them. And those who wish to express their disapproval through shaming others must be restrained from doing so.

The rise of alternative accounts of liberal democracy is therefore destabilizing. The very meaning of the term "liberal democracy" has become much more ambiguous and contested. The resulting instability provided yet another challenge to liberal democracy's self-confidence in its confrontation with totalitarianism.

This problem, like the problem of illiberal movements such as Romanticism, stems from the absence of a shared community religion in liberal democracy. Without a shared worldview, it has become difficult for liberal democracy to maintain a consensus on the philosophy that justifies liberal democracy. Again, since liberal democracy originally sought to build on the moral rules that were shared in common across multiple worldviews, it has struggled to provide a positive moral vision. That has left the door open for new philosophies of liberal democracy to challenge the original natural-law justification of the system.

THE INNER CIRCLE

Karl Barth, though Swiss by birth, was a theology professor in Germany when the Nazis came to power. Barth was alarmed at the number of Christians and Christian leaders in Germany who sympathized with the Nazis and expressed support for their racial ideology; even before Hitler took power, these leaders were organized, calling themselves the "German Christians." When the Nazis took power, Barth sought to rescue the church from subordination to the regime. In 1934 he organized the signing of the Barmen Declaration, in which he and like-minded Christians declared their refusal to put the church in the service of the state, or to preach any doctrine other than what was revealed in the Bible. When he refused to swear an oath of allegiance to Hitler, Barth was expelled from his professorship in 1935 and returned to his native Switzerland.

In his political writings, Barth is responding primarily to the problems of sympathy for Nazi ideology on the one hand, and the weak resistance to Nazi ideology due to pietism (which had been particularly strong in Germany) on the other. Barth's goal is to justify Christian involvement in politics against the pietists, while not allowing politics to corrupt the mission of the church along with the so-called German Christians.

The starting point of Barth's political thought is his rejection of the traditional idea of general revelation. He argues that humanity can know God only through the Bible. The revelation of God through nature described in Romans 1 and other biblical passages, Barth argues, must be understood as a merely potential revelation—one that does not reach completion in human consciousness. God displays himself in nature, so he is revealed, objectively speaking. But humanity cannot see God; it does not receive the revelation.[6]

Along the same lines, Barth reverses the traditional Protestant ordering of the law and the gospel. Traditionally, Protestants held that knowledge of the law must come first, preparing the way for the gospel by showing people what God wants from them and convicting them of their sinful refusal to obey. The gospel of salvation comes only after a person knows him- or herself to be a sinner who needs saving. For Barth, the situation is reversed: it is only through knowledge of the gospel that we come to know the law. As he wrote in a 1935 address published under the title "Gospel and Law," a provocative reversal of the traditional phrase "law and gospel": "From what God does for us, we infer what he wants with us and from us."[7] Barth defines sin not as resistance to God's law, but as resistance to God's grace.[8] He hastens to add that resistance to grace does imply resistance to the law; nevertheless, identifying sin as being fundamentally resistance to grace rather than to law is a reversal of the traditional understanding.

This reversal shapes Barth's account of what moral law means apart from the saving work of Christ. Traditional natural-law doctrine had always taught that humanity's natural knowledge of the moral law is distorted by sin. Barth, however, goes much further. When sinful humanity tries to understand the law apart from the gospel, Barth argues, it is exercising its resistance to grace; in other words, it is sinning. Apart from Christian faith, even the attempt to understand right from wrong is merely an exercise in moral blindness. Apart from faith, the law becomes only a tool of each person's own self-glorification; people latch on to parts of the law and use it to self-righteously puff themselves up, discarding the rest.[9] "The service of the law, robbed of promise [i.e., the gospel] and

---

[6]For a discussion of Barth's rejection of natural revelation as it relates to the debate over natural law, see Stephen Grabill, *Rediscovering the Natural Law in Reformed Theological Ethics* (Grand Rapids: Eerdmans, 2006), pp. 21-53.

[7]Karl Barth, "Gospel and Law," sec. 2; in Karl Barth, *Community, State, and Church: Three Essays*, introduced by David Haddorff (Eugene, Ore.: Wipf & Stock, 2004).

[8]See, e.g., Barth, "Gospel and Law," sec. 3.

[9]"Now man certainly does pounce, one on this, another on that letter and shred of the law, with the entire passion of his caprice, victorious and left to itself by God, and at the same time with the entire passion of his bad conscience and surely, absolutely surely, taking the line of least resistance.

thereby dishonored and emptied—in plain language but in the most concrete seriousness—represents the relapse out of belief in the one living God into the impoverished heathen worship of the elements."[10] To believe in moral law apart from the gospel is a disguised form of nature worship.

Barth extends this theology into the political realm in the 1938 essay "Church and State." He holds that the tendency of sinful human nature to abuse the law was limited in Christian natural-law thinkers, because their knowledge of the moral law was really informed by their faith, although they mistakenly attributed that knowledge to human nature. But where the human understanding of justice is truly detached from justification in Christ, people seek to "construct a secular gospel of human law and a secular church, in which, in spite of emphatic references to 'God,' it would inevitably become clear that this deity is not the Father of our Lord Jesus Christ, and that the human justice which is proclaimed is in no sense the justice of God." This, he says, is the "sterility of the Enlightenment," which was ultimately produced by separating human justice from the gospel, a separation that originated in Christian natural-law doctrine. "Pietistic sterility" grows from the same source, among Christians who accept the separation between human justice and the gospel but focus on the latter rather than the former.[11]

The key words in the passage quoted above are "in no sense." Traditional natural-law doctrine holds that the natural human understanding of justice is distorted by sin but is still a reflection of the image of God in humanity: this natural understanding still retains—in its overall outline, if not in all its particulars—the shape of divine justice. But Barth holds that the natural human understanding of justice is "in no sense" the justice of God. His radical break from natural-law thought is not in his assertion

Each pounces on that portion which he thinks he can best use and each with the triumphant thought that he, with his letter and shred in hand, sooner or later brings about—at least in the eyes of men—a kind of special justification of his existence. . . . In what direction can one not plunge if he once ignores and bypasses the faith which God in Jesus Christ demands for himself and himself alone? There are then a thousand works of the law, the law torn into a thousand shreds, a thousand servitudes to which we subject ourselves, a thousand letters on each of which some little man or even many at the same time can cling in order to sip their own righteousness from it" (ibid.).
[10]Ibid.; earlier in the passage, Barth specifically invokes "natural law" as one example of "our pretended obedience to the law for our own self-justification."
[11]Karl Barth, "Church and State," introduction, in *Community, State, and Church.*

that sinful humanity uses the law selfishly as a tool to serve its own ends, but in his assertion that apart from the gospel, nothing else but this selfish distortion remains.

In the 1946 essay "The Christian Community and the Civil Community," Barth follows these principles to their logical conclusion by constructing a political theory from his understanding of the Bible. He depicts the church—that is, the community of all Christian believers—as the "inner circle" of Christ's kingdom, and the state—the community of all citizens—as the "wider circle" around it.[12] Both circles embody the rule of Christ, but in different ways. Christ rules over the inner circle openly, through revelation; he rules over the wider circle secretly, through his providential control of events. There would be no state at all if God did not graciously resist human sin by arranging events to maintain the state's existence, which he does in order to sustain the social conditions necessary for the preaching of the gospel. This is how he rules those who do not recognize his explicit rule over the church in Christ.[13]

Nevertheless, although the wider circle of the state "shares a common origin and a common center" with the inner circle of the church, the state is not the church and is not Christian.[14] Christian people may run the state, but because it embraces all people, Christian and non-Christian, who live within its territory, the state as such is ignorant of the gospel and cannot preach it or depend on the Bible in any way. "No appeal can be made to the Word or Spirit of God in the running of its affairs. The civil community as such is spiritually blind and ignorant."[15] The state's spiritual blindness does imply that the church makes an important contri-

---

[12]Karl Barth, "The Christian Community and the Civil Community," sec. 5, in *Community, State, and Church.*

[13]"However much human error and human tyranny may be involved in it, the state is not a product of sin but one of the constants of the divine providence and government of the world in its action against human sin: it is therefore an instrument of divine grace. The civil community shares both a common origin and a common center with the Christian community. . . . It is the sign that mankind, in its total ignorance and darkness—which is still, or has again become, a prey to sin and therefore subject to the wrath of God—is not yet forsaken but preserved and sustained by God. It serves to protect man from the invasion of chaos and therefore to give him time: time for the preaching of the gospel; time for repentance; time for faith" (ibid., sec. 6).

[14]Ibid.

[15]Ibid., sec. 2.

bution to the state, since it is good for the state that human selfishness be restrained, but the spiritually blind state cannot restrain it.[16] Nonetheless, precisely because of its spiritual blindness, the state cannot recognize that the church plays this role.

The state cannot know the true reason it exists—because it embodies God's rule over humanity—and therefore it inevitably justifies itself by some other ideology, such as natural law. Though public belief in this ideology is inevitable, it is false, and Christians must not accept such natural-law ideology as their own standard. "To base its policy on 'natural law' would mean that the Christian community was adopting the ways of the civil community, which does not take its bearings from the Christian center and is still living or again living in a state of ignorance. The Christian community would be adopting the methods, in other words, of the pagan state."[17]

Instead of falling for the pagan idea of natural law, Christians should take the church as their model for reforming the state. Barth emphasizes that this does not mean the state should be Christianized. The state can never be Christian, can never be a church. Rather, Christians should seek to promote qualities in the state that are analogous to the qualities of the church: Christians should promote qualities in the state that reflect the qualities of the church, but in a manner appropriate to the state. Barth provides a series of examples: the church acknowledges God's claim over all things, and therefore Christians should support equality under the law in the state; the church is based on God's saving love for sinners, and therefore Christians should support a special care for the poor in the state; the church is a fellowship built on love and not compulsion, and therefore Christians should support liberty in the state; and so on.[18]

Barth's list of qualities that the state should possess includes freedom of religion; freedom of speech; women's equality; and even the separation of legislative, executive and judicial powers. As Barth himself acknowledges, the policies he endorses generally coincide with those

---

[16]Ibid., sec. 7.
[17]Ibid., sec. 11.
[18]Ibid., secs. 15-27.

endorsed by traditional natural-law theory, and in particular with the imperatives of liberal democracy. Skeptical readers might take this as evidence that Barth is really just reading his own preference for liberal democracy into the Bible, especially since his reasoning relies so heavily on analogies, which are not subject to rigorous logical analysis. Analogical arguments from the Bible have been used through history to justify all kinds of radically different political policies; for example, medieval monarchists argued that since Christ is king of the church, the state ought to have a king as well. Barth, however, argues that the coincidence between his theory and traditional natural-law theory is not surprising. Rather, it is evidence of God's providential control over the state. Though the natural-law philosophy is false, by a divinely ordained coincidence it generally reaches the right policy conclusions anyway, because those are the conclusions God wants the state to possess.[19] Barth also acknowledges the coincidence between his theory and the imperatives of liberal democracy, commenting that it is not in liberal democracy as such that the similarity lies, but in the moral goals that liberal democracy strives for.[20]

Barth's own political ideology remained relatively undeveloped. He was focused on addressing a single urgent crisis, and his general account of politics only goes as far as is needed to provide a basis from which to address that crisis. However, Barth's rejection of natural law was widely influential: it served as the starting point from which numerous other Christian thinkers built their own political ideologies in the twentieth century.

JUSTICE AND MORE THAN JUSTICE

Where Barth was responding to the double threat of totalitarianism and pietism in Germany, the American theologian Reinhold Niebuhr was responding primarily to naive idealism in the countries that could have stopped Germany. Since the social gospel movement of the nineteenth century, with its emphasis on social reform, the clergy of the mainline Protestant denominations had been predominantly shaped by a liberal

---

[19]Ibid., sec. 28.
[20]Ibid., sec. 29.

optimism; these church leaders were optimistic about the perfectibility of society and the power of reason and religious fervor to produce improvement by themselves, without the use of force to suppress evil. Niebuhr himself was a liberal, both politically and theologically, but he argued that Western liberals—of both the religious and irreligious variety—were too credulous about how much moral improvement was really possible in politics.

At first many liberals did not welcome Niebuhr's dour realism about the stubbornness of political evil. One scholar, now an editor of Niebuhr's works, recalls that in 1932, when he was thirteen years old, his father—a "liberal, social-gospel minister"—exploded out of his study, waving a copy of Niebuhr's *Moral Man and Immoral Society* and shouting, "Reinie's gone crazy!"[21]

But the events of the 1930s and 1940s would prove that Reinie was not so crazy. His warnings about the rise of fascism and communism, along with the inadequacy of prevailing political attitudes to deal with this challenge, were revealed as prescient. The popularity of his political thinking helped make Niebuhr the most widely known American theologian of the mid-twentieth century.

The central thesis of *Moral Man and Immoral Society*, Niebuhr's most important political work, was that we must follow different ethical imperatives when evaluating and directing the collective behavior of groups than we do when we evaluate and direct the behavior of individuals. Christian ethics requires individual human beings to achieve total unselfishness, but this is not the appropriate standard for collective entities such as societies, governments, economic classes and so forth. Groups do not and cannot behave in the same way that individuals do: they are less capable of transcending their self-interests. "Every effort to transfer a pure morality of disinterestedness to group relations has resulted in failure."[22] We should not give up on the idea of having a collective morality, Niebuhr argued, but we must be realistic in our expectations. That means developing a different set of moral

---

[21]Langdon Gilkey, "Introduction," in Reinhold Niebuhr, *Moral Man and Immoral Society* (Louisville, Ky.: Westminster John Knox, 2001), p. xii.
[22]Niebuhr, *Moral Man*, chap. 10.

expectations for government, and different ethical requirements for our interactions with it.

Niebuhr identifies two major factors that encourage people to greater moral sensitivity: rationality and religion. Unfortunately, both of these factors are stronger in the life of an individual than they are in the life of a collective group such as a society. By contrast, humanity's sinful desires are easier to exercise collectively than they are individually.

Greater rationality encourages greater moral sensitivity because our degree of rationality "determines the degree of vividness with which we appreciate the needs of other life, [and] the extent to which we become conscious of the real character of our own motives and impulses," among other reasons. On the social level, rationality strips away the lies and false justifications that excuse abuses of power. For these reasons, the liberal political theory that prevailed in the early twentieth century placed great confidence in the power of rationality to reform society.

However, while an individual always has a single coherent mind, in a group "a common mind and purpose is always more or less inchoate and transitory." Groups must therefore rely on shared emotions—Niebuhr calls them "impulses"—to drive their collective behavior. And impulses regularly overrule the influence of rationality. More often than not, reason becomes a tool of our impulses rather than its master. "Even the most rational men are never quite rational when their own interests are at stake," he writes; and a society is like a man who is not very rational to begin with and whose interests are always at stake.[23]

Religion encourages moral sensitivity because it forces people to hold themselves to an absolute moral standard, and to conceive of morality as an obligation they owe to a person (God) rather than an abstraction. On the social level, religion implies an equal standard of justice and provides increased hope that political reform may succeed. This is why, as Niebuhr points out, moral reformers in every age have hoped for a religious revival that would overcome political obstacles and sweep their agenda into effect.

But religion is a double-edged sword. There is bad religion as well as good—a point that Jesus made rather forcefully regarding the Pharisees and

---

[23]Ibid., chap. 2.

Sadducees—and that continues to have relevance for the way many Christians fail to live their own faith. For example, people use religion to transform their personal desires into the absolute commands of God, or religion can cause people to focus so much on God that they neglect to improve their own behavior. And religion is more likely to go bad at the social level than it is at the individual level. "If nations and other social groups find it difficult to approximate the principles of justice, as we have previously noted, they are naturally even less capable of achieving the principle of love, which demands more than justice. The demand of religious moralists that nations subject themselves to 'the law of Christ' is an unrealistic demand, and the hope that they will do so is a sentimental one."[24]

But while these good influences become less powerful at the social level, other influences become more so. By its very nature, collective life provides constant temptations to indulge our wickedness. The sinful individual who cannot get much of the power and pleasure that he craves in his own life can get them vicariously through the triumph of his group over other groups. "The frustrations of the average man, who can never realize the power and glory which his imagination sets as the ideal, makes him the more willing tool and victim of the imperial ambitions of his group. His frustrated individual ambitions gain a measure of satisfaction in the power and the aggrandizement of his nation."[25] Moreover, sinful individuals feel the need to excuse their sin by inventing moral justifications for it, and collective life provides more plausible excuses. By transferring his selfish ambitions from himself to his country, he can disguise their essential selfishness from himself more effectively.[26]

As a result of these facts, politics can never reach a very elevated moral level. In particular, reason and religion will never be able to remove the need for force and violence at the heart of politics. "The selfishness of human communities must be regarded as an inevitability. Where it is inordinate it can be checked only by competing assertions of interest; and these can be effective only if coercive methods are added to moral and ra-

[24]Ibid., chap. 3.
[25]Ibid., chap. 1.
[26]See ibid., chap. 4.

THE CONTESTED PUBLIC SQUARE

tional persuasion."[27] Niebuhr critiques at length the pacifistic tendencies of thought that led liberal-democratic societies to appease totalitarianism for so long.[28]

More broadly, Niebuhr writes that while in individual life "unselfishness" is the proper goal, in social life the less ambitious goal of "justice" is appropriate. However, he hastens to add that the corrosive effects of social life will undermine even the goal of justice if the individuals who make up the society do not aim at something higher: "Any justice which is only justice soon degenerates into something less than justice. It must be saved by something which is more than justice."[29] We must maintain a difficult balancing act, remembering that the state is not capable of doing better than mere justice, while also remembering that we must never allow mere justice to become the moral standard that really matters to us as individuals.

Niebuhr calls for "a frank dualism in morals," warning against any attempt to permanently reconcile the conflicting imperatives of individual and social morality.[30] The right balance must be struck in each particular situation, and in each case the appropriate policy depends on historical circumstances, which will change. It is dangerous to set up some practical compromise that works in one particular situation as the transcendently right policy. As Niebuhr would remark in another book, "There is no justice, even in a sinful world, which can be regarded as finally normative. The higher possibilities of love, which is at once the fulfillment and the negation of justice, always hover over every system of justice."[31]

Here we come to Niebuhr's objection to traditional natural-law doctrine. Niebuhr accuses natural-law philosophers of being overly optimistic in the power of reason to work out the one right solution to political problems, saying that they have tended to take the practical solutions that worked in their own circumstances and set these up as natural laws.

---

[27]Ibid., chap. 10.
[28]See esp. ibid., chap. 9.
[29]Ibid., chap. 10.
[30]Ibid.
[31]Reinhold Niebuhr, *The Nature and Destiny of Man: A Christian Interpretation*, 2 vols. (New York: Scribner's, 1941-1943), vol. 1, chap. 10, sec. 4.

He attributes this optimism to the influence of classical Greco-Roman rationalism.[32]

Nevertheless, for Niebuhr the problem of politics remains centered on understanding human nature as it is revealed to us in history and experience, rather than on scriptural analysis. The appropriate solutions to political problems may change as circumstances change; but according to Niebuhr, what does not change are the qualities of human nature that define these political problems. Unlike most natural-law theorists, Niebuhr refuses to acknowledge any significant points of continuity between Christian and non-Christian conceptions of human nature; his attack on the great natural-law philosophers for their alleged Greco-Roman optimistic rationalism is one example of this element of his thought. Yet human nature is still the basis of Niebuhr's argument, and to justify his analysis of politics he can appeal—and in fact he almost always does appeal—to his reader's lived and observed experiences of human nature rather than to scriptural quotations. This is a sharp contrast with someone like Barth, whose political writings appeal almost exclusively to Scripture.

In other words, Niebuhr retains much of the basic concept of natural law even as he rejects the full teaching of historic natural-law doctrine. He draws a sharp line between the Christian and non-Christian understandings of human nature, acknowledging no overlap. However, he justifies the Christian understanding by appealing not to Scripture but to knowledge that is common to all humanity; he argues that the Christian understanding is the only one that adequately accounts for all the known facts of human history and experience.[33] So there is one sense in which he builds on common ground between Christians and non-Christians, and another sense in which he does not.

THE ETHICAL VACUUM

When Barth and Niebuhr began writing against totalitarianism in the 1930s, both understood themselves to be in the minority when they criticized the established dominance of natural-law doctrine. In fact, as hindsight would later make clear, by then confidence in natural law had

---

[32]Ibid., vol. 2, chap. 9, sec. 5.
[33]See ibid., esp. vol. 1, chaps. 1-3.

already been badly shaken in all the ways described earlier in this chapter. Amid the catastrophic events of the 1930s and 1940s, the idea of natural law was widely seen as having been discredited. Thus when C. S. Lewis, an English literary critic and apologist for Christianity, wrote against totalitarianism in the early 1940s, he understood his *defense* of natural-law doctrine to be a minority viewpoint.[34]

In a series of works written between 1941 and 1943, Lewis laid out a case for natural law that would continue to define his views on the subject for the rest of his career. He argued that our awareness of moral law cannot be derived from any other part of our nature (such as an "instinct" to preserve the species) that is not in itself a moral law, or from anything that we receive through the senses (such as hearing the gospel). Either of these views would imply that we could start out with no moral awareness and then acquire it—by following our instincts, by hearing the gospel, or in some other way. But a person who truly started out with no moral awareness could never acquire it, just as a person who started out with no rational thoughts could never acquire them. To be meaningful, moral law must be accepted on the same basis on which we accept the validity of the laws of logic, such as the law that if X = Y and Y = Z, then X = Z. We cannot prove logic to be valid, because in order to prove anything, we must begin by assuming that logic is valid. We accept the validity of logic because our minds will not work any other way; it is simply our nature to think logically, and to think any other way is self-contradictory.[35] Similarly, we cannot prove that the laws of morality are obligatory, because the very act of proving something to be obligatory requires us to assume the laws of morality.

In an essay titled "On Ethics," Lewis argues that if we try to evaluate whether a moral code is obligatory, we must assume that while we are doing so, we are in what he calls an "ethical vacuum," standing outside morality in order to evaluate it. And if we are in an ethical vacuum, no moral code or anything else can be obligatory. "It cannot, while we are

---

[34]Lewis would not be known as a novelist until later, though in 1933 he had published a philosophical novel titled *The Pilgrim's Regress: An Allegorical Apology for Christianity, Reason and Romanticism* (London: J. M. Dent & Sons, 1933).

[35]Lewis most famously made this argument in the first three chapters of his book *Miracles: A Preliminary Study* (New York: Macmillan, 1947).

in the vacuum, be our duty to emerge from it. An act of duty is an act of obedience to the moral law. But by definition we are standing outside all codes of moral law. A man with no ethical allegiance can have no ethical motive for adopting one."[36] And any code that is not obligatory is not a moral code. Hence, if we were ever really to enter a moral vacuum, we could never leave it. "We never start from a *tabula rasa* [blank slate]; if we did, we should end, ethically speaking, with a *tabula rasa*."[37]

Hence we can never prove moral law or derive it from anything. As with logic, so with morality: we must simply assume it or go without it. "The ultimate ethical injunctions have always been premises, never conclusions. Kant was perfectly right on that point at least: the imperative is categorical. Unless the ethical is assumed from the outset, no argument will bring you to it."[38] Or as Lewis put it in another essay, "We have only two alternatives. Either the maxims of traditional morality must be accepted as axioms of practical reason [moral reasoning] which neither admit nor require argument to support them and not to 'see' which is to have lost human status; or else there are no values at all."[39] In other words, we must accept the basic principles of morality the same way we accept the basic principles of logic—absolutely and without needing any justification—or else abandon them.

This does not mean that our awareness of morality comes from nowhere. It comes from God—but it comes to us directly from God, so to speak, not through some other medium. God implants it in us when he creates us.[40] Morality is a fundamental part of our human nature, in the same sense in which rational thought is a fundamental part of human nature. A person who does not know the moral law is cut off from humanity, just as a person who cannot think rationally is cut off from humanity.

According to Lewis's argument, people do not realize that moral knowledge is inherent in human nature largely because they believe that the world contains

---

[36]C. S. Lewis, "On Ethics," in *The Collected Works of C. S. Lewis* (New York: Inspirational Press, 1996), pp. 205-6; this essay was not published in Lewis's lifetime but is believed to have been written in the period from 1941 to 1943.

[37]Ibid., p. 209.

[38]Ibid. Lewis is not endorsing Kant's broader theory of "the categorical imperative," but he is agreeing with Kant that the imperative of moral law must be a categorical one: one that is assumed as an axiom rather than justified by argument.

[39]C. S. Lewis, "The Poison of Subjectivism" (1943), in *Collected Works*, p. 225.

[40]On this subject see chaps. 4-5 of *Miracles*.

an endless bewildering variety of radically different moral codes. If each society has its own unique morality, as is popularly believed, then morality must be artificial. Lewis points out that this does not square with the facts of history:

> And what of the . . . objection that the ethical standards of different cultures differ so widely that there is no common tradition at all? The answer is that this is a lie—a good, solid, resounding lie. If a man will go into a library and spend a few days with the *Encyclopedia of Religion and Ethics* he will soon discover the massive unanimity of the practical reason [moral reasoning] in man. From the Babylonian *Hymn to Samos*, from the Laws of Manu, the *Book of the Dead*, the Analects, the Stoics, the Platonists, from Australian aborigines and Redskins, he will collect the same triumphantly monotonous denunciations of oppression, murder, treachery and falsehood, the same injunctions of kindness to the aged, the young, and the weak, of almsgiving and impartiality and honesty. He . . . will no longer doubt that there is such a thing as the Law of Nature. There are, of course, differences. There are even blindnesses in particular cultures—just as there are savages who cannot count up to twenty. But the pretence that we are confronted with a mere chaos—[that] . . . no outline of universally accepted value shows through—is simply false and must be contradicted in season and out of season wherever it is met.[41]

In his 1943 book *The Abolition of Man*, Lewis provides an appendix of quotations from the religious and philosophical works of the major civilizations in world history—from ancient Egypt, Babylon and China through modernity—and shows the breadth of agreement among them on the basic principles of morality.

Lewis is careful to add that he is not saying that people or societies cannot make moral advances, or have their moral knowledge corrected and improved. However, this process never consists of an old, false morality being replaced by a new, true one; to transfer our allegiance from one morality to a different morality would require us to evaluate one morality as better than another—which we could only do by entering the fatal "ethical vacuum." Instead, when a person or a society corrects a moral error or improves a moral deficiency, it is only realizing more fully and more consistently the consequences of the moral knowledge it already possesses.

---

[41]Lewis, "Poison of Subjectivism," pp. 226-27.

For example, Lewis points out that the ancient Roman Stoics and Confucius had both advocated the law "Do not do to others what you would not have them do to you." When Jesus later advocated the law "Do to others what you would have them do to you," this was a moral advance—but the advance consisted in giving existing moral principles a more full and consistent application.[42]

Lewis was writing in opposition to both religious and irreligious alternatives. On the irreligious side were modern subjectivist theories seeking to replace the traditional notion that right and wrong are objective facts with an imperative to preserve the human species, an imperative that was said to arise from a subjective source: instinct. Against this view, Lewis argues that people do not, in fact, have a natural instinct to preserve the human species, and even if they did, the mere fact that we have an instinct to do something does not make it obligatory. Lewis argues that if a society omits the starting assumption of objective right and wrong, it must end in tyranny and potentially in totalitarianism, because without that assumption no moral law is possible, and without moral law the rulers can have no obligations to their subjects.[43]

Lewis also anticipates two objections from Christian opponents of natural law who take a Barthian view. The first is the claim that natural-law doctrine is "trusting our own reason so far that we ignore the Fall"; the second is that it is "retrogressively turning our absolute allegiance away from a person [i.e., God] to an abstraction."[44] Against the first, Lewis responds that Scripture affirms natural knowledge of moral law—though not sufficient natural goodness to obey it—even among sinful humanity.[45] And he further argues that to deny all natural knowledge of moral-

---

[42]See C. S. Lewis, *The Abolition of Man* (London: Oxford University Press, 1943), chap. 2.

[43]This is the primary argument of *Abolition of Man*. In "On Ethics" (p. 211), Lewis also comments about those who claim that new moralities can replace traditional morality: "Their activity is always in the long run directed against our freedom." In "Poison of Subjectivism" (p. 223) he notes that subjectivism can take other forms besides "the power philosophies of the totalitarian states," but he argues that it is subjectivism that "has given these power philosophies their golden opportunity."

[44]Lewis, "Poison of Subjectivism," p. 227; these two anticipated objections parallel Barth's two claims that moral law cannot be known by sinful human nature but only through the gospel, and that any claim to natural knowledge of morality amounts to "heathen worship of the elements."

[45]Lewis states: "As regards the Fall, I submit that the general tenor of Scripture does not encourage us to believe that our knowledge of the law has been depraved in the same degree as our power to

ity drains the gospel of its moral basis. If we do not start out possessing some standard of goodness by which we can evaluate that God is good, we cannot worship God for his goodness, and our religion will be mere worship of power. "If once we admit that what God means by 'goodness' is sheerly different from what we judge to be good, there is no difference left between pure religion and devil worship."

Similarly, in response to the second objection, while Lewis agrees that our allegiance to God must be ultimate and unconditional, he insists that our allegiance to good over evil must be equally ultimate and unconditional: "If good is to be defined as what God commands, then the goodness of God himself is emptied of meaning and the commands of an omnipotent fiend would have the same claim on us as those of the 'righteous Lord.'"[46] Lewis argues that the only solution is to assume that the appearance of our having two ultimate allegiances (to goodness and to God) must be an illusion. We perceive two ultimates, but in the transcendent and unimaginable reality of the divine nature, these two must really be one, on a level we cannot understand, just as the three persons of the Trinity are really one superpersonal being, though in a mode that is unimaginable to us.

Lewis's analysis also provides a defense of natural law against Niebuhr's most important line of criticism. Niebuhr had treated Christian and non-Christian understandings of human nature as radically distinct, evaluating historic natural-law doctrine in terms of "Christian" elements that ought to be kept and non-Christian "rationalist" elements that ought to be purged. Lewis's argument implies that this way of putting it is too simple. If one worldview is better than the other—and Lewis agrees with Niebuhr that the Christian worldview is better than that of the ancient Greco-Roman philosophers—this implies that we are relying on some common moral standard shared among all humanity, by which we can judge dif-

---

fulfill it. He would be a brave man who claimed to realize the fallen condition of man more clearly than St. Paul. In that very chapter (Romans 7) where he asserts most strongly our inability to keep the moral law he also asserts most confidently that we perceive the law's goodness and rejoice in it according to the inward man. Our righteousness may be filthy and ragged; but Christianity gives us no ground for holding that our perceptions of right are in the same condition. They may, no doubt, be impaired; but there is a difference between imperfect sight and blindness" ("Poison of Subjectivism," pp. 227-28).

[46]Ibid., p. 228.

ferent worldviews. Otherwise we fall afoul of the ethical vacuum. And if there is a common moral standard among humanity, then we should not speak of a tug of war between "Christian" moral principles and "rationalist" moral principles. Rather, we should say that Christianity does a better job than other worldviews of giving a full and consistent expression to the moral knowledge that is shared among all. And if, as Niebuhr alleges, natural-law thinkers have tended to take the practical moral solutions to the problems of their own eras and set them up as though they were absolute principles for all time, that need not represent the incursion of a non-Christian "rationalist" philosophy into Christian thought. On Lewis's terms, it is more easily explained in terms of the personal moral failings of those natural-law thinkers: shortsightedness is a character flaw, not a philosophy.

To Be Continued

The philosophies described above only provide a small sample of the enormous range of political ideas that have created, and have emerged from, the current crisis in political thought. The very nature of the crisis is a multiple breakdown of consensus: a breakdown of consensus in favor of liberal democracy, a breakdown of consensus about the basis of liberal democracy among those who still favor it, and a breakdown of consensus among Christian thinkers on how to cope with these breakdowns. In this environment, the number of viewpoints that clamor for our attention is practically limitless. There is no space for all the critiques of liberal democracy, the new theories of liberal democracy, and Christian ideas about the best way forward. The ideas presented in this chapter are only a sort of highlight reel.

The crisis is nowhere near resolution, and it would be foolish to venture any predictions. All the ideas outlined in this chapter continue to exercise widespread influence. There are strong arguments both for and against the prospects of liberal democracy's survival; for and against the prospects of natural-law thought as the animating idea of liberal democracy; and for and against the prospects of Christians ending up building a new consensus around something resembling the ideas of Barth, Niebuhr, Lewis or any one of a dozen other thinkers for whom we have no space here. The tail end of a book that covers almost twenty-five hundred years of history is not the place to begin evaluating the prospects for the next twenty-five hundred.

The last chapter of a historical survey never ends well, because history is a story to which we do not yet know the ending. It is disappointing not to be able to offer a pithy summary of where the events of the last century have left us and to project what they are leading to. The most it seems safe to say is that, since the crisis shows no sign of resolution, the next century is bound to be as eventful as the last one. That is not a cheering assessment for anyone who looks at what the last century produced, but there is no reason not to hope—and pray—that ultimate good will once again be brought out of the transitory evils of human politics, as it has so many times before.

CONCLUSION

Things did not have to be this way. In summing up the results of history, the great temptation is always to attribute a kind of inevitability to events that they never really possess. Let us avoid this error. At every one of the major historical junctures covered in this book, Christian political thought had numerous alternatives available. History is just people making choices, and so—without commenting on the mysterious relationship between divine omnipotence and human free will—we should at least say that, humanly speaking, our history could have been different in any number of ways.

Nonetheless, people do not make choices at random. They do what they do for reasons. To understand the choices that were made in the events covered by the preceding eight chapters, we must understand the reasons those choices were made—or at least a few of the most important reasons, since the total psychologies of the people involved are unavailable for our inspection.

Christianity is one of the few major religions in the history of humanity that claims to be simply true: not that it is true in the sense of providing a picture or allegory or metaphor of cosmological truths, like the world's various mythological systems; not that it is true in the sense of laying out a formula or diagram or deduction of abstract truths, like the world's various philosophical systems; not that it is true in the sense of guiding people into living out the deeper truths of their own natures, like the world's various ethical systems; not that it is true in any particular *sense* at all—just that it is *true*. And since it claims to be simply true, it cannot be the truth of one people or of one segment of society. It is either the truth, and therefore rightfully everyone's truth, or else it is no truth at all.

This was what made the encounter between Christianity and the ancient Greco-Roman world so transformative, not only for the Greco-Roman world but for Christianity as well. On the one hand, Christianity was not something that one could simply add to the existing stew of mythologies and philosophies the way Rome kept endlessly adding new foreign gods to the pantheon and new schools of thought to its philosophical debating clubs. The gods of the world could stand side by side in the pantheon because each of them claimed only a local and limited affiliation: Athena was the goddess of Athens, not of the universe. The philosophical schools could stand side by side in the marketplace because none of them expected the whole world to follow it: Plato was the teacher of the Platonists, not of the great uneducated masses toward whom he rarely showed anything better than condescension. (He famously had the words "Let no one ignorant of geometry enter here" written above the door of his school; this is often cited for what it says about his high view of the importance of geometry, but it says even more about his low view of the importance of ordinary people.) But Christ could not be the god of only one city or the teacher of only one school.

On the other hand, for precisely the same reason, Christianity did not claim to have no points of contact with natural human life, including its mythologies and philosophies. Paul began his famous speech on the Areopagus by observing that the Athenians had built an altar to an "unknown god," telling them that he had come to reveal their unknown god to them (Acts 17:23). Mythology and philosophy both claimed to offer access to deeper truths; Christianity was claiming to fulfill both of their fundamental purposes. This is why Christianity ultimately took up into itself both the mythological and the philosophical impulses of the society that embraced it. The mythmakers and philosophers became Christians, but the Christians also became mythmakers and philosophers. The influence of the Greco-Roman mythologizing impulse on later Christian thought is not a subject of central relevance to this book.[1] The philosophical impulse,

---

[1]For a profound reflection on the relationship between Christianity and pre-Christian myth, see C. S. Lewis, "Myth Become Fact," in *The Collected Works of C. S. Lewis* (New York: Inspirational

however, must take center stage in any consideration of how Christianity has confronted the questions of politics.

Closely related to Christianity's claim to be simply true was its unique claim about the church. The community of people whose lives had been transformed by Christianity was utterly unlike either the religious communities of mythology or the schools of philosophy. It claimed to be an eternal community; it claimed that God was not only saving individuals from their sins, but also building up a social organization that would outlast the universe itself.

This claim about the church stands behind the whole history of Christian understandings of the nature of the state. If all social organizations are essentially worldly, then their importance can only be judged in worldly terms; and obviously on those terms, the state must be the most important social organization. The claim that the church is eternal made it thinkable to reduce the state's importance in our conception of what matters most for human life. In some periods of time, Christians took this too far and tried to set up the church as an alternative state, exercising political power. But that was not the original intention, as the New Testament makes clear, and the church's foundation in an otherworldly mission ultimately drew it back from entanglement with worldly power. The removal of politics from the center of human life, however, has not been diminished by this correction.

Similarly, if all social organizations are worldly rather than eternal, then religion must be promoted through a worldly institution and by using worldly means. The natural tendency of humanity has therefore been to promote religion through the state. Christianity partook of this same universal tendency after the conversion of the Roman Empire. Over time, however, the church's unique claim to be eternal counteracted this tendency. The contrast between the worldliness of the state and the otherworldliness that is appropriate to the preaching of the gospel eventually became too great to ignore.

Press, 1996); see also chap. 14 of C. S. Lewis, *Miracles*, in *The Complete C. S. Lewis Signature Classics* (San Francisco: HarperCollins, 2002); and idem, *The Pilgrim's Regress*, in *Collected Works*. But Lewis sometimes minimizes the damage done to Christian thought by the mythologizing impulse of the ancient Greco-Romans; for a sobering corrective, see B. B. Warfield, *Counterfeit Miracles* (New York: Charles Scribner's Sons, 1918), chap. 2.

All these consequences of the Christian claim drive Augustine's political thought. Augustine carefully sifts through the mythology and philosophy of pre-Christian Rome, seeking to refute all that is false in it, and more generally to demonstrate the superiority of Christianity for explaining the human experience. Yet at the same time he is careful to maintain the deep connection between Christianity and natural human experience, because God is the God of human nature. Augustine wishes to show that the Bible does not simply sweep away human wisdom and replace it root and branch, but corrects its errors and elevates it—one might even say regenerates and sanctifies it. Moreover, Augustine rebukes those Romans for whom the glory of Rome was the most important thing there was. The state serves an important purpose, but only a worldly purpose. For ultimate meaning, we must look elsewhere.

The consequences of Augustine's thought in turn reach their fruition in the natural-law philosophy of the Middle Ages. The very term *natural law* comes to us from Augustine, and the central concepts of natural-law doctrine are all implicit in Augustine's thought. But they are only implicit, and it was the genius of the medieval scholastics to systematize this doctrine—which is just another way of saying that they uncovered what was implicit and made it explicit, in order to better understand it and trace out its consequences.

Indeed, if not for the Reformation, the gradual development of Augustine's ideas within the traditions of natural-law doctrine might have ended up supplying the bulk of the history of Christian political thought. But the great cataclysm of the Reformation introduced a new spectrum of problems with their own history, though those problems do intersect with the questions that drive natural-law doctrine.

The Reformation was not the first lasting division between Christians, nor was it the first great dispute over fundamental doctrine. But it was the first time those two things (doctrinal dispute and lasting division) were joined together. Each of the great controversies over fundamental points of doctrine in the early church was settled, at least for the most part, within a century. Arianism lingered on well after the Council of Nicaea, and Pelagianism lingered after the Council of Carthage, but there was no question of Christianity itself dividing; the only question was how long it would take for the holdouts to either recant their views or leave Christianity entirely. On the other hand, while the great eleventh-century schism between East and West did divide Christianity, it did so on the ecclesiastical level rather than on the deeper level of fundamental doctrine. Important as that division was and is, it is not the same thing as a disagreement over the grounds of salvation. The Reformation, by contrast, represents precisely a disagreement over the grounds of salvation. It has divided Christianity not only in its institutional organization, but also in the roots of its faith.

This division has forced a major problem off the back burner of Christian political thought, where it had sat during the Middle Ages as other questions received greater attention. The scholastics could afford to be sanguine about the tensions created by mixing the worldly power of the state with the otherworldly power of the gospel. They were by no means ignorant of these tensions, but they were far more worried about the possible consequences of separating the worldly and otherworldly powers more fully. It would have been a risky thing to attempt, and in the Middle Ages there was no pressing urgency to attempt it. It seemed safer to stick with the old ways.

And then suddenly it was not safe anymore. With the benefit of hindsight, we can now see that the entanglement of worldly and otherworldly power in the Middle Ages was more dangerous than the scholastics realized. When a lasting division over fundamental doctrine arose within Christianity, that entanglement resulted in political disaster. After a period of compromise under the policy of *cuius regio, eius religio*, Christians gradually came to the conclusion that the risky separation of worldly power from otherworldly power had to be attempted. Hence they undertook the bold experiment that we now call religious freedom.

Meanwhile, the development of natural-law philosophy continued. The doctrine that governments have natural duties led by implication to the doctrine that individuals have natural rights. In particular, the doctrine that might does not make right—that the mere possession of coercive power cannot by itself entitle the possessor to the rightful authority of government—led by implication to the doctrine that governments can, in certain narrowly defined circumstances, forfeit their entitlement to obedience. And the Augustinian appreciation for the fallenness of human politics, combined with the systematic empirical investigation of what systems have best served to restrain that fallenness, formed the basis of what Hamilton called the Enlightenment's "science of politics." From the combination of these developments, we received the system known as liberal democracy.

Now these two great culminations—religious freedom and liberal democracy—are in crisis again. Some are discontent with the way they reduce the state to no more than a cold, calculating caretaker of worldly affairs. Others support religious freedom and liberal democracy but dislike their historic basis in natural law, wishing to reinvent them according to other philosophies. Each of these two fault lines has produced numerous alternatives to the historic understandings of religious freedom and liberal democracy grounded in natural law. The societies where these systems first emerged are now divided among multiple political philosophies, and no one is sure what theory governs.

As I have suggested in the preceding chapters, the most obvious culprit in this crisis is what I have called "the problem of public virtue." That is, how do we maintain political adherence to the moral laws necessary for politics (do not kill, do not steal, keep your promises, etc.) without a shared community religion? The early advocates of religious freedom, especially Locke, seemed supremely confident that this would not be a problem. Yet even the strongest supporters of religious freedom must admit that it has turned out to be a very serious problem. Western societies maintained a strong consensus around natural-law doctrine for about fifteen hundred years. Now, in what is historically a very short time, that strong consensus has vanished, replaced by a cacophony of competing philosophies. No doubt there are many causes at work, but the removal of a shared community religion as the basis of social consensus on political philosophy would seem to be the most obvious candidate for the leading factor. Even those who love religious freedom must not be blind to its consequences, or they will not be able to preserve it.

At the end of the last chapter, I resolved to offer no predictions. But it seems safe enough to say that if we do not figure out some way to forge a social consensus on political philosophy, the end result must eventually be disastrous. We can coast for a long time on cultural inertia and messy compromises, but we cannot survive that way forever. Lincoln predicted that persistent internal disagreements about the meaning of liberty must ultimately shatter a political community, and he was proved right. Are our disagreements any less fundamental than the ones Lincoln confronted?

All paths now lead to danger. If we wish to preserve religious freedom, we must somehow find a way to build social consensus around the moral laws that politics requires without going back to dependence upon a shared religion. Locke's confidence that this would happen simply on its own has proved to be misplaced. Tocqueville gave us what is probably the most penetrating analysis of the problem, and in the end he did not even pretend to offer a clear solution. To the contrary, he warned us that all of the tools available for preserving the moral foundations of democracy can easily become subverted and end up undermining those foundations instead. All of the greatest defenders of religious freedom since Tocqueville have joined him in confessing that its preservation in the face of this challenge is uncertain. But what is the alternative? Even if we were inclined to declare the experiment in religious freedom a failure, how would that help us? Attempting to restore a shared community religion as the basis of government policy would only deepen our divisions and exacerbate our conflicts. And if the entanglement of worldly and otherworldly power caused unthinkable slaughter between Protestants and Catholics in the sixteenth and seventeenth centuries, what would it do now, when our societies are even more radically divided over religion?

I do not know the answer to this crisis. However, I do know that the first step to finding an answer is understanding the question. We are going to have to do a better job of understanding the real nature of the crisis. If we do achieve that insight, we still might not succeed; but if we do not even try to achieve it, we will have lost before we even begin.

That is what has driven me to write this book. If it has been any help to you, please join me in giving thanks to God and in praying he will give us the wisdom we need to preserve such justice as we have in this fallen world.

Index

Academy (in Athens), 52, 54
Achilles, 49-50, 50n.
Adams, John, 173-74
Adams, Samuel, 173, 174
Aeschylus, 46
Albert of Mainz, 108, 109, 136
Alexander the Great, 56, 62, 79
Ambrose, 66
American Revolution, 174, 178
American Revolutionary War, 178, 195, 197, 201
Amsterdam, 153, 154
Anselm of Canterbury, 87, 118n.
Antigone, 46
Apollo, 44, 47, 51, 53
Areopagus, 44, 244
Aristophanes, 46
Aristotle, 14, 34, 54, 56, 57-58, 58n., 92, 115, 126n., 204
    and *Metaphysics*, 58n.
    and *Nicomachean Ethics*, 56, 58n.
    and *Politics*, 56, 58n.
Articles of Confederation, 205, 207, 208
Athanasian Creed, 15
Athena, 46, 47, 49
Athenians, 54
Athens, 44, 46, 52, 53, 55, 56, 60, 244
Augsburg, Imperial Diet in, 138
Augustine of Hippo, 14, 52, 62, 79, 80, 111, 122, 123, 124, 126n., 177, 179, 191, 191n.
    and *The City of God*, 17, 28n.-29n., 52n., 63-65, 69, 70-71, 70n., 71n, 72-75, 81-83, 131
    and *Confessions*, 66-67, 68
    and the fall of Rome, 69-70, 70n., 76-78
    and the idea of natural law, 88-90

and interaction with Marcellinus, 70-71
    philosophy of, 72-75, 75n., 76, 78
    theology of, 68-69, 160
Babylon, 238
Bacon, Francis, 169
Barmen Declaration, 225
Barth, Karl, 211, 225-30, 235, 241
Basilica of St. Peter, 108, 110, 136
Benedictine Order, 84
Bill of Rights (England), 181
Bill of Rights (United States of America), 165
Boston, 172, 197
Boston Massacre, 172-74
Brandenburg, 136, 142
Britain, 16
Buddhism, 34
Burke, Edmund, 218, 223-24
Calvin, John, 130, 131n., 132, 155, 182, 204
    and *Institutes of the Christian Religion*, 131
    and success of the "two-swords approach," 135
    and view on civil government, 131-35
Carthage, 69
    Council of, 68, 246
Chaerephon, 43-44
Charlemagne, 65
Charles II, 180-81
Chesterton, G. K., 48n.
China, 238
Cicero, 62, 76, 115, 177, 191, 191n.
    and *On the Republic*, 79-80
Clement of Alexandria, 61, 61n., 72
Cleves, 142, 143, 145, 153
Confucius, 34
Constantine, Flavius Valerius Aurelius, 15, 77

Constantinople, 65
Constitution of the United States of America, 199, 204, 205
Continental Congress, 16, 174
Cooper, Anthony Ashley, 179-80, 181
Counter-Reformation, the, 136-37
Creon, 46
Czechoslovakia, 215
Damascus, 43-44
Declaration of Independence, 174, 196, 197
Delphi, 43
Delphic oracle, 44, 51
Descartes, René, 144
Democritus, 57
Dominican order, 85
Donatists, 68
Donatus Magnus, 68
Eck, Johann, 113, 170
Egypt, 55, 63, 213n., 238
Elizabeth I, 152, 169
England, 85, 131, 134, 135, 138, 142, 143, 150, 151, 162, 169, 170, 180, 182, 193
English Civil War, 151, 153, 180
Enlightenment, the, 17, 144, 146, 199, 248
Ephesus, 24
Epictetus, 58n.
Euripides, 46
Europe, 86, 107, 114, 116, 119, 121, 127n., 136, 137, 138, 139, 140, 144, 152, 158, 199
  and religion after the Reformation, 150
  and religion before the Reformation, 148-49
Europe, Eastern, 127, 169-70
Europe, Western, 17, 117-18, 128, 129, 135
Erasmus, Desiderius, 111, 125
Federalist Papers, the, 198, 201n., 203, 207
Filmer, Robert, 17, 176
Fortune, 71
France, 65, 128, 131, 135, 149n., 150, 151, 153, 170, 180
Franciscan order, 85
Frederick the Wise, 108, 115, 118
French Revolution, 178, 218
  and the Reign of Terror, 222
Geneva, 130, 131, 131n., 132, 134, 135, 137
Germany, 65, 107, 111, 120, 121, 131, 135, 138, 139n., 142, 214-15, 225, 230
Glorious Revolution, 178, 181, 182
Greece, 44, 46, 51, 55, 110, 127n., 133, 140
Greeks, 47, 48, 50n., 63
Hamilton, Alexander, 16, 198, 199, 201n., 206, 248
Henry IV, 128
Henry VIII, 181
Henry, Patrick, 165n.
Hippo, 70
Hitler, Adolf, 225
Hobbes, Thomas, 114
Holy Roman Empire. *See* Roman Empire
Homer, 45, 47, 48
Hungary, 120, 127n.
Iliad, 45, 50n.
India, 63
Islam, 92, 127, 127n.
Israel, 27, 94, 94n.
Israelites, 187
Italy, 114, 140
James II, 180
Jan of Leiden, 121
Jefferson, Thomas, 16, 164, 197
Jepthah, 172, 187
Jerusalem, 60, 142, 161
John, apostle, 19, 20
Judea, 94, 94n.

Jupiter, 71
Justin Martyr, 40, 88
Kant, Immanuel, 237, 237n.
Karlstadt, Andreas, 120
Kellogg-Briand Pact, 215
Leipzig, 113
Lincoln, Abraham, 249
Leo III, 65
Leo X, 108
Lewis, C. S., 23n., 166n., 211, 236,
    236n., 237n., 239n.-40n., 245n.
  view on natural law, 236-41
Locke, John, 14, 145, 152, 153, 165,
    167, 176-77, 181, 195n., 249
  and the birth of liberal democracy,
    198
  and Christianity, 156-57
  and the concept of the state of
    nature, 184-86, 184n.
  and *Essay Concerning Human Un-
    derstanding*, 146
  influence on the American Revo-
    lution, 195-97
  and *Letter Concerning Toleration*,
    152, 154-55, 161, 164
  philosophy of, 146-47, 157-58
  and *The Reasonableness of Christi-
    anity as Delivered in the Scrip-
    tures*, 156
  and *Two Treatises of Government*,
    17, 153, 157, 176, 182
  views on religious freedom, 159-
    61, 163-64, 169
  views on revolution, 179, 183-84,
    186-93, 191n.
London, 85
Los Angeles, 74
Louis XIV, 128
Luther, Martin, 14, 111, 113, 115,
    120, 126n., 128, 135, 136, 160
  and *Against the Murderous and
    Thieving Hordes*, 125, 125n.
  and *Appeal to the Ruling Class of*

Germany, 129
  and *Bondage of the Will*, 125n.
  and the concept of natural law,
    125-27
  and *Secular Authority*, 123-24,
    129-30, 169
  and views on society and govern-
    ment, 123-24, 129
Lyceum, 54, 56
Macedonia, 56
Machiavelli, Niccolò, 114, 213n.
  and *The Prince*, 114
Madison, James, 14, 16, 164-65,
    165n., 200, 202, 203, 204
  and *Memorial and Remonstrance
    Against Religious Assessments*,
    165
  and the problem of power 206-7
Magdeburg, 136
Manicheans, 66, 89
Manicheism, 66
Marcellinus, 69
  and interaction with Augustine of
    Hippo, 70-71
Marx, Karl, 213n.
Marxism, 215, 217, 219
Mary of Orange, 181
Massacussetts, 201
Mattijszoon, Jan, 121
Milan, 66
Mill, John Stuart, 153, 220-21, 223-
    24
Montesquieu, Charles, 194-95, 198
Munich, 215n.
Münster, 121, 122, 177
Nantes, Edict of, 128, 151
Naples, 84
  University of, 84
Nazis, 214-15, 225
Nebuchadnezzar, 47
Neo-Platonism, 72
Netherlands, the, 121, 129, 135, 153,
    169, 181

New Testament, 21, 22, 26-27, 29, 31, 35, 40, 74, 111, 155, 164, 169

Newton, Isaac, 146

Nicaea, First Council of, 77, 246

Nicene Creed, 15

Niebuhr, Reinhold, 211, 230-35, 240, 241

Nietzsche, Friedrich, 50n., 219

Nietzscheism, 219

Old Testament, 22, 24, 27, 40, 41, 89, 121, 132, 155, 164, 186

Odysseus, 49-50, 50n.

Odyssey, 45

Oedipus, 46

Orange, Second Council of, 68

Ottoman Empire, 127n., 152

Oxford, 142, 179

Paul, apostle, 14, 24, 29, 30, 31, 32, 35-37, 38, 39, 43, 44, 61, 74, 76, 84, 93-94, 142, 155, 244

Peasants' War, the, 120, 122, 177

Pelagianism, 68

Pelagius, 68, 70

Pennsylvania, 199, 201

Persia, 63

Peter, apostle, 14, 30, 31, 35-36, 38, 39, 107, 116, 209

Pharisees, 232

Philadelphia, 174

Phoenix, 50n.

Plato, 14, 43n., 52, 54, 55n., 57-58, 57n.-58n., 61, 72, 100, 115, 244
    and the *Apology of Socrates*, 51n., 53n., 60n.
    and the *Republic*, 57n., 58n., 92

Plotinus, 17

Poland, 120, 129, 149n., 169-70

Polycarp, 19-20

Porphyry, 17

Portugal, 135

Pythagoras, 58

Radical Reformation, the, 118, 119-21, 175

Reformation, the, 14, 17, 106, 107, 114, 116-18, 120, 122, 131, 133, 134, 137, 138, 141, 147, 158, 165, 169, 246
    sources of 110-11
    theology of 112-13

Renaissance, the, 87

Republic, 52

Roman Catholic Church, 108, 110, 112, 116, 149
    and the Counter-Reformation, 136
    and response to Calvin's "two-swords approach," 135

Roman Empire
    and the adoption of Christianity, 20, 77
    Holy Roman Empire, 17, 65
    and the persecution of Judaism, 20, 37

Romans, 47, 48, 73, 76

Romanticism, 212, 216-17, 219, 221

Rome, 31, 34, 37, 41, 56, 63, 133, 135, 193, 244, 246
    church and state in early Christian Rome, 77
    fall of, 65, 67, 69, 73, 76-78, 110, 111, 112-13, 182

Rousseau, Jean-Jacques, 212-13, 216, 217, 221, 222

Rutherford, Samuel, 196n.

Sadducees, 233

Saxony, 108, 150

Scholasticism, 86

Scholastics, 92

Shaftesbury, Earl of. *See* Cooper, Anthony Ashley

Shays, Daniel, 201

Shays' Rebellion, 201

Sigismund I, 170

Sigismund II, 170

Smith, Adam, 200, 213n.

Smyrna, 19

Socrates, 44, 46, 47, 51-55, 55n., 57,
    59
Sophists, 58
Sophocles, 46
Soviet Union. *See* Union of Soviet
    Socialist Republics
Spain, 135, 149n.
Speyer, Diet of, 138
Sproul, R. C., 16
Stilicho, 65
Stoics, 34, 58
Sweden, 129
Switzerland, 135, 225
Tertullian, 61, 61n., 72
Tetzel, Johann, 107-9, 136
Thales, 54
Thomas Aquinas, 14, 56, 85, 87, 160,
    177, 179
    and Aristotle, 92-93
    and the concept of natural law, 95-
        99, 102-5
    early life of, 84
    and *Summa Contra Gentiles*, 92
    and *Summa Theologica*, 86, 90, 92,
        96n.-97n.
    and view on government author-
        ity, 101
Tocqueville, Alexis de, 167, 220, 249
    and *Democracy in America*, 167,
        220
    and views on democracy and
        religion, 168
Topeka, 74

Transylvania, 170
Union of Soviet Socialist Republics,
    209
United States of America, 164,
    196n.
Vandals, 65
VanDrunen, David, 95n.
Varro, 17
Vienna, 127n., 152
Virginia, 165n.
Visigoths, 65
Volusianus, 69n., 70
Warsaw, 170
Washington, George, 16, 197
Weimar Republic, 215
Westphalia, Treaty of, 139, 140
Whitehead, Alfred North, 52
William of Ockham, 17, 85, 87,
    95, 98, 160, 177, 184, 188
    and the concept of natural law,
        102-6
    and *Dialogue on the Power of the
        Emperor and the Pope*, 100
    early life of, 85
    philosophical career of, 100
William of Orange, 181
Wittenberg, 108, 115, 120
Worms, Imperial Diet of, 113, 115,
    120
Xenophon, 55n.
Zeus, 47, 48
Zurich, 134
Zwingli, Huldrych, 134